LUHMANN ON LAW AND POLITICS

Perhaps more than any other social theorist in recent history, Niklas Luhmann's work has aroused extreme, and often antagonistic, responses. It has generated controversies about its political implications, its resolute anti-humanism and its ambitious critique of more established definitions of society, social theory and sociology. Now, however, a steadily growing number of scholars working in many different disciplines have begun to use aspects of Luhmann's sociology as an important methodological stimulus and as a theoretical framework for reorientating their studies. This collection of essays includes critical and reconstructive contributions by social theorists, political theorists, legal scholars and empirical sociologists. Together, they provide evidence of Luhmann's extensive and diverse relevance to the issues facing contemporary society, and, at the same time, they enhance our understanding of the challenges posed by his theoretical paradigm to more traditional conceptions of social theory.

Oñati International Series in Law and Society
A SERIES PUBLISHED FOR THE OÑATI INSTITUTE FOR THE SOCIOLOGY OF LAW

Titles in this Series

Social Dynamics of Crime and Control: New Theories for a World in Transition edited by Susannah Karstedt and Kai Bussmann

Criminal Policy in Transition edited by Andrew Rutherford and Penny Green

Making Law for Families edited by Mavis Maclean

Poverty and the Law edited by Peter Robson and Asbjørn Kjønstad

Adapting Legal Cultures edited by Johannes Feest and David Nelken

Rethinking Law Society and Governance: Foucault's Bequest edited by Gary Wickham and George Pavlich

Rules and Networks edited by Richard Appelbaum, Bill Felstiner and Volkmar Gessner

Women in the World's Legal Professions edited by Ulrike Schultz and Gisela Shaw

After National Democracy edited by Lars Trägårdh

Healing the Wounds edited by Marie-Claire Foblets and Trutz von Trotha

Imaginary Boundaries of Justice edited by Ronnie Lippens

Family Law and Family Values edited by Mavis Maclean

Contemporary Issues in the Semiotics of Law edited by Anne Wagner, Tracey Summerfield, and Farid Benavides Vanegas

The Geography of Law: Landscapes, Identity and Regulation edited by Bill Taylor

Luhmann on Law and Politics edited by Michael King and Chris Thornhill

Theory and Method in Socio-Legal Research edited by Reza Banakar and Max Travers

Precarious Work, Women and the New Economy edited by Judy Fudge and Rosemary Owens

Luhmann on Law and Politics

Critical Appraisals and Applications

Edited by

MICHAEL KING

and

CHRIS THORNHILL

Oñati International Series in Law and Society

A SERIES PUBLISHED FOR THE OÑATI INSTITUTE
FOR THE SOCIOLOGY OF LAW

OXFORD – PORTLAND OREGON
2006

Published in North America (US and Canada)
by Hart Publishing
c/o International Specialized Book Services
920 NE 58th Avenue, Suite 300
Portland, OR 97213-3786
USA

Tel: +1 503 287 3093 or toll-free: (1) 800 944 6190
Fax: +1 503 280 8832
E-mail: orders@isbs.com
Web Site: www.isbs.com

Hart Publishing is a specialist legal publisher based in Oxford, England. To order further copies of this book or to request a list of other publications please write to:

Hart Publishing, Salter's Boatyard, Folly Bridge,
Abingdon Road, Oxford, OX1 4LB
email: mail@hartpub.co.uk
Telephone: +44 (0)1865 245533 Fax: +44 (0)1865 794882

WEB SITE http//:www.hartpub.co.uk

British Library Cataloguing in Publication Data
Data Available

ISBN 13: 978–1–84113–623–3 (cloth)
ISBN 10: 1–84113–623–9 (cloth)

ISBN 13: 978–1–84113–624–7 (paper)
ISBN 10: 1–84113–624–7 (paper)

Typeset by Hope Services Ltd, Abingdon, Oxon
Printed and bound in Great Britain by
Biddles Ltd, King's Lynn, Norfolk

Contents

Notes on Contributors

John Paterson is Reader in Law at the University of Aberdeen.

Michael King is Professor of Law at Brunel University, UK.

Tim Murphy is Professor of Law at the London School of Economics.

Chris Thornhill is Professor in the Politics Department at the University of Glasgow.

Gert Verschraegen is Research Fellow of the National Fund of Scientific Research, Flanders, and works in the Sociology Department at Leuven University, Belgium.

Samantha Ashenden is Senior Lecturer in Sociology at Birkbeck College, University of London.

Jean Clam is Senior Research Fellow at the CNRS in Strasburg and at the Centre Marc Bloch, Berlin.

Anne Friederike Müller was formerly AHRB Research Fellow at King's College, University of London.

Bernd Hornung is Senior Researcher and Lecturer at the Institute of Medical Informatics, Medical Center for Methodological Sciences and Health Research of the Faculty of Medicine at Marburg University.

Andreas Philippopoulos-Mihalopoulos is Reader in Law at the University of Westminster.

Introduction

MICHAEL KING AND CHRIS THORNHILL

THIS VOLUME REPRESENTS the outcome of a memorable workshop held in September 2003 at The International Institute for the Sociology of Law in Onati, Guipuzcoa, Spain. The theme of the workshop was Niklas Luhmann's Legal and Political Theory. This workshop was conceived as an international forum to facilitate wide-ranging discussion of ways in which aspects of Luhmann's social theory might be applied in contemporary debates in the social sciences, and it attracted participants from Belgium, France, Germany, Holland, Italy, Mexico, New Zealand and the UK. A number of the chapters in this volume were originally presented as discussion papers at this workshop, and others were stimulated by discussions arising during and after the workshop. We are extremely grateful to the staff at the Institute in Onati, particularly Malen Gordoa Mendizabal and Volkmar Gessner, for their help and financial support in organising the workshop. We hope that this volume does justice to the quality of the setting in the *Antigua Universidad* and to the debates between participants during the workshop sessions.

CONTENT, THEMES AND CONTEXT

A steadily increasing number of scholars across many different disciplines are now taking Niklas Luhmann's writings as a major theoretical source for their work. The collection of essays in this volume offers further evidence of this increasingly broad and enthusiastic reception of Luhmann, and it includes contributions from several distinct fields of inquiry—including social theory, political sociology, political theory, legal theory and social anthropology. It also marks a growing discrimination in the understanding of the complexity of Luhmann's ideas and a refined critical appreciation both of their breadth and of their limitations.

Perhaps more than any other theorist in recent history, Luhmann's work has aroused extreme responses and stimulated diverse theoretical receptions. At an earlier stage in the appropriation of his work, particularly during the period of his heated debate with Jürgen Habermas in the 1970s, the status of Luhmann's theory was questioned and debated in the starkest and most polemical terms. At this stage attitudes to Luhmann were closely tied to more generally polarised political stances, and it was assumed that readers of his work either fully embraced his anti-humanist view of the world and accepted all aspects of his systemic sociology, or rejected his work entirely, and opted instead for more normatively inflected accounts of the way that society operates. The publication of this book, however, is a clear indication that times have changed and that the preconditions of debate have been altered. It is certainly not the case that every contributor to this volume would wish to be described as a fervent supporter of Luhmann's theoretical approach, or would express preference for Luhmann's work over all other theoretical perspectives on the social world. Nonetheless, all believe his vision to be original, fascinating and theoretically productive, and all thus insist that it warrants the most committed and detailed consideration. All of them would also accept the view that the theoretical potential of his work can be appreciated and realised without a full subscription to all its implications and preconditions.

We have chosen, for the sake of clarity and thematic coherence, to organise the chapters in this volume according to their thematic focus. The book therefore has three distinct sections: one section comprises chapters that reflect on the relation between theory and practice in law, one section contains chapters that provide commentaries on politics, law and human rights, and one section incorporates chapters that express broader critical reactions to Luhmann's general theory of society.

In addition to the thematic connections between individual contributions, however, many of the chapters in this volume are connected by common methods, concerns and interests, so that three distinct approaches to the interpretation and application of Luhmann's sociology are represented here. First, the volume includes essays which seek to analyse and, in some cases, criticise Luhmann's writings by situating them within the matrix of a particular and distinct academic discipline. These essays also compare his theoretical accounts or methodological principles with those of other writers in order to identify both the strengths, the limitations, and the critical resonances of the theory.

As a sociologist, for example, Bernd Hornung provides a very insightful description of the construction and of the key conceptual features of Luhmann's social theory (or, to use his own terms, *theories*). In so doing, he identifies the concepts and categories which centrally characterise and delineate the four phases of theory building which mark Luhmann's trajectory: these are, Hornung claims, *functionalism*, *complexity*, *autopoeisis and selectivity*, and *semantics*. He examines the interactions between these theoretical phases in Luhmann's development and he shows how his sociology is ultimately constructed through a fusion of these distinct conceptual paradigms. He then proceeds to question whether autopoietic theory can legitimately be applied to social systems. He concludes his chapter with a provocative analysis of the different types and levels of 'statement' contained in Luhmann's writings, and he discusses how these might be used in wider sociological research.

In the field of political theory, analogously, Chris Thornhill critically examines Luhmann's self-styled project of elaborating a *Sociological Enlightenment*.

He assesses whether Luhmann makes good his proclaimed intention of moving beyond the classical Enlightenment of the eighteenth century, and of offering a more persuasive basis for understanding or legitimating political action and political institutions within society. Luhmann, as Thornhill explains, argues that the conception of human rationality as a constant normative and transformative force in human society and history relies on a series of unaccountable and metaphysical presuppositions, and so he denies that any theory which posits the criterion of human reason as its legitimating factor can truly account for the social origins and justifiable functions of power. In these claims, Luhmann sets out a crucial challenge for contemporary political theory, and he demands that political theorists should reflect and refine the categories of analysis and argument which they commonly employ. However, Thornhill is also quick to point out the very controversial practical implications of this approach, not only for the future of political theory and political sociology, but also for Luhmann's own political position. Thornhill thus critically identifies the practical outcome of Luhmann's political thought as an 'implicit attachment to nineteenth century models of administrative positivism and limited legal-statism'.

A further example of these attempts to contextualise Luhmann within a particular academic discipline is the chapter by Anne Friederike Müller. As an anthropologist, Müller reflects on the threat or 'irritation' that Luhmann's separation of human consciousness from society presents for branches of the social sciences whose foundations reside in their ability to study societies through observing and analysing individual and group behaviour. However, after grappling with those aspects of Luhmann's theory which are clearly inimical to an anthropological approach, Müller ends on a conciliatory note by identifying in his distinction between *Autonomie* and *Autarkie* (autonomy and self-sufficiency) a possible basis for applying Luhmannian concepts in an anthropological consideration of the relations between mind, body and society.

The second general approach represented by contributors to this volume involves focusing upon a specific substantive social issue contained in Luhmann's writings and subjecting this issue to close scrutiny both in terms of Luhmann's own account, and in terms of how this account relates to other approaches. Gert Verschraegen, for example, focuses on the topical subject of human rights, and he emphasises how Luhmann's approach to the subject differs from that of other political thinkers. 'As a sociologist,' Verschraegen explains, 'Luhmann is interested . . . in linking human rights to specific societal structures. Human rights are not considered in an ethical or juridical way, but seen *as a social institution with a special function.*'

On these grounds, Verschraegen argues that, conceived in Luhmannian terms, human rights always have a paradoxical character. Rights claim to be founded on natural rights or rights that exist in nature, but 'at the same time . . . rights claims have to be enforced by a state in order to be effective' and so they presuppose an established coercive or constitutional order. In his conclusion, he refers to Luhmann's doubts about the tenability of a notion of 'the state': 'the state', for Luhmann, is no more than a construction of a world political system which organises itself in order to give the impression that solutions to global problems are available through concerted political action. The idea that human rights might be globally secured through 'states' appears, therefore, a rather simplistic and self-serving proposition. However, as Verschraegen points out, Luhmann offers no solution to this problem except to say that our understanding of how human rights are preserved and enforced must still await the evolution of 'suitable forms' of global intervention.

Samantha Ashenden looks at the implications of Luhmann's concept of power for broader questions of political sociology. She takes as her starting point his refutation of the central assumption of liberal constitutionalism, namely that 'political power can and must be curtailed, and that this is possible through the separation of powers within the state and through the separation of state and society'. On Ashenden's account, Luhmann sees the classical-liberal attempt to separate the institutional organs bearing power and, in so doing, to place limits on the application of power, as having an effect which is diametrically opposed to its primary intention; this process actually results in a multiplication of power and in an increasingly diffuse dissemination of power through society. Ashenden recognises the originality of Luhmann's analysis and, in particular, she declares sympathy for his argument that causal models of power-formation and power-transmission support hierarchical conceptions of power. Luhmann's systems-theoretical approach, she explains, allows observers of power to move away from causal models, to 'open up the possibility of looking at complex connections between systems', and so to countenance highly pluralistic and multi-focal interpretations of how power is produced and applied. However, she is not entirely won over by Luhmann's arguments, seeing a number of problems and limitations in his theory of power and a number of unresolved tensions and inconsistencies in the categories of his own analysis.

John Paterson's essay, treating Luhmann's sociology as the basis for an instrumental doctrine of law, also exemplifies an approach to Luhmann which applies his general theoretical framework to specific issues. Paterson's analysis differs, however, from the other chapters, in that Luhmann's theory of law is considered in conjunction and comparison with Gunther Teubner's concept of 'reflexive law'. For Teubner, there are clear, if not obvious, ways in which law is able to influence and even regulate other systems: it can accomplish this, for example, by persuading other systems to accept a process of self-regulation based on legal principles adapted to the particular operations of the target system. When Paterson brings Luhmann to the centre of the debate, it is to demonstrate that nothing in Teubner's scheme of reflexive law actually contradicts Luhmannian theory, and that in certain ways it can be seen to develop Luhmann's ideas, albeit in ways which Luhmann himself might not have intended. While Michael King in his chapter in this book queries such an instrumental application of Luhmann's work, Paterson suggests that the concept of reflexive law may represent a way in which Luhmann's sociology creates options for 'for making better use' of society's as yet untried possibilities.[1]

The third of the approaches to Luhmann's writings that we would identify among the contributors here might loosely be described either as critically interpretive and independently responsive, or as an attempt to expand the content and the application of Luhmann's categories beyond the focus which Luhmann himself used. Although they may tackle specific issues, such as power, race or regulation, these essays do not apply Luhmann's ideas in any instrumental or strategic way, and they are not concerned either with the specific application or the immanent elucidation and/or critique of Luhmann's theoretical concepts. Generally, these essays use Luhmann's social theory as the point of departure for wide-ranging discussions of the nature of modern society, or for interpretations of pressing issues and tendencies in modern society.

Jean Clam, for instance, suggests that his use of Luhmann's theoretical elements 'will remain deliberately very intuitive'. He adds: 'I do not intend to engage in a discussion of the theory itself, but I would like to try to work with some of its theorems, to apply them directly to the question of modern power, and to try to obtain descriptive accounts of it through them.' Clam then uses Luhmannian concepts to analyse transformations in the belief structures and political cultures of contemporary society. During the course of this analysis he discusses the crisis in Western liberal democracies brought about by the growth of different types of fundamentalism and by the at times violent political 'recentration' of societies that the contamination of political operations with religious vocabularies inspires. He criticises what he sees as the '[h]eavy, excessive re-politicisation of democracy', exemplified by the USA in contemporary world politics, and he discusses this phenomenon as 'mobilising, randomly and arbitrarily, an order of order against another order of order which is perceived to be of minor value and strength'. This tendency towards 'recentration', he believes, has destroyed the capacity for 'alterity' which at other times, in other worlds, opened possibilities of social self-reflection, and which allowed societies, through such self-reflection, to accept that its constructed image of 'the other' is precisely merely a constructed image, and nothing more. Although not committed to a literal application of Luhmann's ideas, Clam nonetheless identifies in Luhmann's thought an important set of paradigms for accounting for very recent sociological transformations, and even for explaining the liberating elements which still inhere in modern mental attitudes.

Tim Murphy attempts a similar kind of topology. Taking as his starting point the claim that Luhmann's notion that modern society consists of 'the totality of world communications,' he elaborates a Luhmannian examination of the themes of race equality and human rights. His particular concern is to show that the concept (or non-concept) of 'race' expresses a legal programme which

[1] N Luhmann, 'The Coding of the Legal System' in *State, Law, Economy as Autopoietic Systems*, A Febbrajo and G Teubner (eds), (Milan, Guiffré, 1992), 145–86; 182.

intentionally 'challenges universalism', but which also forms a 'global category or problem'. 'Under the banner of inclusion,' he tells us, 'we are in the process of seeking to carve out equality and sameness on the bedrock of difference. And now the law is being used to valorise this process—to legislate for self-respect.' Murphy deploys a systems-theoretical perspective to confront the paradox which he identifies as race/~~race~~. He sees 'the proliferation of racial distinctions' as largely the result of legislative measures and of the monitoring and enforcement methods that have accompanied them. Neither beliefs about identity nor theories of society built on the basis of human nature are able adequately to offer an analysis of this global paradox: a 'sociological enlightenment' is required, using different tools and a different starting point from the universally imputed 'man', commonly posited as the ground of social inquiry. Murphy, following Luhmann's lead, seeks to provide us with the tools and the starting point to see the problem of race with fresh eyes—even if this new vision, unlike the liberal, human-rights perspective, knows no easy answers.

Finally, in this category, Michael King, in his reply to John Paterson's chapter, asks the question: 'What use is Luhmann's theory?' He finds the answer to this question in the paradoxical argument that Luhmann's usefulness lies in his uselessness. He thus maintains that those who attempt to apply the theory 'as a blueprint for the improvement of social systems' and those who try and make his theory useful or practically beneficial may well be contributing to the theory's ultimate redundancy. King clearly endorses an intuitive approach to Luhmann's theory as it relates to law, and he considers this approach more reflective of Luhmann's own intentions than an interpretation which construes Luhmann's work as a set of tools which might eventually lead to the self-improvement of society or to the more effective regulation of social problems. In setting out this view, he makes it clear that the debate about the practical utility of Luhmann's work should not be construed as a debate between 'practice' and 'theory'. It is rather a debate between an instrumental application of Luhmann which emphasises 'the immediacy of autopoiesis as a critical framework for the analysis of current policies and legal decisions' and one which emphasises the abstract, indeterminate quality of Luhmann's writings—which accentuates 'the possibility of seeing things differently, of completely different understandings of events in the world', and which envisions a future which cannot begin as long as events in society continue to be conceptualised and analysed as they are at present. On King's account, it is this distinction, and not the simple distinction between closed and partly closed systems, that marks the difference between Luhmann's approach to the legal system and that of Gunther Teubner.[2]

In addition to these major categories of analysis and approach, Andreas Philippopoulos-Mihalopoulos' paper is distinct for its performative character and for its interpretation of Luhmann's work as subverting common definitions

[2] See G Teubner, *Law as an Autopoietic System* (Oxford, Blackwell, 1993).

of the role of scientific inquiry and common understandings of the theoretical division of labour—especially the division between theoretical analysis and aesthetic and literary practice. He adopts an approach to Luhmann's ideas which regards the theory as a 'creative, almost playful and artistic development of different knowledge fields',[3] and suggests that the process of concept formation in Luhmann's sociology invariably contains a spontaneous and associative dimension. In this respect, this chapter is an example of a post-modern approach to the study of law and legal texts, which deploys general social and psychological theories in order to render fluid standard preconceptions about legal and ethical categories. Proceeding from the premise that in Luhmann's theory, the traditional question of the fairness of law loses all practical meaning, Philippopoulos-Mihalopoulos considers the fraught relationship between law and justice. In particular, he discusses the propensity of the legal system to deceive or to *cheat* its addressees by promoting fictitious and paradoxical concepts of justice, and exploiting or disclosing the blind-spots of other social systems, while never revealing its own. On these grounds, he also revises and challenges wider conceptions of the role of theory in the law. Theory, he explains, serves both to remind the law of its blind spots and to warn the law not to transgress the limit of the claims which it can make for its own validity. However, theory also does service to the law in providing motives which obscure its blind spots and maintain the paradox and contingency of law's functions. Law, if theoretically informed, thus becomes conscious of the need to cheat without exposing its contingent foundations in public—of the need never to utter the 'unutterable' and paradoxical foundations of its validity.

LUHMANN AND SCIENTIFIC REVOLUTIONS

For all the diversity of their approach and their varying degrees of commitment to Luhmann's sociology as a whole, one conviction which unites all the chapters in this book is that Luhmann's work involves a major change of paradigm in sociology, and in its implications for other fields of scientific inquiry. The question of whether Luhmann's break with the humanist theoretical legacy in the social sciences represents a scientific revolution, and of whether his theory of society contains an entirely new paradigm for sociology, are likely to remain hotly contested issues for some time to come. Some critics deny that Luhmann's work can lay claim to revolutionary status, and they see Luhmann more as an eclectic synthesiser than as an innovator—as one who borrows ideas from others, producing from them a patchwork of different concepts and then claiming that together these represent a radically original social theory. In different ways,

[3] G Teubner, R Nobles and D Schiff, 'The Autopoiesis of Law: An Introduction to Legal Autopoiesis', in J Penner, D Schiff and R Nobles (eds), *Introduction to Jurisprudence and Legal Theory* (London, Butterworths, 2002) 925.

however, all contributions in this volume make a strong case for Luhmann's work on the grounds that it challenges the conceptual foundations and implications of all established perspectives in the social sciences and seeks to revise the discipline of sociology (broadly defined) on new preconditions.

To use Kuhn's vocabulary, a theory constituting a 'scientific revolution' is one which proposes a new theoretical paradigm which extends beyond the existing store of ideas and methods underpinning a distinct discipline, and which therefore offers a model for understanding phenomena which breaks fundamentally with the past. In several key respects, we feel that we are entitled to claim that Luhmann's work constitutes one of the major scientific revolutions in the recent history of the social sciences. We believe this to be the case for the following reasons.

First, unlike classical perspectives in sociological and social-theoretical inquiry, Luhmann abandons the human being as the central unit of theoretical analysis: this means that his work renounces and transforms the central foundation of Western European thought—namely the claim that human society is steered and shaped by human beings and that society is residually formed out of human actions. Instead of this, Luhmann argues that society is made up of contingent communications, and that it cannot be made transparent to any stable or invariable attributes of which all human beings are in possession in like manner. This means, for example, that society is not an agglomerate of interactions and behavioural dispositions, but a sequence of communicative exchanges within demarcated, self-referring social systems. On these grounds, Luhmann challenges us to think about society in categories which refuse to view human interests or orientations as the immediate or remote cause of all social events, and which accept that social evolution is stimulated by many different causes, and is ultimately founded only in its own contingency.

Second, unlike all standard positions in post-Enlightenment philosophical reflection, Luhmann denies that human rationality can act as a normative focus for evaluating and guiding processes of social change. For Luhmann, rationality is not an explanatory or normative resource which is inherent in all human beings, and he argues that the rational principles through which human beings claim to judge and affect their environments are nothing more than selective constructions through which systems give plausibility to their operations and communications. There are, in short, *many types of rationality* in modern society, and there are no uniform or perennial criteria to help us determine which rationality produces the most reliable insights and which leads most securely to experiences of progress and social improvement.

Third, although Luhmann has commonalities with Parsonian functionalism and post-1945 German institutionalism, his account of social systems as *operatively closed*—that is, as autonomously constructing their own operations through which they generate both their own environment and their identity, their self-image within that environment—marks a radical departure from previous positions in a functionalist tradition of sociology. This shift of paradigm has profound implications for our understanding of how society exists and evolves and for our conception of the role of regulation and steering in society.

Fourth, Luhmann's assertion that all knowledge claims must necessarily be based on the drawing of a distinction creating a marked and an unmarked space also fundamentally modifies common socio-epistemological preconditions, and it profoundly challenges the widely accepted cognitive foundations of sociological method. It is true that Luhmann derives this concept from the otherwise little-known mathematician, George Spencer Brown.[4] However, Luhmann adapts the theory in a way that was never envisaged by Spencer Brown, applying it in particular to 'social and conscious systems' in order to demonstrate their inherently paradoxical nature—their inability to treat as knowledge anything which lies on the unmarked side of the distinction marking their own creation and their utter inability to recognise this limitation. On this principle, only observers of the system are able to see the system operating within its limited marked space and to acknowledge the existence of the unmarked space. Yet every observer needs to draw a distinction in order to observe and in doing so creates his or her own marked and unmarked space. This is what Luhmann means by 'self-reference' and 'other-reference' (or 'external reference'). As Luhmann himself puts it:

> If one accepts the distinction of reference into self-reference and external reference, then the problem of reference poses itself on two levels. Reference itself is nothing but the achievement of an observational designation. Each observation designates something (traditionally speaking: it has an object). The opposite concept here is simply operating. In contrast to referring, operating is an objectless enactment. In the observation, the difference between observation and operation can be reformulated in an innovative way as the distinction between self-reference and external reference. Self-reference refers to what the operation 'observation' enacts. External reference refers to what is thereby excluded.[5]

This conception casts deeply questioning reflexes on commonplace accounts of how social observation relates to the objects of its inquiry, it undermines and relativises widely held ideals of objectivity and neutrality in sociological method, and it promotes a multi-perspectival understanding of social communications.

On these grounds, therefore, this book seeks to add weight to the growing conviction that Luhmann's work represents a ground-breaking moment in the broad terrain of social-scientific inquiry. Above all, this volume hopes to correct the belief that Luhmann's works form a monolithic system or edifice, against which readers must position themselves either in total negation or in derivative emulation and assimilation. As with all important theoretical paradigm shifts, naturally, Luhmann's work poses distinct challenges to its interpreters and to

[4] G Spencer Brown, *Laws of Form* (London, Alan & Unwin, 1969).

[5] N Luhmann 'The Modernity of Science' in W Rasch (ed), *Theories of Distinction*, K Behnke (trans) (Stanford Ca, Stanford University Press, 2002) 61–75; 65.

those who enter into critical discourse with it, and those participating in the reception of such work have to be able modify and rethink the categories of their own methodologies. However, this book hopes to promote an engagement with Luhmann's work which will appreciate the resonances of his theory in a multitude of scientific disciplines, which will acknowledge the deep reorientation which his theory stimulates, but which will also test out new theoretical vocabularies against Luhmann and not be fearful of articulating informed critique.

I.

Theory and Practice in Law

1

Reflecting on Reflexive Law

JOHN PATERSON

> Every command executed is always one of an immense number unexecuted. All the impossible commands inconsistent with the course of events remain unexecuted. Only the possible ones get linked up with a consecutive series of commands corresponding to a series of events, and are executed . . . So that examining the relation in time of the commands to the events, we find that a command can never be the cause of the event, but that a certain definite dependence exists between the two.[1]

> There are few bases for being able to radically change whatever society one is living in. There are many bases for making better use of its possibilities.[2]

INTRODUCTION

IT IS PERHAPS appropriate that Niklas Luhmann, who insisted on a polarised view of autopoiesis, admitting of no intermediate degrees of closure,[3] should provoke polarised views on the implications of the theory for law. In a recent critique Capps and Olsen bemoan the fact that autopoietic law is the 'antithesis' of Roscoe Pound's characterisation of the ongoing relationship between law and society as 'a continually more efficacious social engineering'.[4] For King and Thornhill, however, Luhmann's 'refutation of the belief that the legal system can be viewed as an effective vehicle for social engineering' represents one of his 'most enduring additions to contemporary legal and political thought'.[5] At first glance Capps and Olsen would appear to be on firmer ground. There is surely something counterintuitive—if not, indeed, perverse—in suggesting that law cannot be used to effect social change. Those of us educated as lawyers or political scientists have certainly been led to believe otherwise.

[1] L Tolstoy, *War and Peace* (vol 3) (London, Everyman's Library, 1992) 501–2.

[2] N Luhmann, 'The Coding of the Legal System' in G Teubner and A Febbrajo (eds), *State, Law and Economy as Autopoietic Systems* (Milan, Guiffré, 1992), 145–186; 182.

[3] N Luhmann, 'Closure and Openness: On Reality in the World of Law' in G Teubner (ed), *Autopoietic Law: A New Approach to Law and Society* (Berlin, de Gruyter, 1987), 335–348; 346.

[4] P Capps and H Palmer Olsen, 'Legal Autonomy and Reflexive Rationality in Complex Societies' in *Social and Legal Studies* 547 at 547.

[5] M King and C Thornhill, *Niklas Luhmann's Theory of Politics and Law* (Basingstoke and New York, Palgrave, 2003) 224.

So what does Luhmann mean? Is this rather startling suggestion simply a conceit to draw attention to the fact that law's record in respect of social change is less than perfect? Is he simply trying to provoke lawyers and political scientists out of a perceived complacency? In fact he means much more than this. For Luhmann, it is not just that law is not very good at producing social change, it is also that law itself is under threat when it is deployed in this way. More precisely, tendencies such as social engineering endanger law's autonomy by endangering its binary code, forcing decisions to be taken on the basis of differences other than that between legal and illegal.[6] For some, no doubt, the idea that law might take account of softer notions such as benefit and harm in reaching decisions would be welcome, an indication of law's responsiveness to social need. For Luhmann, however, this is to be seduced by apparent short-term gains at the expense of long-term harm not only to law, but also to society as a whole. If law is not to be a political tool in the pursuit of social objectives, it nevertheless does perform a vital social function within Luhmann's account of society, that of stabilising expectations.[7] If this function were to be jeopardised, then society as a whole would count the cost. To that extent, then, for all the intuitive appeal of the critique by Capps and Olsen, it is King and Thornhill who surely reach the correct conclusion.

As the polarisation of these assessments implies, however, the conclusion one reaches on the implications of autopoiesis for law depends very much on whether one finds the theory convincing in the first place. If one does, then the implications for law flow naturally and inevitably. If one does not, then those implications can appear not only counterintuitive, but also downright dangerous. As Roger Cotterrell, one of the theory's more measured critics, has recently observed, autopoiesis certainly 'dramatises our deep disappointment that more cannot be done with law to effect social regulation', while the picture it presents of 'contemporary positive law's autonomy is, in important respects, plausible', but much of what it 'offers beyond this is harmful in so far as it is used to guide socio-legal inquiry'.[8]

Paradoxically, however, those legal theorists who have done most to develop the idea of autopoiesis in the domain of law, such as Gunther Teubner[9] and Helmut Willke,[10] while not infrequently criticised in the same breath as Luhmann,[11] also find themselves attacked from the opposite direction. Thus, as

[6] N Luhmann, 'Closure and Openness', above n 3 at 347.

[7] N Luhmann, 'The Unity of the Legal System' in G Teubner (ed), *Autopoietic Law: A New Approach to Law and Society* (Berlin, de Gruyter, 1987) 12–35; 27.

[8] R Cotterrell, 'The Representation of Law's Autonomy in Autopoiesis Theory' in J Přibáň and D Nelken (eds), *Law's New Boundaries: The Consequences of Legal Autopoiesis* (Aldershot, Ashgate-Dartmouth, 2001) 80–103; 89–90.

[9] See especially, G Teubner, *Law as an Autopoietic System* (Oxford, Blackwell, 1993).

[10] For example, H Willke, 'Political Intervention: Operational Conditions for Generalised Political Exchange' in B Marin (ed), *Governance and Generalised Exchange: Self-Organizing Policy Networks in Action* (Frankfurt/Boulder, Campus/Westview, 1990), 235–254.

[11] See, for example, P Capps and H Olsen, 'Legal Autonomy', above n 4.

well as being accused of endangering law's role as an instrument of social change by the opponents of autopoiesis, they have also come under fire from Luhmann for essentially giving in to a desire to see a continued role for law in social engineering.[12] Despite the fact that such theorists have explicitly identified their new model of law, *reflexive law*, as post-instrumental[13] and as taking account of the autopoiesis both of law and of the systems it purports to regulate,[14] Luhmann is concerned that what the model claims to be able to do is theoretically impossible.[15] Nor have the opponents of autopoiesis been slow to perceive logical contradictions in the account of reflexive law.[16]

The concern in this chapter, then, is not to respond (again!) to the critics of reflexive law who are also critics of autopoiesis.[17] Rather the request is that they should suspend their theoretical disbelief for a moment and join us in considering whether reflexive law is actually consistent with autopoiesis. For, as the criticisms just outlined above indicate, the position of reflexive law is a rather complicated one. If writers such as Teubner are right, then for all the apparent pessimism of autopoiesis vis-à-vis the possibility for social change effected by law, some form of social engineering remains possible—albeit radically different from what is envisaged under more traditional paradigms of law. If, on the other hand, Luhmann is right, then reflexive law proceeds from false premises, and, whatever it offers, it tells us nothing about what we might hope to do with law in the context of a society composed of autopoietic subsystems. Indeed, if Luhmann is right, it may well be that the proponents of reflexive law have fundamentally misunderstood what his account of society and his project of sociological enlightenment imply. Dreams of social change through law—even in its autopoietically-aware, post-instrumental orientation—must remain simply that.

It is, therefore, important to know precisely what Luhmann's understanding of law is and whether the proponents of reflexive law have properly grasped it. These are the issues to be examined in the following two sections of this chapter. Thereafter, in the final section, it is a question of considering whether when reflexive law, either explicitly or implicitly, transgresses against Luhmann's account of autopoiesis and law's place within a society composed of autopoietic

[12] See especially, N Luhmann, 'Some Problems with Reflexive Law' in G Teubner and A Febbrajo (eds), *State, Law and Economy as Autopoietic Systems*, above n 2, 389–415.

[13] G Teubner, 'After Legal Instrumentalism: Strategic Models of Post-Regulatory Law' in G Teubner (ed), *Dilemmas of Law in the Welfare State* (Berlin, de Gruyter, 1985) 299–325.

[14] Teubner, *Law as an Autopoietic System*, above n 9 at 69.

[15] N Luhmann, 'Some Problems with Reflexive Law', above n 12 at 411.

[16] See, for example, J Habermas, *Between Facts and Norms: Contributions to a Discourse Theory of Law and Democracy* (Cambridge, Polity Press, 1996) 53–55.

[17] See instead, for example, S Smith, 'Beyond "Mega-theory" and "Multiple Sociology": A Reply to Rottleuthner' (1991) 19 *International Journal of the Sociology of Law* 321; G Teubner, 'Social Order from Legislative Noise' in G Teubner and A Febbrajo (eds), *State, Law and Economy as Autopoietic Systems*, above n 2, 609–49; G Teubner, 'Regulatory Law: Chronicle of a Death Foretold' (1992) 1 *Social and Legal Studies* 451; J Paterson, 'Who is Zenon Bankowski talking to? The Person in the Sight of Autopoiesis' (1995) 8 *Ratio Juris* 212.

subsystems, such transgressions are fatal to the concept. The tentative conclusions drawn are that they are not—and in particular because it turns out that, despite raising serious problems for reflexive law, Luhmann also provides it with indications for the direction of its future development. The question then, of course, is whether such development beyond the realm of theory is theoretically, let alone practically, possible. In reflexive law, it seems, as in social engineering, 'It is difficult, almost impossible, to abandon the notion of steering and to let the future come as it comes'.[18]

LUHMANN ON SOCIETY AND LAW

Niklas Luhmann's account of society as a whole and of law's place within it in terms of autopoiesis theory is rich and dense, and evolved gradually over time. To attempt to do anything like justice to it within the space available here would clearly be impossible.[19] Instead the focus will be upon those aspects that have the most direct bearing upon law, especially its function within an autopoietic account of society and its ability or otherwise to influence other social subsystems. This will allow us in due course to make an assessment of the claims made for reflexive law.

Perhaps the key element of Luhmann's understanding of law that it is necessary to grasp in this context is its *function*. In a society composed of autopoietic subsystems, law serves to stabilise normative expectations over time—nothing more and nothing less. 'Law consists of the exploitation of conflict perspectives for the formation and reproduction of congruently (temporally/objectively/socially) generalised behavioural expectations'.[20] The ability to perform this function depends upon the fact that autopoiesis implies normative (or operational) closure and cognitive openness. This apparently contradictory definition has been the source of a great deal of confusion, criticism and well-meaning attempts at improvement.[21] But as even some critics have noticed, this formula cannot be altered without fatal damage to Luhmann's account.[22] For law, normative closure means that 'only the legal system can bestow normative quality on its elements and thereby constitute them as elements'. But the legal system is also simultaneously cognitively open since in the constant reproduction of its

[18] N Luhmann, 'Limits of Steering' (1997) 14 *Theory, Culture and Society* 141; 141.

[19] Faithful and accessible introductions are provided by M King and A Schütz, 'The Ambitious Modesty of Niklas Luhmann', (1994) 21 *Journal of Law and Society* 261, and more comprehensively by M King and C Thornhill, *Niklas Luhmann's Theory of Politics and Law*, above n 5.

[20] N Luhmann, 'The Unity of the Legal System', above n 7 at 27.

[21] For example, D Zolo, 'The Epistemological Status of the Theory of Autopoiesis and its Application to the Social Sciences' in G Teubner and A Febbrajo (eds), *State, Law and Economy as Autopoietic Systems*, above n 2, 67–124; 118, where he insists that one must actually speak of 'normative openness'.

[22] R Lempert, 'The Autonomy of Law: Two Visions Compared' in G Teubner (ed), *Autopoietic Law: A New Approach to Law and Society* (Berlin, de Gruyter, 1987) 152–190; 178.

elements it needs to be able 'to determine whether certain conditions have been met or not'. Thus, normative closure is all about the 'self-continuation [of the system] in difference to the environment' while cognitive openness 'serves the coordination of this process with the system's environment'.[23] For the rest of society, normative closure means simply that it is able to determine in advance whether something will be legal or illegal. For some, this will seem like an almost absurdly attenuated role for law, but for Luhmann this represents a significant achievement in the evolution of functionally differentiated modern society.[24] (That should not, of course, be taken to mean that Luhmann has a normative objective in view: his theory is evolutionary not evolutionist.)[25] The alternative would be that for every planned conduct, society would be unable to determine in advance whether that conduct would become an issue for law, and, if it would, what the attitude of law towards it would be. The stultifying effects on society are easy to imagine. In Luhmann's terms such a situation would involve everything being determined at the level of cognition, on the basis of ongoing experience, as opposed to the level of normativity.

With this picture of law in mind, it is then necessary to examine some of the consequences. Put at its simplest, if law is normatively closed and cognitively open, this means that information is not transferred from it to other social subsystems nor vice versa. As each system makes selections on the basis of its own binary code so it constructs its own reality, produces information internally. This does not mean that there is no connection with the world outside the system, only that it now becomes necessary to substantially modify our understanding of causality:

> a system creates its own past as its own causal basis, which enables it to gain distance from the causal pressure of the environment without already determining through internal causality what will occur in confrontations with external events.[26]

It certainly does not mean that law can get by without society. As Luhmann puts it, the 'legal system for its part is probably more dependent than any other subsystem on receiving impulses . . . from interaction systems with other functional orientations'.[27] But those impulses do not mean that law is simply at the mercy of society; law itself will make selections on the basis of its own binary code. And by the same token, just as society 'needs' law to stabilise normative expectations, so this does not mean that other subsystems are in some sense con-

[23] N Luhmann, 'The Unity of the Legal System', above n 7 at 20; see also N Luhmann, 'The Self-Production of Law and its Limits' in G Teubner (ed), *Dilemmas of Law in the Welfare State* (Berlin, de Gruyter, 1985) 111–127;113–114.

[24] N Luhmann, *Social Systems* (Stanford California, Stanford University Press, 1995) 332–334.

[25] On this distinction, see E Blankenberg, 'The Poverty of Evolutionism: A Critique of Teubner's Case for "Reflexive law"' (1984) 18 *Law and Society Review* 273; and G Teubner, 'Autopoiesis in Law and Society: A Rejoinder to Blankenburg' (1984) 18 *Law and Society Review* 291.

[26] N Luhmann, *Social Systems*, above n 24 at 41; see also N Luhmann, 'Closure and Openness', above n 3, 335–336.

[27] N Luhmann, 'Communications about Law in Interaction Systems', in K Knorr-Cetina and AV Cicourel (eds), *Advances in Social Theory and Methodology: Toward and Integration of Micro- and Macro-Sociologies* (Boston, Routledge & Kegan Paul, 1981) 234–256; 246.

trollable by law; they too will make selections on the basis of their own binary codes: 'the operational mode of self-referential systems changes into forms of causality that to a large extent reliably prevent it from being steered from outside.'[28] Society for Luhmann is not, then, composed of mutually indifferent, solipsistic communicative realms, but nor is it composed of open systems susceptible to deterministic analysis and intervention.

Such an understanding of law and society has implications for how the various subsystems operate, how they achieve and maintain operational closure. The importance of binary codes has already been touched upon, but these cannot be the end of the story if autopoiesis is taken seriously. The drawing of distinctions between system and environment on the basis of such a code inevitably entails a paradox. For law, this is the question of why its own binary code is not applied to itself. Operationally, the answer is that to do so would risk the viability of the system,[29] but the question is then how to avoid coming into contact with that foundational paradox. The answer for Luhmann is that the legal system develops ways of concealing the paradox so that it appears as if its operations are not in fact based on self-reference. In other words, the system develops means of deparadoxification.[30]

It is clear that the legal system could not rely on its binary code alone to achieve deparadoxification. Something else is needed, and in Luhmann's approach this is the *programme*. Whereas a system's code is invariant (and thus to change code is to change system), its programmes can change. As King and Thornhill express it, 'programmes are able to give the impression of incorporating universality, finality or perfection by reconstructing them within the legal system.'[31] In short, programmes define what is 'correctly' legal and 'correctly' illegal.[32]

It is in the discussion of programmes that we approach most directly the limits of law with regard to social engineering that have become such a contentious aspect of Luhmann's work, and which in turn have spawned the debate on reflexive law. Insisting on his view of law's function as being concerned solely with the stabilisation of normative expectations over time, Luhmann is clear that law cannot be interested in such questions as whether law has produced intended societal effects beyond that basic functional requirement. It is a matter of indifference to law that the expectations were disappointed. It is precisely this ability on the part of law to hold firm in the face of disappointment that allows society to avoid the stultifying effects of continuously being thrown back on experience, on cognitive as opposed to normative learning. Law is able to hold

[28] N Luhmann, *Social Systems*, above n 24 at 41.

[29] N Luhmann, 'Law as a Social System', (1989) 83 *Northwestern University Law Review* 136; 145.

[30] N Luhmann, 'The Third Question: The Creative use of Paradoxes in Law and Legal History' (1988) 15 *Journal of Law and Society* 153.

[31] M King and C Thornhill, *Niklas Luhmann's Theory of Politics and Law*, above n 5 at 60.

[32] N Luhmann, 'The Coding of the Legal System', above n 2 at 171–2.

this line because it operates on the basis of conditional programmes, that is, on the basis of programmes of the form 'if *x*, then *y*'. 'Legal decisions do not lose their validity if the future falsifies the prediction inherent in them'.[33]

Problems arise, however, when law is increasingly instrumentalised by politics. This shift in the orientation of law was already evident to Max Weber, whose observations about the materialisation of law[34] have influenced a variety of different strands in the debate on the appropriate direction for law in contemporary conditions.[35] For Luhmann, the issue is that whereas law operates on the basis of conditional programmes, politics operates on the basis of purposive programmes. Whereas a conditional programme immunises, as it were, the legal system against the potentially negative effects of disappointed expectations, purposive programmes stand or fall on the basis of whether the expectations they generate are met. The consequences for politics of the disappointment of purposive programmes are clear and accepted: they produce pressure on government to perform better and, in the ultimate, can lead to the loss of power. The political system itself, however, is not adversely affected. The same cannot be said for the legal system. It is true that Luhmann has pointed to the fact that law does not directly apply purposive programmes, but rather 'nests' them in conditional programmes,[36] but he is nonetheless concerned about the consequences for law. When law is used in an attempt to achieve the desired ends of purposive programmes the picture is clouded and 'the "natural" order of the genesis of law is reversed'.[37] The shift towards the legislature and away from adjudication entailed by this reversal signals 'a new primacy of cognitive over normative considerations' which means that 'we are lucky if [law] nevertheless remains able to fulfil its own societal function'.[38] The increasing instrumentalisation of law may be understandable as politics tries to compensate for the loss of control that is the inevitable side-effect of functional differentiation, but 'including the desired result, in spite of all risks, in the normative framework of law, contributes unavoidably to overstrain'.[39] Perhaps the clearest example of this overstrain is in the increasingly all-consuming field of risk. The point of a norm is to stipulate how individuals should behave in the future. That in turn implies that one *knows* how they should behave in the future. With risk issues, however, that is precisely what one does not know. The normative structure, accordingly, is simply not well adapted to deal with risk, and yet it is to norms—to law—that politics almost feels compelled to turn in the face of ever-increasing

[33] N Luhmann, 'The Unity of the Legal System', above n 7 at 118.

[34] M Weber, *Economy and Society* (Berkeley, University of California Press, 1978) 333ff.

[35] For example, J Habermas, *Between Facts and Norms*, above n 16, 392ff; G Teubner, 'Substantive and Reflexive Elements in Modern Law', (1983) 17 *Law and Society Review* 239.

[36] See the discussion in M King and C Thornhill, *Niklas Luhmann's Theory of Politics and Law*, above n 5 at 62–63.

[37] N Luhmann, 'The Unity of the Legal System', above n 7 at 28.

[38] N Luhmann, 'The Self-Production of Law', above n 23 at 119.

[39] *Ibid* 124.

demands to deal with risk.[40]

However persuasive the example of risk may be in highlighting the problems facing law when it is instrumentalised, it is nevertheless the case that there is an intuitive feeling that law cannot be as powerless as Luhmann's analysis seems to imply. Is regulatory failure inevitable? Is regulatory success unthinkable? Luhmann answers both questions in the negative, but insists that success and failure must be understood in a different way to the assumptions underpinning law as a political instrument of social change. Although each social subsystem constructs information on the basis of its own distinctions, it is nevertheless the case that when the same event is selected by different systems this can produce 'extremely close relationships between system and environment'. This 'structural coupling' or 'twofold membership of events' in various subsystems can certainly exist within society, albeit only 'occasionally'.[41] Nor should we expect too much in terms of law's ability to produce change in other systems by means of such structural coupling. Since information 'is nothing but selection exclusively internal to the system', there is no guarantee that the same event will be processed as information by the different systems. And, beyond that, 'the surprise value of one and the same event differs in different systems'.[42] There may, therefore, be something that *looks* like regulatory success, but this will have been the result of the rather precarious and by no means controllable or predictable mechanism of structural coupling.

REFLEXIVE LAW?

It is against the backdrop of this challenging account of society and of law's place within it that the concept of reflexive law has been developed. It is important to stress, however, that reflexive law has not emerged simply as a response to Luhmann's approach to society as composed of autopoietic subsystems. Its genesis is somewhat more complicated. Max Weber's observations on the materialisation of law have already been mentioned, and it is impossible to understand reflexive law without placing it in the context of a Weberian account of the evolution of law.[43]

In the classical liberal state of the nineteenth century, law, for Weber, was characterised by its *formal* orientation. The state played what Adam Smith described as a 'night-watchman' role, deploying law so as to provide a minimal framework within which individual and corporate actors could regularise the

[40] N Luhmann, *Risk: A Sociological Theory* (Berlin and New York, Walter de Gruyter, 1993) 59. For a discussion, see J Paterson, 'Trans-science, Trans-law and Proceduralization', (2003) 12 *Social and Legal Studies* 525.

[41] N Luhmann, 'Closure and Openness' above n 3 at 342.

[42] *Ibid* 343.

[43] See also G Bechmann, 'Reflexive Law: A New Theory Paradigm for Legal Science?' in G Teubner and A Febbrajo (eds), *State, Law and Economy as Autopoietic Systems,* above n 2, 417–434; 423.

social (and especially economic) relationships they chose to enter into. The key form of law was, of course, the contract. This could itself be understood as a minimal framework within which the actors in a given relationship could construct detailed provisions relating to their respective rights and obligations. The state would provide the means by which contracts could be enforced, but (beyond some minimal rules) would not be concerned with their content. This bourgeois conception of law was, of course, closely related to the dominant liberal economic rationality, which assumed that the unfettered operation of the market would ensure a rational distribution of goods.[44]

That this assumption was flawed became clear already (and perhaps especially) in the context of the industrialisation that was one of the most striking achievements of the liberal state. Even economics began to recognise that the operation of the market produced negative externalities, that the privity of contracts was not well adapted to cope, that it was not always (or ever) possible to assign a monetary value to social costs.[45] Problems such as these led to demands for the state to respond, which in turn led it away from the minimal role it had previously performed and towards ever greater intervention in an attempt to correct so-called market failures. This led to the instrumentalisation of law by politics as the latter sought to achieve solutions for the problems with which it was increasingly confronted. Reaching its fullest expression in the welfare state, this *substantive* or *material* orientation of law was dependent for its success on the ability of science (natural and social) to provide politics both with adequate explanations of societal problems and adequate tools and techniques for their solution.[46]

In more recent years, of course, a considerable literature has emerged on the apparent failure, even crisis, of the welfare state.[47] As regards the legal dimension of the welfare state, this literature has naturally focused on the problems facing substantive law. At its most basic, attention has been directed to the practical difficulties facing prescriptive or command-and-control regulation.[48] The response to these difficulties has largely been two-fold. On the one hand, there has been a call to deregulate, to lift the regulatory burden—in short to regain the advantages of the formal orientation of law.[49] On the other hand, the prescription has been to bolster regulation, to provide more resources, better information, stronger enforcement—in short to keep faith with the substantive orientation.[50] The danger of a vicious circle here is obvious.

It is to this supposedly sterile debate between the adherents of two apparently

[44] M Weber, *Economy and Society*, above n 34 at 333ff.

[45] For a discussion, see RJ Pierce Jr, *Economic Regulation* (Cincinnati, Anderson, 1994).

[46] M Weber, *Economy and Society*, above n 34 at 392ff.

[47] Perhaps most famously, J Habermas, *Legitimation Crisis* (Boston, Beacon Press, 1975).

[48] R Stewart, 'Regulation, Innovation and Administrative Law: A Conceptual Framework' (1981) 69 *California Law Review* 1259.

[49] In politics, of course, this reached its zenith in the 1980s with Reaganomics and Thatcherism.

[50] Very broadly speaking, the Democratic or socialist opponents of the neo-liberal agenda in the 1980s could be said to have preferred this approach.

discredited paradigms of law that a number of third alternatives have offered their contributions.[51] Going by a range of more or less exotic names, including the procedural paradigm,[52] contextual proceduralisation,[53] and reflexive law,[54] they have sought to break the vicious circle and to offer something distinct from formal and substantive law that is capable of coping with contemporary conditions. Each of these alternatives is influenced by Weber's account of the evolution of law, but its precise nature depends very much upon the particular theoretical understanding of contemporary conditions upon which it is based. For the procedural paradigm, this is the colonisation of the lifeworld by, for example, administrative power as proposed by Habermas, which in turn produces a prescription based on the theory of communicative action.[55] For contextual proceduralisation, it is the inadequacy of the epistemological presuppositions underpinning traditional modes of governance, which in turn leads to a prescription in terms of an increase in 'the "reflexivity" of our forms for the governance of collective action, both at the level of its institutional arrangements and at that of the actors involved'.[56] And for reflexive law, of course, this is the account of functionally differentiated modern society provided by Luhmann, which in turn leads to a prescription in terms of an orientation of law which is aware of the double contingency of the situation it finds itself in.[57]

Focusing as we are on reflexive law, the question, then, is whether in the context of a society composed of autopoietic subsystems it is possible to envisage a new orientation or paradigm of law that respects the various limits laid down by the theory, including law's function of stabilising normative expectations over time, the necessity for law to maintain its deparadoxifying strategies, and the constraints of structural coupling. To say that this is a tall order is a considerable understatement.

In terms of what is sought, this might succinctly be expressed as a matter of 'establishing patterned connections between a system and external interventions in spite of the "inner-directedness" of systemic processes' or of coupling 'different sequences of events in order to arrive at concerted action and intelligible interaction'.[58] In this regard, Gunther Teubner has put forward the most ambi-

[51] Politically, the analogue would be the Third Way, much discussed but little explained by Blair and Clinton in the 1990s. See also A Giddens, *The Third Way: The Renewal of Social Democracy* (Cambridge, Polity Press, 1998); and A Giddens, *The Third Way and its Critics* (Cambridge, Polity Press, 2000).

[52] J Habermas, *Between Facts and Norms*, above n 16.

[53] J Lenoble and M Maesschalck, *Toward a Theory of Governance: The Action of Norms* (The Hague, London, New York, Kluwer Law International, 2003).

[54] G Teubner, *Law as an Autopoietic System* above n 9; H Willke, 'Political Intervention' above n 10.

[55] J Habermas, *The Theory of Communicative Action* (vols 1 and 2) (Cambridge, Polity Press, 1986 and 1989).

[56] J Lenoble and M Maesschalck, *Toward a Theory of Governance*, above n 53, 319. See also J Lenoble, *Droit et Communication* (Paris, Cerf, 1994).

[57] G Teubner, *Law as an Autopoietic System* above n 9; H Willke, 'Political Intervention' above n 10.

tious and most elaborated proposal. In the earliest statement of the concept he was at pains to locate reflexive law in relation to formal and substantive law. Thus, he suggested that reflexive law 'shares with substantive law the notion that focused intervention in social processes is within the domain of law, but it retreats from taking full responsibility for substantive outcomes'.[59] There is an apparent normative dimension when Teubner goes on to claim that such an approach 'is justified by the desirability of coordinating recursively determined forms of social coordination',[60] but it would presumably be possible to argue that this is not inconsistent with Luhmann's own view of law's function.

Reflexive law thus appears to succeed in distinguishing itself from substantive law. At first glance, however, it might nevertheless be open to the criticism that it looks very like a reformalisation of law, a return to the paradigm of the classical liberal state, but Teubner counters this critique by suggesting that it 'does not merely adapt to or support "natural social orders" . . . but searches for "regulated autonomy" '.[61] That might have been expected to quieten such critics (although in fact it has not), but it does raise the question of whether this is still compatible with Luhmann's theoretical account. Doubts in this regard are only heightened when Teubner goes on to describe the external social functions of reflexive law as being 'to structure and restructure semi-autonomous social systems . . . by shaping both their procedures of internal discourse and their methods of coordination with other social systems' and to facilitate 'integrative processes within a functionally differentiated society'.[62] This looks to have transgressed some of Luhmann's boundaries until Teubner clarifies that the means by which reflexive law achieves these ends are indirect and abstract and involve fostering 'mechanisms that systematically *further the development of reflexion structures within other social subsystems*'.[63] Quite what these indirect and abstract means might be remains to be seen, but it is possible to note at this point one key area in which Teubner has departed from Luhmann's theory, namely in proposing that systems can be 'semi-autonomous', a point we will return to in due course.

In the next development of the concept of reflexive law, Teubner stays close

[58] H Willke, 'Societal Guidance through Law?' in G Teubner and A Febbrajo (eds), *State, Law and Economy as Autopoietic Systems*, above n 2, 353–387; 377–378.

[59] G Teubner, 'Substantive and Reflexive Elements', above n 35 at 254.

[60] *Ibid.* To this extent, the critique by writers such as Bechmann (that reflexive law reveals a continuing desire for control) or Van Seters (that reflexive law seems to need some conception of purpose) loses its sting. See G Bechmann, 'Reflexive Law', above n 43, 423; and P Van Seters, 'Law and Purpose' in G Teubner and A Febbrajo (eds), *State, Law and Economy as Autopoietic Systems*, above n 2, 435–450; 450. Rehbinder is thus closer to the mark when he notes that the 'innovation' of reflexive law lies in the 'focus of intervention'; E Rehbinder, 'Reflexive Law and Practice: The Corporate Officer for Environmental Protection as an Example', in G Teubner and A Febbrajo (eds), *State, Law and Economy as Autopoietic Systems*, above n 2, 579–608; 582.

[61] G Teubner, 'Substantive and Reflexive Elements', above n 35 at 254.

[62] *Ibid*, 255.

[63] *Ibid*, 275, emphasis in original.

to Luhmann when he proposes that substantive law inevitably fails insofar as it 'does not conform to the conditions of the "structural coupling" of law, politics and society' and thus faces what he terms the regulatory trilemma: the incongruence of law, politics and society; the over-legalisation of society; or the over-socialisation of law.[64] He again seeks to reassure when he speaks of reflexive law as being concerned with 'the external support of self-referentiality', and identifies three dimensions of reflexive law as autonomy, externalisation and coordination.[65]

An indication of how reflexive law could operate comes when Teubner reminds us that structural coupling 'as such leads only to transitory structural changes'. Such tangential responses between law and other social subsystems can, however, become 'epidemic', as it were, when 'linkage institutions are evolving that are responsible for the duration, intensity, and quality of structural coupling'.[66] In other words, it may be said that reflexive law seeks in some sense to *enhance* the structural coupling of law and other subsystems, which Luhmann identified as merely occasional and precarious. It thus seems clear that Teubner has identified the one area in Luhmann's theoretical account where it would be at all possible to conceive of reflexive law. It is a question, however, whether once the ambition is translated into some concrete programme it does not itself end up transgressing the boundaries of structural coupling and itself confronting the regulatory trilemma.

How Teubner proposes to develop the concept of reflexive law becomes clearer in due course when he suggests three possible approaches: mutual or reciprocal observation; coupling through interference; and communication via organisation.[67] In a more recent statement (with the present author) on reflexive law as it relates to what may be termed regulatory situations, however, four 'scenarios' are offered: tangential response; bifurcation and attractors; synchronising difference reduction; and binding institutions.[68] Of these latter four alternatives, two map fairly readily on to the previous tripartite arrangement, while tangential response and synchronising difference reduction appear as new additions.[69] In what follows each of these will be considered in turn to see whether it remains within the boundaries established in Luhmann's theoretical account, and, if not, where and to what extent it crosses them.

[64] G Teubner, 'After Legal Instrumentalism', above n 13, 386–387.

[65] *Ibid*, 389ff.

[66] G Teubner, 'The Two Faces of Janus: Rethinking Legal Pluralism' (1992) 13 *Cardozo Law Review* 1443; 1458.

[67] G Teubner, 'Social Order', above n 17, 622; and especially G Teubner, *Law as an Autopoietic System*, above n 9.

[68] J Paterson and G Teubner, 'Changing Maps: Empirical Legal Autopoiesis' (1998) 7 *Social and Legal Studies* 451; 474–479.

[69] There is an argument for separating bifurcation and attractors from coupling through interference, but they are dealt with together here because of the common dependence on the concept of interference.

Tangential response.

Of the now five alternatives for reflexive law, this is the one that adheres most closely to Luhmann's account. In this case, faced with evidence that substantive regulation is unsuccessful, the response of the legal system is to abandon any attempt to 'establish stable structures in the regulated area' and instead to try only 'punctual interventions' on a sort of trial-and-error basis 'until the regulated area has moved somewhat' in the desired direction. There is no attempt here on the part of law to recontextualise the response of the 'regulated' area as anything other than unpredictable and thus no attempt to impose social objectives in anything like the way that political purposive programmes assume to be possible. Insofar as Teubner suggests that we can 'talk of reflexive law if, and only if, the legal system identifies itself as an autopoietic system in a world of autopoietic systems and faces up to the consequences',[70] then tangential response seems to represent the purest possible form. But insofar as it is the form least likely to offend against Luhmann's account (though even that must remain open to question, as we shall see in due course), it is equally the form that is most likely to upset those who want law to continue to be understood as a tool for social engineering. While 'tangential response' might be an adequate way of characterising the 'interventions' of central banks in currency markets and national economies, even reflexive law's proponents are concerned that the sort of trial-and-error approach implied here looks irresponsible in the face of the sorts of problems society faces, for example, with regard to technological risk issues, and call for a stronger form of structural coupling.[71]

Reciprocal or mutual observation.

Albeit that this form of reflexive law offers something more than the tangential response model, it does not represent a very much stronger form of structural coupling. The advance here is that instead of simply recontextualising the response of the regulated area as unpredictable, the legal system adopts a stance of second-order observation in which it 'reconstructs the self-reference of the observed system'.[72] This remains 'a highly indirect form of regulation', insofar as it attempts no more than the deliberate increase of 'possibilities for variation

[70] G Teubner, *Law as an Autopoietic* System, above n 9, 69.

[71] J Paterson and G Teubner, 'Changing Maps', above n 68 at 475.

[72] G Teubner, *Law as an Autopoietic* System, above n 9 at 80. Teubner thus also deals with Deggau's concerns about introducing reflection as a new control principle given the closure of autopoietic subsystems; H-G Deggau, 'Identity, Reflection and Control in the Legal System' in G Teubner and A Febbrajo (eds), *State, Law and Economy as Autopoietic Systems*, above n 2, 451–481; 470. The claim made is no stronger than the reconstruction of the observed system's self-reference. As Teubner stresses elsewhere, autopoietic closure excludes the possibility of one system's taking part in the autopoiesis of another; G Teubner, 'Social Order', above n 17 at 618.

within the law' and thereby to influence the co-evolution of law and other social subsystems.[73] Assume, for example, that health and safety regulators confronting a complex industry observe that the regulated area itself observes not on the basis of the legal binary code but rather on the basis of the economic binary code. In other words, they observe that the operation of a given technology is not driven by whether or not a given practice is 'legal', but rather by how it affects payment or non-payment. In such circumstances, the regulators would be prompted to abandon any too simplistic, linear causal or deterministic model of the implementation of regulations and to consider instead how any given regulatory signal might appear on the screens of the regulated area. It does not take too much imagination to see that this might produce a distinctively different approach to regulation—and, importantly, one that does not simply coincide with what might be proposed by the economic analysis of law. Despite the new approach that this variant of reflexive law opens up, it nevertheless once again appears to respect Luhmann's theoretical account, doing no more than building on the operation of observation, and in particular, *Verstehen*.

Coupling through interference or 'bifurcation and attractors'.

This alternative appears to mark a definite departure from Luhmann's account insofar as the concept of *interference* is one developed by Teubner. Whether this concept nevertheless remains compatible with Luhmann's theory is the question. 'Interference is a bridging mechanism whereby social systems get beyond self-observation and link up with each other through one and the same communicative event'.[74] By making use of this interference it is suggested that it would be possible to 'probe for sensitive "intervention points" which will provoke the desired instability' and move the regulated system from its existing attractor state into one compatible with the aims of the legal system.[75] One way in which this probing might be carried out would be by means of an 'option policy'.[76] For example, consider the recently published Basel II Framework for capital adequacy in banking.[77] In contrast to the previous arrangement—the 1988 Basel Capital Accord, which prescribed a simple uniform standard—the new framework allows banks to choose from three different approaches to the calculation of minimum capital. These range from the Standardised Approach (which envisages an institution using external measures of credit risk in the calculation of regulatory capital), through the Foundation Internal Ratings-Based Approach (which allows a bank to use its own measures of

[73] G Teubner, *Law as an Autopoietic System*, above n 9 at 82.
[74] *Ibid*, 86.
[75] J Paterson and G Teubner, 'Changing Maps', above n 68 at 475.
[76] G Teubner, *Law as an Autopoietic System*, above n 9 at 93–95.
[77] Basel Committee on Banking Supervision, *International Convergence of Capital Measurement and Capital Standards: A Revised Framework* (Basel, Bank for International Settlements, 2004).

Probability of Default but to rely on supervisory measures of other risk components), to the Advanced Internal Ratings-Based Approach (which allows an institution to provide its own measures for more of the risk components used in the calculation of regulatory capital, such as Loss Given Default and Exposure at Default). Each higher level of approach requires more sophisticated risk measurement and management techniques but offers the opportunity for a bank to reduce the amount of capital it is required to maintain and thus to make the most efficient use of its assets. Banks are free to choose an approach, subject to its appropriateness for the complexity of their business and their ability to utilise it. In each case, however, the regulator is attempting to move the institution towards an attractor state of reduced risk without compromising its ability to maximise the efficient use of its assets.[78] At first sight, the concept of interference looks very similar to Luhmann's account of structural coupling. This is especially so when Teubner indicates that this 'bridging mechanism' is possible because the subsystems all use the same 'basic stuff', that is, meaning; they all develop on the basis of the same elementary operations, that is, communication; and most importantly because 'all forms of specialised communication within any subsystem are also at the same time forms of general societal communication'.[79] Nevertheless, Teubner insists that something more is intended here and that his description of interference is different from Luhmann's account of the materiality continuum.[80] Whereas the emergence of social systems from the substratum of the materiality continuum involves the emergence of something entirely new, this is not the case with regard to the differentiation of social subsystems within the broader social system.[81] This argument certainly has some force, but it is then a question of whether in defining interference, Teubner has done no more than to claim more from structural coupling than Luhmann allows. If that is the case, of course, it then becomes a question of whether that claim is nevertheless justified. There may, however, be another objection to this particular approach to reflexive law. This relates to the apparent challenge that the probing for sensitive intervention points or an option policy mounts to law's function of the stabilisation of normative expectations. Teubner is aware of this, but suggests that the advantages of such an approach should not be overlooked. He stresses, for example, that it takes seriously the evolution of other subsystems. We could also mention that even in a non-reflexive regulatory model there is often de facto optional regulation, with systems responding to those that are in some sense attractive and ignoring others, while the similarly

[78] For a discussion see J Tanega and P Bonisch, 'Basel II: Avoiding Regulatory Failure', Paper presented at the International Conference on Global Risk and Emerging Markets, Centre for the Study of Emerging Markets, Westminster Business School, University of Westminster, London, 11–12 June 2004.

[79] G Teubner, *Law as an Autopoietic System*, above n 9 at 93–95.

[80] N Luhmann, 'Closure and Openness', above n 3, 338.

[81] G Teubner, *Law as an Autopoietic System*, above n 9 at 87.

flexible approach of regulators has also been documented.[82] Furthermore, Teubner seeks to dispel fears about optional regulation and indeed to deal with the problems facing even non-reflexive regulation by suggesting that an option policy could equally stipulate that among the options available one must be chosen and that opting out is not an option.[83]

Communication through organisation or binding institutions.

The idea here is that the different communicative subsystems 'are channelled parallel to each other' in a formal organisation that acts as a 'binding institution' with the aim of producing 'systematic effects' through the need for the different subsystems to be 'compatible with each other'.[84] One example of this is 'intra-organisational juridification' where 'organisational processes are legally reconstructed in such a way that they themselves become sources of law'.[85] What such a binding institution thus seeks to achieve is a close structural coupling of law and the other subsystems channelled through the organisation. It may be possible (and indeed fruitful) to understand the use of Safety Cases and Safety Management Systems in the regulation of complex high-technology industries as an example of this approach to reflexive law. This development first of all sees regulations *setting goals* with respect to safety rather than *prescribing how* technological processes should be operated. It then places the emphasis on the regulated to justify (or make the case for) the safety of the precise operational approach that they adopt. Finally, it requires that the regulated adopt a Safety Management System, which integrates the disparate elements of the complex whole, encouraging them, as it were, to be 'compatible with each other', rather than pulling in different and potentially dangerous directions.[86] Insofar as this approach does no more than build on structural coupling it seems not to transgress Luhmann's account. The only caveats—by no means insignificant—would be, firstly, that there is no guarantee that the establishment of the formal organisation itself would not fall foul of the regulatory trilemma, and, secondly, that there is once again an apparent risk to the function of law in stabilising expectations insofar as the organisational processes can become sources of law.

[82] See, for example, R Cranston, *Regulating Business: Law and Consumer Agencies* (London, Macmillan, 1979); G Rhodes, *Inspectorates in British Government: Law Enforcement and Standards of Efficiency* (London, George Allen and Unwin, 1981); K Hawkins, *Environment and Enforcement: Regulation and the Social Definition of Pollution* (Oxford, Clarendon Press, 1983).

[83] G Teubner, *Law as an Autopoietic System*, above n 9 at 132–133.

[84] J Paterson and G Teubner, 'Changing Maps', above n 68 at 477.

[85] *Ibid*, 477.

[86] For a discussion, see J Paterson, *Behind the Mask: Regulating Health and Safety in Britain's Offshore Oil and Gas Industry* (Aldershot, Ashgate-Dartmouth, 2000).

Synchronising difference reduction.

This last proposed model of reflexive law is derived from a particular understanding of programmes within Luhmann's theory. Because all information is constructed internally by the autopoietic subsystems, any societal steering that they try to achieve (for example, via the purposive programmes of the political system) can only ever be *self*-steering. This is because any steering attempts can only be directed at the system's environment which is itself internally constructed. The steering itself is understood as the minimisation of a difference. All steering, whether discussed in autopoietic terms or otherwise, can be defined in this way. In autopoiesis, however, the difference to be minimised, between the current direction and the desired direction, is also internally produced. The 'problem' and the 'solution' identified by a purposive programme, therefore, are both constructs of the political system and the programme itself is the means by which the system seeks to minimise the difference between them.[87] This deepens our understanding of programmes, but it does not at first sight seem to offer anything particularly new to reflexive law inasmuch as it appears to constitute no more than another account of the operational closure of social subsystems and, accordingly, of the impossibility of social engineering. Tantalisingly, however, Luhmann raises the possibility of being able to influence the self-steering of another system. Specifically, this is a matter first of all of observing how the other system works,[88] an approach that does not seem far removed from the most indirect forms of reflexive law, such as reciprocal observation. Before social engineers get too carried away, however, Luhmann reminds them that the observation of the operation of the other system can only be carried out on the basis of the 'steering' system's own distinctions, but this comes as no surprise to the proponents of reflexive law who would not claim otherwise. The question, now, however, is whether something more than reciprocal observation can be achieved on the basis of this understanding of programmes as self-steering programmes. The proposal is that when 'several differences are minimised simultaneously they will partially reinforce and partially sabotage each other'. Law's self-steering cannot, of course, impose new programmes in other subsystems. But 'the regulatory messages' constituted by law's difference minimisation programme 'are re-read, re-constructed and recontextualised' by those other subsystems. Among the possible difference minimisation or self-steering programmes available in the other subsystems, these regulatory messages 'may make one . . . much more costly, or produce incentives for another one'. Accordingly, 'systematic control results' may occur 'in the critical case when self-regulation processes in different social fields tend to work in the same direction and thus reinforce each other'. In case there is any concern that here the

[87] See N Luhmann, 'Limits of Steering' above n 18; and J Paterson, 'An Introduction to Luhmann' (1997) 14 *Theory, Culture and Society* 37.

[88] N Luhmann, 'Limits of Steering', above n 18 at 54.

proponents of reflexive law have overstepped the most basic mark in autopoiesis, they quickly seek to reassure by adding: 'Some might call this coincidence effectiveness of law and attribute it to causal processes'.[89] An example of such an approach might be the requirement by regulators in the context of complex, high technology industries, that the regulated utilise quantified risk assessment as a key component of their Safety Case for the operation of a given site or installation. Coupled with a requirement that risks to safety must be reduced to a level that is as low as reasonably practicable, this subtle approach does not involve the regulator in an attempt to impose a different self-steering programme on the regulated area. Rather, because the regulated must now be explicit about assumptions and uncertainties in the calculation of risk relative to their operations, it seeks to make it difficult for programmes that increase risk to survive because they become difficult to justify in terms of quantified risk assessment.[90] This approach to reflexive law, accordingly, is certainly a variant of reciprocal observation but it focuses the attention of the observing system very directly not only on the distinction drawn by the other system (code), but importantly also on the differences it constructs and attempts to minimise (programme). Once again, of course, there is no suggestion that such observation escapes the limitations of being based on the distinctions drawn by the observing system, but the suggestion is that such observation, by taking account not only of double contingency but also of the specific self-steering programme of the observed system, has a better chance of achieving a more adequately complex picture of the environment.

REFLECTING ON REFLEXIVE LAW

If we try to sum up the position we have now arrived at, it might be suggested that reflexive law as proposed by Teubner (and also by the present author) endeavours by and large to stay within the confines of autopoiesis theory as Luhmann has developed it. It is explicitly concerned with defining law that is aware both of its own autopoiesis and that of the other social subsystems it purports to regulate. There are times when, as the proponents readily admit, there are obvious clashes with Luhmann's account, specifically when Teubner insists on degrees of autonomy and where there is reliance upon the concept of interference. Perhaps surprisingly, however, it is possibly easier to deal with these issues than with some others. As regards the question of degrees of closure, for example, it is possible to avoid a conflict by looking to see whether any of the suggested models of reflexive law depend upon something less than autopoiesis in order to be able to operate as the proponents intend. The answer is that they do not. In each case the models proceed on the basis that both the 'regulating'

[89] J Paterson and G Teubner, 'Changing Maps', above n 68 at 476.

[90] See J Paterson, *Behind the Mask*, above n 86.

and the 'regulated' subsystems are autopoietic. There is certainly a debate to be had about the 'rigid inflexibility' of Luhmann's approach to autopoiesis as opposed to Teubner's understanding of social autopoiesis as 'merely a special case of social autonomy',[91] but it is not, as it turns out, directly relevant to a consideration of reflexive law. Similarly with interference—although this is a concept that does not appear in Luhmann's account, we have seen above that it is possible to view this as only a slightly more ambitious reading of structural coupling. The question of the justification of that reading, assuming that it turns out to be too much more ambitious to remain comfortably associated with structural coupling, remains—but for present purposes we can give it the benefit of the doubt.

Lest it be thought that as an acknowledged proponent of reflexive law I am guilty of engaging in a self-justificatory whitewash of the concept, let me clarify that I am dealing with these admitted divergences from Luhmann's account so rapidly because I believe that the real problems for reflexive law in the context of that account of autopoiesis lie elsewhere.

Much more problematical, for example, is the proposal of an 'option policy' which is admitted to represent a challenge to law's function of stabilising expectations. One can defend the options approach at a practical level—especially where it includes the stipulation denying any opt out—not least on the basis of historical precedent. Did not the Normans following the Conquest achieve the uniform application of the King's justice throughout England, not by imposing it by force but by offering it as an option to indigenous local justice? The challenge to the normative function of law does not thereby disappear however. Nor is it only the option policy that faces problems in this regard. It looks as if it may also confront binding institutions where organisational processes can become sources of law. And even the less 'interventionist' approaches to reflexive law are not immune. Synchronising difference reduction, reciprocal observation and even tangential response may also offend here insofar as they still envisage law being utilised to achieve purposive programmes, albeit that these are always qualified as indirect. Does reflexive law, therefore, inevitably throw society back on cognitive learning? One solution may be that reflexive law could be nested within conditional programmes, just as Luhmann has suggested purposive programmes can be. Thus, even where reflexive law results in other subsystems apparently challenging law's function of stabilising expectations, the risks to both law and the wider society associated with such a shift could be minimised by ensuring that the norms produced would still rely upon law with regard to their validity.[92] Luhmann has noted, of course, that attempts to respond to the 'polycontexturality of modern life' at the level of law's programmes results in

[91] G Teubner, *Law as an Autopoietic System*, above n 9 at 75–76.

[92] Coincidentally, this approach could also be used to deal with the problem that arises closer to home for reflexive law's proponents of the concept's failing to respect the limits of structural coupling and thus ironically falling foul of the regulatory trilemma, or the 'reflexive trilemma' as Rehbinder has termed it; Rehbinder, 'Reflexive Law and Practice', above n 60 at 586–587.

'vagueness, situation dependence and fluctuation'.[93] The question is, however, whether reflexive law programmes would fall foul of this objection. As Teubner has observed:

> Legal doctrine is still bound to the classical model of law as a body of rules enforceable through adjudication. The legal order lacks a conceptual apparatus adequate for the planning and social policy requirements that arise in the interrelations among specialised social subsystems.[94]

Similarly, Luhmann has noted that what is missing is:

> A conceptual system oriented towards social policy which would permit one to compare the consequences of different solutions to problems, to accumulate critical experience, to compare experience from different fields, in short: to learn.[95]

Could reflexive law constitute such a conceptual apparatus or conceptual system adequate to the challenges facing law in the context of functional differentiation? Might the nesting approach, as a consequence, prove unnecessary? Reflexive law cannot, therefore, necessarily be dismissed on this theoretical basis, however problematical it might appear. Rather, the possibility that reflexive law might constitute a significant evolution at the level of doctrine, which may have implications for law's function, becomes an empirical question. We will return to this point below.

Luhmann, however, raises a much more fundamental problem, one that calls into question the very possibility of reflexive law. It is all very well for Teubner to insist that we can 'talk of reflexive law if, and only if, the legal system identifies itself as an autopoietic system in a world of autopoietic systems and faces up to the consequences',[96] but this assumes that the legal system is actually capable of this task. Luhmann, for one, is not sure that it is. He wonders, for example, 'to what extent the theoretical apparatus of the legal system . . . is capable of perceiving and taking into account autopoietic systems in its environment'. [97] Before we even get to the question of law and politics instituting some programme of reflexive law, therefore, there is a prior problem of law's cognitive competence in this regard: 'if [law] must make indications with the aid of this distinction [legal/illegal] then what limits are thereby imposed on insight into the autopoiesis of environmental systems?'[98] Luhmann suggests that reflexive law can only be self-reflexive law and can thus 'only reinforce the self-sensitivity of law to its actual social conditions', although he concedes that 'even this is a great deal'.[99] He later goes so far as to suggest that reflexive law 'point[s]

[93] N Luhmann, 'The Coding of the Legal System', above n 2 at 176.
[94] G Teubner, 'Substantive and Reflexive Elements', above n 35 at 271.
[95] N Luhmann, 'Evolution des Rechts' (1970) 3 *Rechtstheorie* quoted in G Teubner, 'Substantive and Reflexive Elements', above n 35 at 264.
[96] G Teubner, *Law as an Autopoietic System*, above n 9 at 69.
[97] N Luhmann, 'Some Problems with Reflexive Law', above n 12 at 393.
[98] *Ibid*, 393–394.
[99] *Ibid*, 398.

in the right direction', but this does not change the fact that 'the question still remains of how the systems involved, and how in particular the legal system, will cope with the burdens of reflection which [reflexive law] implies'.[100] Specifically, the problem is that this 'reflection confronts the system with the paradoxicality to which it owes its existence.'[101]

And that in a nutshell is the fundamental problem that reflexive law faces. Its proponents may be able to produce answers to the other problems, but unless they can deal with that one, then all those efforts will count for nothing. If reflexive law implies an unavoidable catastrophic confrontation of the legal system with its foundational paradox, then the concept is dead in the water.

This looks serious, but all may not yet be lost. After all, law, in common with all of the other functional subsystems, has always had to develop strategies of deparadoxification. The challenge may now be greater, but that does not mean it is impossible. Unless, of course, there is something qualitatively different about a legal orientation that includes knowledge about the autopoietic nature of the system. Doesn't this make the process of deparadoxification itself paradoxical? In other words, is reflexive law a paradox too far? Or might some further creative use of this paradox evolve?

Luhmann himself (paradoxically!) may provide an answer here. He is clear, for example, that it is not necessary 'to risk the glance into paradoxicality'; rather, it is 'sufficient to develop thoughtful procedures for observing observation, with a special emphasis on that which, for the other, is a paradox and, therefore, cannot be observed by him'.[102] As regards law, however, can this be a task for law itself, or only for legal sociology? There are times when Luhmann appears to restrict it to the latter, but even then there are indications that he sees this sociological observation feeding through by way of legal training to correct the problems he perceives there. [103] At other times, however, it appears clearer that law itself could evolve in such a way as to deparadoxify even the paradox that reflexive law appears to present:

> if the assumption holds that there is always a primary necessity to avoid the paradox, there may be different ways to do so. In many ways the forms of deparadoxifying the paradox depend on conditions of social acceptability, and these conditions change with the transformations of the social system of the society. They depend on social structures and are therefore historical conditions.[104]

Further, in discussing the difficulties legal theory confronts in grasping 'the positive quality of law in the absence of any conception of an external . . . justification' he suggests that 'the theory of autopoietic systems offers at least

[100] *Ibid*, 411.

[101] *Ibid*, 411–412.

[102] N Luhmann, 'Sthenography' (1990) 7 *Stanford Literature Review* 133; 137.

[103] N Luhmann, 'The Sociological Observation of the Theory and Practice of Law', in A Febbrajo (ed), *European Yearbook of the Sociology of Law* (Milano, Guiffré, 1988) 23–42; 26.

[104] N Luhmann, 'The Third Question', above n 30 at 154.

the possibility of an adequate description'.[105] Importantly, however, he continues: 'Whether this description can be introduced into the legal system itself (ie, used as its self-description) must be left an open question (which means, left to evolution)'.[106] Could, then, law evolve (or, indeed, have already evolved) to a point where it has indeed included its own autopoiesis as its self-description? Discussing the epistemological consequences of autopoietic closure, Luhmann certainly does not exclude the possibility:

> If an autopoietic system observes autopoietic systems, it finds itself constrained by the conditions of autopoietic reproduction . . . and it includes itself in the fields of its objects, *because as an autopoietic system observing autopoietic systems, it cannot avoid gaining information about itself.*[107]

This, too, then, becomes an empirical problem. And, of course, for years the critics, and even those with a more open mind, have been complaining that empirical proof or demonstration is precisely what the adherents of autopoiesis and the proponents of reflexive law have failed to produce.[108] The obvious problem in this regard is that the theory does not seem to lend itself to empirical research. Some work has been done, however, with the point being made that while autopoiesis changes everything when it comes to empirical work—'research questions, the phenomena to be identified, the concepts to be made operational and the analytical instruments' as well as the very role of empirical research—it certainly does not preclude it.[109] Indeed, it appears to offer a means of resolving some of the problems facing contemporary legal theory and legal sociology.[110] These are all big claims, but empirical work informed by autopoiesis has begun to be done in the field of law and regulation.[111] And it should by now be clear that the focus of such work must not just be on the search for and demonstration of reflexive law as distinct from law's formal and substantive orientations, but also on the question of reflexive law's compatibility with the theory of autopoiesis and on what its emergence may tell us about law's evolution.

Even if it is clear, then, that reflexive law has an analytic status, the question remains as to whether it also has a normative one. In other words, irrespective of whether it turns out to be possible to demonstrate the evolution of law in the direction of reflexivity, would it be possible to propose reflexive models as a means of responding to perceived regulatory problems? Teubner is clear in this

[105] N Luhmann, 'Law as a Social System', above n 29 at 149.

[106] *Ibid*, 149.

[107] N Luhmann, 'The Autopoiesis of Social Systems', in F Geyer and J van der Zouwen (eds), *Sociocybernetic Paradoxes: Observation, Control and Evolution of Self-Steering Systems* (London and Beverly Hills, Sage, 1986) 172–192 at 186, emphasis added.

[108] For example, H Rottleuthner, 'The Limits of Law—The Myth of a Regulatory Crisis' (1989) 17 *International Journal of the Sociology of Law* 273; 281; WT Murphy, 'Systems of Systems: Some Issues in the Relationship between Law and Autopoiesis' (1994) 5 *Law and Critique* 241.

[109] J Paterson and G Teubner, 'Changing Maps', above n 68 at 452.

[110] *Ibid*, 452–455.

[111] J Paterson, *Behind the Mask*, above n 86.

regard that reflexive law does have a dual character 'as both normative and analytic',[112] allowing both 'empirical analyses of the historical position of law in society *plus* normative evaluation and choice of strategies'.[113] One thing is clear, however: the effects of any such efforts would not be predictable. (Of course, if the outcome should happen to look like reflexive law, some might call this coincidence the effectiveness of legal theory and legal sociology and attribute it to causal processes.)

Would Luhmann approve of such normative efforts? The last word is with him: 'There are few bases for being able to radically change whatever society one is living in. There are many bases for making better use of its possibilities'.[114]

[112] G Teubner, *Law as an Autopoietic System*, above n 9 at 69.
[113] G Teubner, 'Social Order', above n 17 at 612, emphasis in original.
[114] N Luhmann, 'The Coding of the Legal System', above n 2 at 182.

2

What's the Use of Luhmann's Theory?

MICHAEL KING

ONE OF THE difficulties that confront anyone trying to explain the importance of Luhmann's ideas on social systems to lawyers and policy-makers lies in their understandable requirement that social theories need to be *useful*. Useful, in this context, usually means that it is able to provide answers to legal and policy questions or, at the very least, point in the direction where these answers are to be found. Other theories about society and about people as social beings are useful, because from lawyers' perspectives they appear to be able to perform one or more of these tasks. Jurisprudence represents a body of principles, values and understandings many of which are useful to law and lawyers and legislators. But jurisprudence, as we know, is much closer to philosophy than to social theory. Its abstract nature means that established principles and values may seemingly be transformed into effective social policy and legal decisions by applying them to the facts of any social situation. It can tell us that treating unequals equally may be unjust, or that laws should be formulated for the general benefit of citizens, but legal and policy decisions always require some empirical input to identify who are unequal and what will be of benefit to citizens in every given situation.

Empirical social research applied to legal and policy issues is by definition useful. It reveals how the legal system is actually working in practice. It is able, in other words, to provide 'the facts' for lawyers and policy-makers. These facts may point out discrepancies, deficiencies and inequalities in the way that the law operates and so pave the way for reforms. Yet facts on their own are like bricks without a structure to give them a form or without mortar to hold them in place. So, as constructivist sociologists tell us, every empirical study undertaken on the operations of the legal system in different social spheres necessarily occurs within the framework of some prior understanding about society, whether or not this framework is made explicit. This is so whether the research involves marital relationships, economic organisations, human rights, intellectual property or any other area of social life. The purpose of useful social theory from the point of view of decision makers and practitioners is to give some coherence and structure to empirical research, so that its results may be used with relative ease in formulating and justifying social policies and legal arguments and decisions. A simple example could be that of social theories which postulate a causal link between poverty and crime. These may provide the framework for research into family income levels and delinquency, the results of which, in turn may be used as a justification for making financial allocations to poorer families or for court decisions which show leniency to young offenders from such families. On the other hand there are social theories that are not at all useful to practitioners in any immediate or direct way. These may well provide a framework and the cement for empirical observations, but they do so, for example, by identifying structures and relationships between social events which may well have no resonance in the taken-for-granted world of lawyers, politicians and policy-makers. Luhmann's theory, I would suggest, is one of these.

For the practically minded, therefore, sociological theory exists somewhere between the abstractions of jurisprudence and moral philosophy and the factual observations of empirical research, and its usefulness lies entirely in its apparent ability to transform abstraction into a framework for understanding policies and decisions in terms of their impact on society. These sociological frameworks for understanding may, of course, also be useful to critics of social and legal decisions as well as to the decision-makers themselves.[1] Yet, where social theories are too abstract or general, too remote from accepted ways of seeing the world, or too complex to be simply transformed into decisions, practising lawyers, politicians or civil servants are quite capable of ignoring them and proceeding with their business as if they had never been formulated. What is more, the lawyers, judges, law commissioners and parliamentary draftsmen who apply principles to 'the facts' are more than content to proceed as if there were nothing to confuse the issues or interfere with their task of drawing up legislation or formulating judgements in ways that they, working within a widely accepted framework of understanding and drawing upon empirical research, believe will protect its members against injustice and threats to social stability and security. If they refer to social theories at all, therefore, it is likely to be in a way that does not confuse issues which for them are relatively clear and straightforward; they might refer, for instance, to theories that reinforce the advantages of democracy or restrain what are seen as the excesses of a free market economy. Those theories that draw attention to the socially corrosive nature of racial discrimination or emphasise the importance of human rights are ideal for their purposes. The same is true of social theories that give a clear guidance as to what forms of regulation are most effective—preferring, for instance, self-regulation over governmentally imposed regulation, or welfare intervention over punishment. This may involve legislation or legal decisions that are designed to encourage socially desirable or restrain socially undesirable aspects of human nature. For them to admit social theories such as Luhmann's into the consciousness of decision-makers could be quite counter-productive to their daily task of drafting legislation, presenting arguments in court and judging cases. It

[1] See Marx, Foucault, feminist and anti-racist theories.

is much easier for them to ignore sociology altogether than grapple with ideas which are likely to make their difficult tasks even more difficult.

Society's decision-makers do not have the time to engage in games of intellectual sifting, discovery and interpretation. More often than not, it is left to academic observers of law and politics to make connections between obscure and difficult social theories and the practical world of law and politics. And so it is that we enter the scholarly world of political sociology and the sociology of law, with its erudite, arcane analyses, its debates and its controversies. It would be a wild fantasy to suggest that those who make the law or formulate the policies that are put into legislation read these learned books and articles and even more of a fantasy to make believe that they are in any direct way influenced by them. Those of us who write the books, the articles for learned journals and the chapters in edited collections may convince ourselves that our influence on society is more subtle and indirect. Perhaps then it is our students—that future generation of lawyers, administrators and politicians—who will take on board our difficult ideas and put them into practice. Yet, unfortunately it seems to be increasingly the case that we assume a thirst for knowledge and understanding of complex ideas that precious few students today have the time or inclination to acquire. Those few that do acquire them are much more likely to become theoretical scholars themselves than participate in the world of practical decision-making. The rest tend to regard all our scholarship as useful only for passing exams and as lacking relevance to their lives beyond the examination hall. And yet we continue to write as if the health of society and even its future existence (and that of humankind) depended upon our efforts. Much of our work risks becoming meaningless once we ask ourselves for whom precisely we are writing if not for other scholars like ourselves, and what effects we expect our ideas to have beyond the closed circle of academics who read about them and (in some cases) respond to them. Yet, it is precisely questions such as these which lie at the heart of the issue of Luhmann's usefulness and that need to be answered.

The thrust of this essay, therefore, could be seen as presenting two opposing ways of 'making Luhmann useful'. The first is to transform the theory so that it starts to have some relevance, some practical importance, in the management of society and the solution of social problems. The second is to remain aloof and rely upon a belief that it may be not in itself be at all bad for society if a group of people choose to remain sufficiently detached from the hurly-burly of public life to analyse and interpret social events in a very different way from those actually involved in them or those who have to make decisions based on precise expectations as to what is and what is not acceptable as reality.

It is, of course, a truism that the more abstract and generalised theories about law become, the further they move away from the daily concerns of lawyers and policy-makers. However, it is worth stating nevertheless, because much of the discussion among those who take the view that Luhmann can have an immediate impact upon legal decision-making seems to deny implicitly any discontinuity between the 'law' or 'the legal system' about which they generate ideas, connections, beliefs, assumptions, and the 'law' or 'legal system' in which or through which practitioners (whether lawyers, judges, politicians or administrators) formulate arguments and counter-arguments, assess risk, weigh up the evidence, and make decisions.[2] This denial is, of course, self-serving in the impression it gives or is supposed to give that their work has immediate relevance and importance for current legal and political decisions. Yet at the same time this denial risks replicating within the world of social theory that very taken-for-granted reality of practical policy and decision-making. As the gap between theory and practice closes, there is always a price to pay in terms of alternative realities that have to be sacrificed at the altars of practicality and expediency. I hasten to add that this should not be seen as a complaint that theorisers who adapt their theories to the demands of the 'real world' have lost touch with reality, although I concede that this may be the message that comes across to those readers unfamiliar with Luhmannian theory's notion of an inaccessible reality. The concern is rather that the virtual reality in which these scholars carry out their research and publish their writings becomes very different from the virtual reality of those other scholars who wish, in their terms, to retain their intellectual integrity. Yet, I would also suggest that, despite their efforts to make their theories accessible and useful on a practical level, the virtual reality of practical theorists may well be very different from the virtual realities of the practitioners of law, politics and social administration. Attempting theoretically to replicate, for example, the world of judges and lawyers risks, in David Nelken's words 'constructing a sociological approach to law, which ends up creating law in its own image.'[3] In other words, the gap between the theorist's version of the way the legal system works and that of the version that lawyers themselves recognise as reality still remains, even if some theorists operate under the impression that they have captured social reality.

If I come down eventually in this essay on the side of the intellectual purists, of Pericles, rather than 'the plumber'[4] it is not because I want to denigrate or belittle those who want to offer autopoietic theory as a useful guide for more effective policy and legal decision-making. I wish to suggest only that they may be deluding themselves into believing that their attempts to make the theory lawyer-, or policy-maker-, friendly are likely to have any, impact upon what happens outside the closed circle of academics who write for one another. The debate is not then between 'practice' and 'theory' but between two academic interpretations of Luhmann's original ideas—the one emphasising the immediacy of autopoiesis as a critical framework for the analysis of current policies and

[2] See the debate between Roger Cotterrell and David Nelken, for example: R Cotterrell 'Why Must Legal Ideas Be Interpreted Sociologically?' *Journal of Law and Society* 171 and D Nelken, 'Blinding Insights? The Limits of a Reflexive Sociology of Law', (1998) 3 *Journal of Law and Society* 407.

[3] D Nelken, 'Blinding Insights?', above n 1 at 407.

[4] See W Twining, *Blackstone's Tower: The English Law School* (London, Sweet and Maxwell, 1994).

legal decisions, the other pointing out that this approach detracts from the originality of the theory and from the possibilities that it opens up for seeing things differently.

THE PROBLEMS WITH LUHMANN

The aspects of Luhmann's social theory that made it so attractive and interesting to me in the first place are probably also those which make it so unattractive and uninteresting for practitioners. I refer here to the acknowledgment of complexity, the rejection of the claim that human rationality is capable of solving social problems, the refusal to accept the taken-for-granted world as the only reality or authoritative attribution of causes as having universal validity and a total scepticism concerning the ambitions of law and politics to regulate social behaviour in a reliable and predictable manner. For reasons that I shall explain later these appear to be the very attributes of the theory that John Paterson in his contribution to this volume tries so hard to overcome.

Throughout his works, Luhmann specifically rejects a belief in law's capacity to make good individual or collective desires to improve society, control populations, or engage in social engineering. This is entirely consistent with his overriding aim to create a sociology which reflected the complex, fragmented and functionally differentiated nature of modern society—to create, that is, a new sociological enlightenment. Indeed, Luhmann's choice of the faintly ironic title *Soziologische Aufklärung* for the six volumes of his miscellaneous essays was intended to signify a final rejection of the Enlightenment project of improving society through the deployment of human rationality, while at the same time, offering the enlightenment of systems theory as an antidote to the worst excesses of the Enlightenment legacies of social scientific positivism, moral rationalism and progressivism, and social welfarism.[5] In the place of an image of society as the supreme achievement of human endeavour, Luhmann offers us the improbability of society's existence and its utter fragility. Instead of the ordered identification of causes and effects, Luhmann gives us contingency, the unpredictability of social events, explicable only in retrospect and then only by using one or other of the available social systems. Far from the notion of progress being achievable through knowledge, Luhmann emphasises the random, contingent nature of social evolution—the idea that everything could have happened differently; everything could be otherwise.[6] Yet now, just five years after Luhmann's death, we see some socio-legal scholars who are admirers of his work and who claim autopoiesis as their preferred theoretical framework,

[5] For a fuller discussion of Luhmann's sociological enlightenment, see Chris Thornhill's chapter in this volume.

[6] N Luhmann, 'The Autopoiesis of Social Systems' in F Geyer and J van der Zouwen (eds), *Sociocybernetic Paradoxes: Observation, Control and Evolution of Self-Steering Systems* (London and Beverly Hills, Sage, 1986), 171–92.

trying hard to reinterpret his ideas in a way that reinforces, or, at the very least, is compatible with, a vision of law as a force for progress in society, an effective or potentially effective instrument for regulating and controlling events in the world.

THE PATERSON/TEUBNER REHABILITATION OF LUHMANN

I have in an earlier essay given examples of what I term the 'assimilation' of Luhmann's theoretical ideas in ways that confer upon them the appearance that they conform to one side or another of prevailing debates among academic lawyers and legal sociologists. At its most extreme this has even led to one eminent socio-legal scholar welcoming Luhmann as a supporter of a notion of legal autonomy unfettered by politics[7] and to another applauding his apparent endorsement of a dynamic (as opposed to conservative) law which is in full control of its own operations.[8]

John Paterson's attempt in this book, to rescue Luhmann from the depths of his own pessimism and scepticism, however, is far more sophisticated. Drawing on Gunther Teubner's modified version of autopoiesis where different systems have differing degrees of closure or autopoiesis, Paterson argues that reflexive law has both a 'normative and analytical' character,[9] and that its capacity for analysis represents the capacity of the legal system to learn. Its learning, he suggests, could include 'knowledge about the autopoietic nature of the [legal] system'.[10] Although Paterson expressly excludes any predictable outcomes occurring from law's self-improvement, the message is still clear: it is possible for law to become a better regulator of social behaviour by being more reflexive. He manages to pick up a few crumbs of comfort from snatches of Luhmann's writings which appear to support this contention and tries to reconcile the seemingly irreconcilable position of Luhmann's closed systems with that of the rather more or potentially more open systems of Gunther Teubner.

I do not want to get involved here in the debate between Luhmann and Teubner over the degree to which social systems may be open, although I do share David Campbell's concern that, 'while Teubner has always insisted on the radical separateness of social systems . . . he then wants to bring [them] into dialogue'.[11] In terms of the possibilities for social control or regulation, however, the point is surely either that events are random, arbitrary and contingent or

[7] See my discussion of Richard Lempert's treatment of Luhmann in M King, 'The Construction and Demolition of the Luhmann Heresy', (2001) 12 *Law and Critique*, 1; 13–15.

[8] *Ibid*, 15–17.

[9] G Teubner, *Law as an Autopoietic System* (Oxford, Blackwell, 1993) 97.

[10] See J Paterson's chapter in this book.

[11] But, as Campbell points out, 'of course, the possibility of dialogue implies some common ground between the systems, and this destroys the radical separateness that is the distinguishing mark of his form of systems theory.' See D Campbell, 'The Limits of Concept Formation in Legal Science' (2000) 9 *Social and Legal Studies* 439; 442.

they are capable of being regulated or controlled. They cannot be both at the same time. Or can they? One of Luhmann's greatest contributions to social theory was to demonstrate empirically how social systems are able to give the impression of order, progress and controllability within a world that is essentially chaotic and contingent—where things happen because other things happen. Social systems, according to Luhmann, are able to project an impression of control through their becoming self-referential or autopoietic. This is achieved not only by referring to their own norms in order to guide their present behaviour, but, much more significantly for our purposes, by creating within themselves a version of their external environment—be it society, the world or the universe—which has no reality outside the system itself. The system constructs an environment for itself in which it can appear as capable of achieving all its ambitions (*deparadoxification*). Within this environment any problems, any obstacles to the fulfilment of these ambitions are seen as surmountable wherever the system simply improves its performance. Furthermore, the system cannot admit within the external reality that it has constructed any hint of the random, contingent nature of social events, because to do so would bring it face to face with the paradox of its own existence—the fact that what passes for reality is only reality *for the system* created *by the system*.

This leaves two clear choices for sociologists of law or socio-legal scholars. Either you observe it from the inside, accepting law's version of reality, the social world and all the *a priori assumptions* that this involves—or you observe it from the outside, in which case not only will you be able to see the legal system operating within an external environment, but that environment may well be very different from that which the legal system itself is able to observe. Of course, your observations of law and its environment are no more 'real' or 'factual' than those generated by the legal system. They too will be dependent upon fundamental *a priori* assumptions about the nature of reality and law's role in this reality, but what you are not doing is accepting the world as it is portrayed in legal communications.

Unfortunately, John Paterson wants it both ways. He wants to believe in a theory of autopoietic systems with all its contingency, its randomness—the possibility that things could always be different—while at the same time observing ways in which law might improve its performance through better relations with other systems. For him, the secret of better regulation or more effective control lies within law's own grasp and above all a grasp of how other systems see themselves. This is his reality. It could also be law's reality since it presents no challenge to law's paradoxical situation, but it is not Luhmann's reality.

Let me look briefly at some of the implications of his argument for autopoietic theory, for the sociology of law, and for social theory in general. Paterson draws upon Teubner's highly complex account of the ways that law might 'understand' other systems and so be better able to regulate them. He then goes on to argue that, despite Luhmann's clear rejection of the notion of reflexive law, there is, after all, not so much distance between his version of autopoiesis and that of Teubner. In other words, it may well be possible for law to improve its performance by making it better equipped to see other systems in the way that they see themselves. This seems to me to be a clever way of normalising and neutralising the theory of autopoietic systems, bringing it into the fold of what Luhmann called 'the "liberal" tradition of modern Europe'.[12] In this way Luhmann's unique, distinctive (and, some would say deeply pessimistic) contribution to social thought becomes reconciled with the up-beat vision of a society which has the potential to guarantee its own future performance by learning self-improvement. Although hidden behind technical terms, such as 'reciprocal observation' 'coupling through interference' and 'communication via organisation', what we have here is nothing other than a spectacular return of the very enlightenment values, of humanism and progress through the exercise of rationality and the accumulation of knowledge, that Luhmann believed he had jettisoned.[13] In place of the quest for 'real causes' the legal system now 'probes for sensitive "intervention points" '. Instead of relying upon universal human rationality, law is now able 'to build upon the operation of [second order] observation, and in particular *Verstehen*'.

The fact is that throughout his major work on law, *Das Recht der Gesellschaft*,[14] Luhmann never once mentioned the possibility that the legal system could operate in a reflexive way and in his contribution, 'The Problems of Reflexive Law', to the *European Yearbook of the Sociology of Law* he devoted twenty five pages to demonstrating that it could not. Moreover, throughout his writings over many years he derided what he saw as simplistic, idealised and ideological accounts of society that depended upon universal rationality or upon some *a priori* notion of human nature. All this appears to have been forgotten somewhere along the line or, if not forgotten, then supplanted or overshadowed, in Paterson's account, by the conviction that Luhmann may in his concepts of 'structural coupling' and 'system programmes' have left open the possibility 'of one system being able to influence the self-steering of another system'. There is also, of course, Luhmann's single, enigmatic line at the end of one of his articles, which John Paterson quotes to round off his own piece: 'There are many bases for making better use of possibilities'.[15]

[12] N Luhmann, 'Some Problems with "Reflexive Law" ' in G Teubner and A Febbrajo (eds), *European Yearbook of the Sociology of Law* (Milan, Guiffrè, 1992) 390–415.

[13] 'The theory of autopoietic systems compels us to abandon this concept. For in it action is the result of an observation of autopoietic processes.' N Luhmann 'Some Problems with Reflexive Law', above n 12, 390–415.

[14] Now recently translated as *Law as a Social System* (Oxford, Oxford University Press, 2004).

[15] N Luhmann, 'The Coding of the Legal System' in A Febbrajo and G Teubner (ed), *State, Law, Economy as Autopoietic Systems* (Milan, Guiffré, 1991) 145–86; 182. As it happens, Luhmann was not here referring to reflexivity as a way of law regulating other systems more effectively, but to the 'very many problems [which are] insoluble in particular systems'. A problem which is insoluble for law 'can be steered back to politics or the church. Undecidabilities can be tolerated better, as only temporary, if one can point to the progress in science or political consensus making, or in jurisprudence that may clarify and improve the decision-making position.' The 'many bases for making better use of society's possibilities' would appear to refer, therefore, not to the dual 'normative and

THE PERSONIFICATION OF LAW

There is a further point to be made here. There seems to be a tendency among some socio-legal scholars towards a humanising of autopoietic theory, turning it into 'a lawyer-friendly theory', in spite of all the nasty things that Luhmann may have said about law and that lawyers may have said about Luhmann. This is often accompanied with a tendency to humanise law, albeit in a rather different sense: law itself becomes anthropomorphised and the persona, the human attributes, that it takes on reflects the Paterson-Teubner position that inter-connectivity leads to better decisions. Perhaps it is the persona of Dworkin's Hercules—'a judge with unlimited intelligence, knowledge and time to think out problems'.[16] Perhaps it is that of a benign family court judge who believes that his potential for helping solve the family's problems is greatly increased by acquainting himself with the private lives of the litigants and their children or perhaps it is that of the intelligent civil servant who believes that an understanding of global economic forces will enable her to draft more effective legislation for regulating multi-national corporations. The point I wish to make here is that the image of the 'tuned-in' legal system does not seem far removed from that of a 'tuned-in' human decision-making agent. Both hold out the hope of inter-connectivity working to improve their task of regulation, even if the connections exist only in their own heads or in the particular models of human relationships or economic activity that they choose to deploy.

The same cannot be said of Luhmann's theory of autopoietic social systems. Not only did Luhmann (as Teubner and Paterson claim to do) reject the human being as the unit for sociological analysis or social action,[17] but he quite simply was not in the business of prescribing ways of improving the regulatory operations of law and politics. One could even question whether he was in the business of developing a *sociology of law* or a *political sociology*. He certainly never made such a claim, but always maintained that his ambition was to create a theory of *modern society* in its entirety, a society consisting of all social communication systems, which included legal and political communications. Here, I believe, lies a fundamental problem with John Paterson's attempt to compare (and ultimately to reconcile) Teubner and Luhmann. The difference between

analytic' character of reflexive law, but far more modestly to the capacity of modern society to tolerate states of uncertainty by leaving the problems in other systems rather than resorting to the legal certainties of lawful or unlawful.

[16] J Penner, 'Law and Adjudication: Dworkin's Critique of Positivism' in J Penner, D Schiff and R Nobles (eds), *Jurisprudence and Legal Theory: Commentary and Materials* (London, Butterworth's Lexis-Nexis, 2002) 335–84. See R Dworkin, 'Hard Cases' (1979) 88 *Harvard Law Review* 1057.

[17] N Luhmann, 'The Individuality of the Individual: Historical Meanings and Contemporary Problems' in T Heller, M Sosna and DE Wellbery (eds), *Restructuring Individualism: Autonomy, Individuality and the Self in Western Thought* (palo Alto, Ca, Stanford University Press, 1986) 313–25; 318.

them is not so much that one believes in reflexive law and the other does not. It is rather that the one is increasingly interested in finding ways of enhancing the performance of the legal system, while the other had absolutely no ambitions in this direction.

THE ARGUMENTS AGAINST REFLEXIVE LAW

As I stated earlier, I do not wish to replicate here the Luhmann-Teubner debate on reflexive law. I am much more concerned with the wider issue of the usefulness of autopoietic theory or a version of the theory as a vehicle for discovering ways of improving social control through law. However, two of the arguments that Luhmann sets out in his article on reflexive law apply to this wider issue and merit consideration here. The first is that reports of past success in regulation by law are not necessarily sound evidence in favour of inter-connectivity between law and other social systems and, therefore, evidence against Luhmann's rigid notion that systems are normatively closed and unable to 'understand' other systems (except within the narrow limits available through their coding). If one looks hard enough, one can always find what appear to be *ex post facto* examples of law working as an instrument for social control. Often these examples involve a coincidence of economic and legal interests. An airline company, for example, may obey safety regulations, because failure to do so could result not only in illegality, but also, in the worst case scenario, in a disaster or, slightly less drastically, in the revocation of its licence and serious financial loss. From such situations one might conclude that aviation law and the airline industry have become 'structurally coupled', but this is not, to my mind, a particularly helpful way of describing the relationship between them.

The problem that the legal system faces is, as Luhmann points out, its incapacity to regulate any conduct that may be a factor in its effectiveness but is not amenable to a lawful/unlawful determination. He gives the simple example of *not getting caught* in relation to criminal law.[18] If burglars believe that their chances of getting caught are very slim, nothing that the criminal law can do will effectively control the incidence of burglary. Law, as a social communication system, simply has no way of understanding *getting caught/not getting caught* through its lawful/unlawful coding. All that the law may do is to encourage burglars to own up to the times when they did not get caught by making it lawful for courts to take them into account in sentencing and in doing so rule out any future prosecution. But this, of course, depends upon the burglar *getting caught* in the first place. Furthermore, there may well be other factors which could reduce the number of burglaries, such as improved home security, better police detection, more police officers, neighbourhood watch etc, but these are invisible

[18] N Luhmann 'Limits of Steering', chapter 10 of *Wirtschaft der Gesellschaft*, (1997) 14 *Theory, Culture and Society* 41.

to the law, which sees only what it can see using the restricted vision of its coding. Even if individual judges are astute enough to understand these limitations, as judges operating within the legal system, there is precious little that they can do to change them, except voice their dissatisfaction in court or in their written judgment and hope that someone is taking notice.

Returning to the example of air safety regulations, which appear to work well because they are obeyed, all that one can safely deduce from this is that law has succeeded in obtaining compliance with regulations. The only projection into the future that is possible is what Luhmann refers to as a 'future perfect' prediction—if the behaviour will have changed at some time in the future in the desired direction, then one can claim that the law has worked effectively. One can learn from the history of aviation that compliance with regulations is no guarantee of air safety in the future; aircraft crash for reasons which are beyond the control of regulations and, without doubt, they will continue to do so. All that law can do is to regulate what can be regulated through law, and, while this is no mean achievement, it leaves vast areas of activity which could affect air safety quite invisible to law. It is very possible that some of these will become visible in the future, when more is known about, for example, pilot error or metal fatigue, and these too may become subject to regulation. Yet this process is not, as the Paterson-Teubner account suggests, one which depends upon legal reflexivity. Law remains as normatively closed as it ever was. It has only two ways of responding to perturbations from its environment—one is not to recognise the issue as relevant to law; the other is transform it into an issue which can ultimately be resolved through law's coding of lawful/unlawful. Its structural coupling with the problem generating system may well make it more likely that this transformation into legal communications will occur; however, there is no reason to believe that the form of regulation or control that emerges will be any more effective. There are countless examples of the legal system dealing with problems arising in other systems by transforming them into legal issues. Take courts' efforts to protect children by deciding to remove them from their families or to protect consumers against unscrupulous retailers by determining that a breach of an implied contract term had occurred. In each case one could not seriously argue that the legal system had effectively regulated or controlled child abuse or the sale of faulty goods. It is not a continuing process, a matter of one system steering another, which is after all what is understood by regulation or control.

This leads to a second problem in the relationship between law and other systems, which Luhmann identified. This concerns the concept of time. Here he distinguishes between movement, progress or experience of change on the one hand—that is, between time indicated, for example, by the hand of a watch—from, on the other hand, 'the constitution of time as a generalised dimension of meaningful reality'.[19] Since systems process events simultaneously, no one

[19] N Luhmann, 'The Future Cannot Begin: Temporal Structures in Modern Society' (1976) 43 *Social Research* 130; 135.

system is able to control time for the others. It is this second meaning of time—time constructed by systems to give meaning to their own operations which concerns us here.[20] Law, for example may organise time according to whether something occurred before or after a court decision, the bringing into force of a statute or the deadline for filing a claim. Yet, the financial markets, family relations, scientific advances, technological innovations, a government's term of office, wars and global warming do not stand still while lawyers count the days to the hearing of their case or legislatures struggle to fit in all outstanding bills before the end of a parliamentary session.

If reflexive law meant simply that law was able to lend its forms—such as contract or the rules of natural justice—or its programmes—such as the arbitration of disputes—to other systems, and leaving them entirely free to use them for their own purposes, there might be some case for ignoring the problem of simultaneity. But, as John Paterson freely admits, if law is to regulate other systems in a reflexive way, it is not sufficient for it simply to understand how those other systems work. There has also to be some clear mechanisms whereby the legal system can actually influence their self-steering. Indeed, understanding of the other system would appear in the Paterson-Teubner model to be a necessary step, but only the first step towards influencing self-steering. For control or regulation to occur there has to be some way for the legal system to ensure that the other system will operate them in a way that satisfies legal norms or, at least, make such conformity more likely than not to happen. There has, in other words, to be some ongoing 'quality control' and this assumes that it is possible to coordinate time in the one system with time in another. I would suggest that on empirical evidence alone this assumption simply does not hold true. Whatever the area of activity that law seeks to regulate, it is quite unable to structure time in a way that meets the needs of other systems. There are plenty of examples in my own specialist interest area of child law where changes in the family relations, the family's situation or in the child's development undermine any attempts by the court to exercise control over the relationship between children and their carers.[21] In the area of environmental control Luhmann himself pointed out the continual difficulties that legal regulation encounters when changes in scientific knowledge render obsolete regulations that the law is still obliged to enforce.[22] As Luhmann puts it, 'simultaneity of all occurrence means the uncontrollability of all occurrences.'[23]

I fully understand why socio-legal scholars, such as Paterson, want to make autopoietic theory appear useful for law (and so for society). I can appreciate that for them it is inconceivable that a social theory that can be so insightful

[20] Ibid.

[21] See M King, *A Better World for Children? Explorations in Morality and Authority* (London, Routledge, 1997) chapter 1.

[22] N Luhmann, *Ecological Communication* (Oxford, Polity, 1989) chapter 11.

[23] N Luhmann, *Observations on Modernity* (Stanford, Cal, Stanford University Press, 1998) 109.

about the workings of the legal system could ultimately offer nothing of value to those who wish to use it in an instrumental way to make things work better. It flies in the face of a tradition of jurisprudence, political philosophy and socio-legal scholarship that starts with a problem—the premise that 'things could be better'—and then sets out, firstly, to identify what has gone wrong and, secondly, to make things work better in future. The legal journals are full of such well-intentioned diagnoses, prognoses and proposed remedies. I have no wish to mock or belittle their efforts or to cast doubts over their sincerely held beliefs about justice, efficiency, equality, children's interests or the good of society or the planet. It was not so long ago that I counted myself among them. My problem, as I hope I have made clear throughout this essay, is with those who attempt to co-opt autopoietic theory into this enterprise in the mistaken belief that they are doing society and the theory a huge favour, when in fact the opposite is the case. The only sure consequence of using the theory in this instrumental way is that the theory becomes diminished.[24] While they may believe that they are applying a theory of closed systems of communication to solve problems involving the legal system and other systems in its environment, what emerges invariably is a personification of law, a law with human, and possibly also humane, attributes, and not Luhmann's law: that is, a law which can only see only what it can see, only understand what it can understand, only control what it can control, only regulate what it can regulate—all by applying its reductive, astringent, uncompromising code of lawful/unlawful. Inevitably and ironically, in promoting the theory as a new asset for the advance of legal thought and legal action, they are trying to make law do just what the theory says it cannot do—control other systems. They are also helping to contribute to the dedifferentiation of law and so of other social systems, which Luhmann, in his one clear normative statement, identifies as the greatest threat to modern society.[25]

A ROLE, AFTER ALL, FOR ACADEMIC SCHOLARS

As a final word, in true self-referential manner, I should like to return the spotlight to those academic scholars (and I include myself among them) who seek to relate Luhmann's social theory to the practice of law and politics. Rather than pretending that our views have enormous significance for what is actually happening or what can be made to happen within the legal and political systems,

[24] Teubner, Schiff and Nobles appear to agree with this remark when they write: 'There is something in legal culture which cannot be reduced to the narrow view of law as a manipulative political and economic instrument': G Teubner, R Nobles and D Schiff, 'The Autopoiesis of Law: An Introduction to Legal Autopoiesis', in J Penner, D Schiff and R Nobles (eds), *Introduction to Jurisprudence and Legal Theory*, (London, Butterworths, LexisNexis, 2002) 897–954; 925.

[25] M King and C Thornhill, *Niklas Luhmann's Theory of Politics and Law* (Basingstoke, England, Palgrave/Macmillan, 2003) 225.

it might be more modest to admit that we are writing for one another without any realistic expectation that our ideas are of such earth-shattering importance that anyone outside the small world of applied social theorists and political and legal sociologists is going to give them any consideration. This is not meant frivolously or disparagingly but rather to put our efforts into some perspective. As far as the future treatment of Luhmann's writings are concerned, however, we do have a modicum of power and influence at least within our miniscule realm of academic scholarship. Those of us who recognise in his theories an originality, a far-sightedness and a depth of vision which has the potential for altering the ways that a wide range of social events are interpreted do have some responsibility for ensuring that they are understood and disseminated rather than abandoned or forgotten.[26]

There seem to be three, or perhaps four, general ways in which legal academics have tended to respond to Luhmann's theory. The first is to dismiss it entirely as beyond serious consideration and in doing so to assert a very different model of the world. Autopoietic law, for example, comes to represent the antithesis of law's or politics' true identity and Luhmann's theory is viewed as a kind of anti-law or anti-political theory, which attempts misguidedly to detract from the usage of law as an instrument for social reform or conservatism, depending upon the political orientation of the writer. I have given examples of this in an earlier article.[27] The second is the opposite reaction—not only to embrace the theory, but to argue that the legal system itself should embrace the theory, since by doing so could lead to major improvements in its performance. I should place John Paterson's chapter in this book and some, but not all of Gunther Teubner's pieces into this category. More recently Teubner, Schiff and Nobles have introduced a third stance that one can take towards the theory. In the coda to their contribution on autopoietic theory in a jurisprudence text book they add an interesting 'aesthetic' dimension to the value of theory. According to them, the theory's central message

> emphasises a creative, almost playful and artistic development of different knowledge fields. This has nothing to do with the instrumental manipulation of actors or systems. . . . social autopoiesis is essentially an aesthetic theory whose main importance is in its analysis of the way new and unexpected worlds of meaning emerge by processes which create their own reality.[28]

While this may well be true, I would suggest that it represents an amusing by-product of Luhmann's work and does not encapsulate or do justice to the theory. New and unexpected worlds of meaning may indeed emerge, but this is not a game that Luhmann plays for his own amusement or the diversion of his readers. It is deadly serious.

[26] JM Balkin, 'Interdisciplinarity as Colonization', (1996) *Washington and Lee Law Review* 949; 960.

[27] M King, 'The Construction and Demolition of the Luhmann Heresy' (2001) 12 *Law and Critique* 1.

[28] G Teubner *et al*, 'The Autopoiesis of Law', above n 24, 295.

Of course, I have left my own use of Luhmann's theory until last. This is to use the theory as a way of emphasising the limitations, self-deceptions and paradoxes of law and politics in their various operations.[29] It shows up the exaggerated claims and pretensions of various ideological movements for what they are—exposing their ambitions for control and change in the ways in which law reconstructs for its own purposes the knowledge and meaning contained in the communications of other systems.

Let me end in typical Luhmannian manner with a paradoxical answer to the question concerning the usefulness of his theory. Starting with social problems rather than social systems, one could from a position within contemporary society identify four hitherto intractable problems which today call out for urgent solutions. These are: (1) The destruction of the environment (2) economic migration from poor to rich countries (3) racial and cultural integration and (4) the depletion of energy and water resources. For Luhmann a society consisting of functionally differentiated sub-systems is simply not capable of conceptualising these problems in ways that offer any possibility of successful solutions. Political, legal, scientific and economic accounts may satisfy the requirements of their own specific system, but these accounts and the solutions that result from them cannot transcend the boundaries established through the system's closure. Each can see only what it can see. It cannot see what it cannot see and, moreover, it has no way of knowing that it cannot see what it cannot see.

If this is indeed the case, then all our efforts, whether as practitioners or academic scholars, are likely to be in vain when it comes to providing solutions to these problems, for, even if as individuals (or as psychic systems) we recognise their futility, there is no way for us to express our concerns at the level of society except within the confines of society's functionally differentiated systems. Put another way, even if there are lawyers, politicians, scientists or economists who believe that they have found the answer to these problems, how do they convince other systems operating different norms, different criteria for validity and legitimacy that their answer is the right one? And even if this is possible, how can power be exercised to enforce this right solution across the whole of society?

Little wonder that John Paterson wants to mitigate Luhmann's cataclysmic vision by promoting law's capacity to understand other systems and, through

[29] M King, 'Against Children's Rights', in R Keightley (ed), *Children's Rights* (Kenwyn, South Africa, Juta, 1996) 28–50; M King, *A Better World for Children? Explorations in Morality and Authority* (London, Routledge, 1997); M King, 'Comparing Legal Cultures in the Quest for Law's Identity', in D Nelken (ed), *Comparing Legal Cultures* (Aldershot, Dartmouth, 1997), 119–34; M King, 'You Have to Start Somewhere', in G Douglas and L Sebba (eds), *Children's Rights and Traditional Values* (Aldershot, Dartmouth, 1998), 1–14; M King, 'Introduction and Images of Children and Morality' in M King (ed), *Moral Agendas for Children's Welfare* (London, Routledge, 1999) 1–32; M King, 'Future Uncertainty as a Challenge to Law's Programmes: The Dilemma of Parental Disputes' (2000) 63 *Modern Law Review* 523; M King, 'An Autopoietic Approach to the Problems presented by "Parental Alienation Syndrome" for Courts and Child Mental Health Experts' (2002) 13 *Journal of Forensic Psychiatry* 609; M King and F Kaganas, 'The Risks and Dangers of Experts in Court' (1998) 1 *Current Legal Issues* 221.

such understanding, regulate them by teaching them to regulate themselves. For progressively minded lawyers to enter Luhmann's apocalyptic world, his vision of modern society is to pass through the gates bearing the Dantean inscription '*Lasciate ogni speranza, voi ch'entrate*'.

Are we then to regard Luhmann as a latter day Cassandra or Jeremiah warning us of the ultimate destruction of society, humanity, the planet, unless we change our ways? Not really, for purposeful change or self-improvement is 'highly improbable' and not within the repertory of social systems. His message is rather that there are other possibilities, other ways for society to organise itself, other ways of conceptualising society and its problems. Solutions which are invisible at present may appear in the future. He therefore states:

> There are no solutions for the most urgent problems but only restatements without promising perspectives. Taking all this into account, success seems to be highly improbable. On the other hand, we can see fascinating possibilities of arriving at a higher level of intelligibility. It requires at present a kind of stoic attitude to stay at the job and 'to do the formulations'.[30]

On the other hand, the downside of Luhmann's message is that continuing to believe that solutions are just around the corner and can be achieved through more effective social regulation or control is paradoxically likely to decrease the chance that these possibilities, these new ways of conceptualising society, will eventually become visible. While practitioners might well be wedded to the task of doing the same things better, there is no reason why we academic scholars should mimic them.[31] Luhmann's *usefulness*, therefore, might well lie precisely in the *uselessness* of his theory as a blueprint for the improvement of social systems and those who try and make his theory useful in this way may well be contributing to the theory's ultimate *uselessness*.

[30] N Luhmann, 'The World Society as a Social System', in *International Journal of General Systems*, 8 (1982), 137.

[31] There is an echo here of Kuhn's normal science and scientific revolutions or changes of paradigm: TN Kuhn, *The Structure of Scientific Revolutions* (Princeton, USA, Princeton University Press, 1962).

II.

Politics, Law and Human Rights

3

From Subject to System: Some Unsystematic Systems-Theoretic Thoughts on Race Equality and Human Rights

TIM MURPHY

> I am a man, and what I have to recapture is the whole past of the world . . . In no way should I derive my basic purpose from the past of the peoples of colour . . . It is not because the Indo-Chinese has discovered a culture of his own that he is in revolt. It is because 'quite simply' it was, in more than one way, becoming impossible for him to breathe . . .[1]

> When Vice President Al Gore translated the motto *E pluribus unum* as 'out of one, many,' he committed a famous gaffe . . . But his faulty translation captured quite nicely the emerging *zeitgeist*.[2]

INTRODUCTION

TRADITIONALLY, LAW—At least in the form of legislation—has been used to prohibit certain types of human conduct.[3] Even an area like tax law, which at first sight requires people to do something rather than not do something, works (or does not work) by way of precise penalties for prohibited conduct (sending your tax return in late) and even Al Capone, notoriously, was jailed for tax evasion. The tax avoidance industry—and 'avoision'[4]—precisely indicate no desire to lean in the direction of 'compliance' if there are other options. People don't pay their taxes, in other words, because

[1] F Fanon, *Black Skin White Masks* (London, Paladin, 1970) 161.

[2] AJ Bacevich, *American Empire: The Realities and Consequences of US Diplomacy* (Cambridge, Mass, Harvard University Press, 2002), 83.

[3] I would like to thank Tatiana Flessas, Michael King and Nicola Lacey for their comments on an earlier draft.

[4] See A Seldon *et al*, *Tax Avoision* (London, IEA, 1979).

they feel they should.[5] There are, as is well known, other typical modes or rationales for enacting new law—so-called facilitative law setting out roadmaps; and a growing body of regulatory law which perhaps lies somewhere in between.[6] In these cases, though, the links with prohibition are often overlooked. In addition, there are 'symbolic' laws setting out the values of a governmental regime or of a 'people' (in the democratic age) usually on issues of morality. Again, usually, these involve the introduction of specific penalties, whether for drugs, under-age drinking, street violence or pedophilia.

From a systems-theoretic perspective, nothing would lead one to suppose that such legal prohibitions are especially successful, unless large resources are devoted to ensuring compliance.[7] In general, one of the few success stories has been taxation (with exceptions of course) because of the effectiveness and the draconian powers of the bureaucracy created for that purpose. But as has long been recognised, enacting laws is a way of achieving several goals simultaneously: communicating within society that problems are recognised and that action is being taken (what is critical here is that 'time' will defer the question until and into the future of whether the action can achieve anything or deal with the problem). It also enables governmental failure (the assumption that government is responsible for nearly everything that goes wrong) to be recast into action and decisiveness. In these ways, everyone 'in charge' is let off the hook (but only for a while) and these familiar processes thereby provide one way of giving the impression that problems are being managed and that society is under control (that society is controlling itself, in fact).[8]

What, though, about the situation where the law is used positively to change human conduct? What about the case where the law is used to say that this is how you should behave or—even more acutely—feel? One can both doubt the attainability of any goals specified in these terms and at the same time seek to explain how these goals have arisen. Systems theory is useful for both of these tasks. This is not because it has an axe to grind (power is bad, domination needs legitimacy etc) but because it provides a powerful, if intimidating, analytical framework for grasping the problems of a modern society. What follows will be somewhat 'theory-lite': few could or can hope to match Luhmann's complex thinking (thinking rather than thought because it was unfinished and never

[5] Although human rights enthusiasts, if we follow S Holmes and CR Sunstein, *The Cost of Rights: Why Liberty Depends on Taxes* (New York, WW Norton, 1999), should support draconian tax enforcement policies to be consistent. Cf: Daunton's definitive study: M Daunton, *Trusting Leviathan; The Politics of Taxation in Britain 1799–1914* (Cambridge, Cambridge University Press, 2001) and *Just Taxes: The Politics of Taxation in Britain 1914–1979* (Cambridge, Cambridge University Press, 2002).

[6] Both depend on the enforcement capacity of the state—failed states can neither facilitate nor regulate.

[7] Even then, the futility of the 'war on drugs', or the example of Prohibition in the US, point to the difficulties when individuals or society do not wish to comply or prefer to do things which the law forbids.

[8] On the displacement of problems see my *The Oldest Social Science: Configurations of Law and Modernity* (Oxford, Oxford University Press, 1997).

stayed the same—Luhmann rarely drew attention to this feature of his work, unlike Foucault, who notoriously flaunted it). And in any event it is not clear that it is necessary to develop social theory to the degree of complexity to which Luhmann aspired in order to address the topic of this chapter.

I wish to explore these questions through the vehicle of the themes of race equality and, to a lesser degree, human rights. These have become societal themes in Luhmann's precise sense of 'world society' not only through the formal mechanisms of international institutions but in the more parochial sense that most national governments have to have policies on these issues and claim to take them seriously. (I leave aside hopelessly failed states that just do not count). A Luhmannian perspective on this area requires us, however, to explore it through the modalities of society, organisation and interaction and this chapter is organised in this way. But to set the scene, a few words are required about the theme of race itself.

~~Race~~

Is this subheading another stupid attempt at emulating Derrida? Not really. It is intended to flag up a real problem with the nature of the theme I have selected as the main focus of this chapter.

'Racism' is a problem which circulates as a theme in social communication. It seems to require the building of organisations to address it as a problem. And race would seem to be embedded as a way of framing observations in interaction systems. Yet it is unclear what it is we are talking about—and it is precisely in terms of 'talk' that the problem is obscure. In the natural sciences, it is now agreed that race is a non-category. Decomposing 'man' into layers—physical, chemical, biological/genetic — it is now the consensus that the concept of 'race' fails to organise any useful data[9]. The distinctions it enables are pseudo-distinctions. In this sense we encounter the erasure of 'race' as a distinction and its replacement by new hierarchically arranged ontological distinctions[10] that layer what humanity essentially is as an object of observation and as a theme of scientific communication. In this sense, race becomes a trace of a distinction, a memory, an erasure—~~race~~.[11] And yet communication continues. Officially, one might say, race lives on as a communicative theme as 'culture',[12] and this

[9] S Jones, *The Language of the Genes: Biology, History and the Evolutionary Future* (London, Flamingo, 1993).

[10] MP Murphy and LAJ O'Neill (eds), *What is Life? The Next Fifty Years: Speculations on the Future of Biology* (Cambridge, Cambridge University Press, 1995).

[11] E Barkan, *The Retreat of Scientific Racism: Changing Concepts of Race in Britain and the United States Between the World Wars* (Cambridge, Cambridge University Press, 1992); See SJ Gould, *The Mismeasure of Man*, revised edn (New York, WW Norton, 1996) on the bell curve.

[12] C Levi-Strauss, *Structural Anthropology*, vol 2 (Harmondsworth, Penguin, 1977), chapter *XVIII*; GW Stocking Jr, *Race, Culture, and Evolution: Essays in the History of Anthropology*, revised edn (Chicago, University of Chicago Press, 1982).

enables new distinctions to be drawn and thereby gives the impression that the discussion is meaningful and important. While such a shift may help to organise otherwise confused experiences, it is not clear that cultural distinctions are sufficiently secure to clear anything up. Indeed, quite the opposite might be the case: freed from biological constraints or the discipline, such as it is, of the laboratory,[13] the process of making distinctions on the basis of 'culture' seems to open up endless possibilities and with it endless problems.[14] Attempts to simplify this situation—as in the Clash of Civilisations—seem exorbitant. At the other end of the spectrum, we just have a litany of difference, alterity, and rather vacuous and ever-more complicated appeals to pluralism.

Race challenges universalism at the same time as becoming a global category or problem (anti-racism knows no geopolitical boundaries). It destabilises ideas of equality and human rights. It fuels what perhaps should be regarded as a human-nature grounded tendency to draw distinctions—not only for cognitive reasons! Some have argued for the desirability of a post-race or postethnic world—an end to distinctions around this theme.[15] Whether or not this strategy is the right one, in the Western world we are proceeding in the opposite direction. Under the banner of labels like 'inclusion' which in fact presuppose distinctions already established and embedded, we are in the process of seeking to carve out equality and sameness on the bedrock of difference. And now the law is being used to valorise this process—to legislate for equal respect.

Systems theory cannot explain *why* this is happening. Nor can it assess whether these plans and projects are achievable. It can however help to analyse or sketch out the nature of the question, so that some degree of rational attention can be given to it. So we turn to the framing distinction of society, organisation and interaction and consider the theme of race in this sequence.[16]

SOCIETY

'A' modern society in Luhmann's sense is the totality of global communications. Many of the papers in this volume hover anxiously around this position but it is a simple concept. World society is not world government. Functional differen-

[13] K Knorr-Cetina, *Epistemic Cultures* (Cambridge, Mass, Harvard, 1999).

[14] See, for example, the role of Belgium in constituting Tutsi and Hutu in Rwanda—A Chua, *World on Fire: How Exporting Free-Market Democracy Breeds Ethnic Hatred and Global Instability* (London, William Heinemann, 2003) 165 ff.

[15] P Gilroy, *Against Race: Imagining Political Culture Beyond the Color Line* (Cambridge, Mass, Harvard University Press, 2000); S Ali, *Mixed-Race, Post-Race: Gender, New Ethnicities and Cultural Practices* (Oxford, Berg, 2003); DA Hollinger, *Postethnic America: Beyond Multiculturalism*, revised edn (New York, Basic Books, 2000).

[16] For Luhmann's use of these categories, see N Luhmann, *The Differentiation of Society* (New York, Columbia University Press, 1982) chapter 4; *Social Systems* (Stanford CA, Stanford University Press, 1995).

tiation means that we do have (allowing for failed states, failed economies, failed cultures etc) at a world or global level a political system, an economic system, a cultural system, a legal system and so on. This does not mean that anyone is 'in charge'—US hegemony may be illusory in some or even all of these systems.[17] For example, Luhmann's theories were not developed on the basis of the internet; but its arrival amply confirms and makes more real (virtually, of course!) what he was arguing.[18] And the example of the internet suggests precisely that society is society and that the world is the world (although nothing but our hopes can confirm the latter truism since the world cannot be more than society's horizon and environment). Society acquires identity through the distinction it makes between itself and the world. This process is somewhat mysterious but also obvious if one thinks about it. We must be careful about the assumptions we make about what is new here, beyond the volume and velocity of communications.[19]

In any event, scholars are increasingly clear that world society is nothing new. It is not just that globalisation preceded the post-World War Two era;[20] it has in fact been with us for a very long time at least in economic and monetary terms. Wedgwood was a strategy of import substitution. Where did the tea and coffee come from—the coffee that fuelled Habermas's Öffentlichheit?[21] Etc. Perhaps the difference is that we now think we live in a global society and that we think this is new. Thinking it is new (because of airplanes etc) doesn't make it new.[22] In other words, sticking with Luhmann, it may be that we have to discard 'Eurocentric' historical perspectives and instead regard the world-historical process in asymmetric terms: ie accept that differentiated world systems emerged at different stages of the historical 'process', though we would then need to recognise (in world terms) that it is state and law (as ideas and as congelations of practices) that arrive rather late on the scene of world society. Since the symposium struggled with the idea of world society, it may be worth addressing a few further remarks to this issue.

[17] E Todd, *After the Empire: The Breakdown of the American Order* (New York, Columbia University Press, 2003) which addresses the issues more intelligently than M Hardt and A Negri, *Empire* (Cambridge, Mass, Harvard University Press, 2000).

[18] S Woolgar (ed), *Virtual Society? Technology, Cyberbole, Reality* (Oxford, Oxford University Press, 2002).

[19] This is a point sometimes forgotten in the rather Habermasian vogue for 'global civil society'. See, for instance, H Anheier, M Glasius and M Kaldor (eds), *Global Civil Society 2001* (Oxford, Oxford University Press) and its successors. Global civil society often seems to mean Amnesty International and other NGOs. The concepts of Organisation and Society are conflated.

[20] H James, *The End of Globalisation: Lessons From the Great Depression* (Cambridge, Mass, Harvard University Press, 2001).

[21] As in J Habermas, *The Structural Transformation of the Public Sphere* (Cambridge, Polity, 1989); TCW Blanning, *The Culture of Power and the Power of Culture: Old Regime Europe 1660–1789* (Oxford, Oxford University Press, 2002).

[22] P Bracken, *Fire in the East: The Rise of Asian Military Power and the Second Nuclear Age* (New York, HarperCollins, 2000) *xi–xxix*.

Part of the problem is one of perspective.[23] For example, were we to adopt an East Asian perspective, this problem could look quite different.[24] We think that the rise of the West is what needs to be explained as if the answer is to be found in something indigenous to the West. We look for endogenous causes, as did Marx and Weber. But what if the rise of the West is a consequence of things happening in other parts of the world? What if, at very least, we juxtaposed a Western perspective with a Chinese perspective in a simultaneous eighteenth century context? Then we would see an idealised vision of a world of concentric circles with the successor to the Yellow Emperor—the unique individual with the Mandate of Heaven—at its centre and the Europeans as a dangerous and uncivilised periphery whose presence in the Middle Kingdom needed to be contained and controlled.[25]

But the issue is not just about ways of seeing the world or about communicating these visions. It is also a matter of communicative flows more generally, and here the frontrunner is the international flow of people, commodities and *specie*—slaves purchased in West Africa with, among other things, Indian and Chinese textiles, silver extracted from the 'new' world, much of which was destined in the end for China, which along with India supplied the luxury goods the West (old and new) required as what we think of as civilisation developed.[26] And along these overland and sea trade routes, other things travelled too: culture being the most obvious example (think of the fashion in Britain for Chinoiserie and the Brighton Pavilion). For a long time society was able to accommodate this situation, partly because of the uneven development of the (nation-)state system in Europe and in due course in the new world and Japan. China's transformation from multi-ethnic empire (explicitly articulated during the Qianlong emperorship but in a sense implicit for long before that throughout the Qing and perhaps the Yuan dynasties)[27] into a nation-state came later and largely as a result of the predations of Western powers and Japan. And this transformation from empire to nation has created a problem of ethnicity in China which is difficult for the Chinese party-state to manage.[28] In other words,

[23] JM Blaut, *The Coloniser's Model of the World: Geographical Diffusionism and Eurocentric History* (New York, Guildford Press, 1993).

[24] R BinWong, *China Transformed: Historical Change and the Limits of European Experience* (Ithaca, NY, Cornell University Press, 1997). See also P Bracken, above n 22, on which transitions really count.

[25] JL Hevia, *Cherishing Men From Afar: Qing Guest Ritual and the Macartney Embassy of 1793* (Durham, NC, Duke University Press, 1995).

[26] K Pomeranz, *The Great Divergence: China, Europe, and the Making of the Modern World Economy* (Princeton, NJ, Princeton University Press, 2000); AG Frank, *ReOrient: Global Economy in the Asian Age* (Berkeley, CA, University of California Press, 1998).

[27] PK Crossley, *A Translucent Mirror: History and Identity In Qing Imperial Ideology* (Berkeley, CA, University of California Press, 1999); ES Rawski, *The Last Emperors: A Social History of Qing Imperial Institutions* (Berkeley, CA, University of California Press, 1998).

[28] F Dikötter, *The Discourse of Race in Modern China* (London, Hurst, 1992); J Howell (ed), *Governance in China* (Lanham, MD, Rowman and Littlefield, 2004); P Hays Gries and S Rosen (eds), *State and Society in 21st-century China: Crisis, Contention, and Legitimation* (London, Routledge Curzon, 2004).

there is no incompatibility between world society and a ‘world’ of nation-states. But a ‘world’ of nation-states is a ‘world’ of ‘~~races~~’ and a mobile migrant ‘world’ in which ‘race’ is thematised as a problem. ‘Nation-state’ is not equivalent to ‘nation’: this is to say that nation-states are realities whereas nations may be and probably are myths.[29]

‘Things’—commodities, *specie*—did not flow without people and sometimes the things which circulated were people. This ‘trade’ perspective,[30] in other words, is not—never was—‘just’ economics but also culture, politics etc. Only tourism makes us forget this, but then even tourism is not exactly new.[31]

Work in what has come to be known as ‘World History’ also strengthens Luhmann’s perspective and suggests that world society existed long before the arrival of ‘modernity’ in the West, although society did not always have maps and when it did they were not always the same. The world is what the world is, but it does not remain the same. At some point society begins and even Luhmann is probably over-cautious about just when. ‘Modernity’ is a (sometimes painful) retro-reflection on this process. But World History also reveals that it was partial, and that the current preoccupation with ‘globalisation’ is largely the result of post-World War Two international cooperation at a political level, ie the emergence of an international political system with all the negotiatory characteristics of domestic political systems. On top of that, of course, is the emergence of a new-style of international law supposedly above the negotiations of nation-states.[32] Contemporary ‘post-Iraq’ ruminations from politicians about this might suggest that the future of international law is itself obscure or in doubt. But this will not diminish the idea of an international legal order (ie the idea that there is one), only the form which it should take. This in turn largely reduces to the question of which nation-states will choose to take part in a project of world policing (motivations can be left to one side but are of course suspicious).

One symptom, perhaps, of recognition of this state of affairs which social theory has long concealed with the complicity of many historians is a current Europe-wide predicament. I focus here on race equality but the same point could be made more broadly in relation to human rights. Both enterprises are self-evidently virtuous, which is to say that you cannot oppose either of them

[29] PJ Geary, *The Myth of Nations: The Medieval Origins of Europe* (Princeton, NJ, Princeton University Press, 2002), 5–6. Cf, B Anderson, *Imagined Communities: Reflections on the Origin and Spread of Nationalism* (London, Verso, 1983); R Vinen, *A History in Fragments: Europe in the Twentieth Century* (London, Little, Brown, 2000). Cf, my ‘Include Me Out’ (2002) 29 *Journal of Law and Society* 342.

[30] K Pomeranz and S Topik, *The World that Trade Created: Society, Culture, and the World Economy 1400 to the Present* (Armonk, NY, ME Sharpe, 1999).

[31] J Elsner and J-P Rubies (eds), *Voyages and Visions: Towards a Cultural History of Travel* (London, Reaktion, 1999).

[32] AWB Simpson, *Human Rights and the End of Empire: Britain and the Genesis of the European Convention* (Oxford, Oxford University Press, 2001); M Koskenniemi, *The Gentle Civiliser of Nations: The Rise and Fall of International Law 1870–1960* (Cambridge, Cambridge University Press, 2002).

and be taken seriously in public. In the UK, new legislation in the race equality area has two origins. A domestic origin is the Stephen Lawrence inquiry and the thematisation which resulted from its findings of institutional racism in the police. (The concept of institutional racism was already much deployed in the domain of social work, especially social work training programmes). The broader origin was in the European Commission. This latter is a fairly typical example of bureaucracies in search of work which utilise the resources at their disposal to pursue moral or ethical campaigns and visions (it is not clear that there is any other way to explain the Equality directives but more on organisations below). But there were also broader themes circulating in society: the problem of race ghettoes and the management of ethnicised social conflict and the issue of Fortress Europe.[33] The economic system desires enlargement, the political system doesn't know how to handle the domestic consequences so responds in part with legal restrictions and stigmatisation of asylum seekers, and in part with morality—the exemplary society, citizenship lessons and moral correction.

I will not discuss any of this law in detail. It is not always correct that the devil lies in the detail; sometimes the devil is in (or is) the animating spirit; whichever is the case, I want to consider this new animating spirit that wants to change human conduct not through prohibition but through legally-based exhortation.

Within political theory Brian Barry has triggered one of those rather inward-looking academic debates about the relative merits of multiculturalism and human rights.[34] The debate is a useful window on to the central problem, not least because each side adopts such theoretical (in the worst sense) positions. Barry argues for the primacy of human rights but on the assumption of an egalitarian economic system so that legal equality is not systemically undercut by inequality in access to resources. I wouldn't disagree with him but since it's not going to happen what's the point? (Luhmann's theories, for good or bad, were never of the 'I have a dream' variety.) Barry's opponents make noise about equal respect and the value of diversity: so far as I can tell, none address the operationalisabilty of any of this. It is therefore essential to repeat a point about the relevance or significance of this theoretical approach—it is geared, in Marx's terms, primarily to understanding the world[35]—the Owl of Minerva approach.[36] It assumes that plenty of people are busy trying to change the world. That is not the problem, precisely because so many people are so busy. In this respect, although the theoretical style of Luhmann is very different, the unintended consequences of the human action problem can be folded into the

[33] On this, see especially B Hepple, 'Race and Law in Fortress Europe' (2004) 67 *Modern Law Review* 1.

[34] P Kelly (ed), *Multiculturalism Reconsidered: Culture and Equality and its Critics* (Oxford, Polity, 2002).

[35] K Marx, 'Theses on Feuerbach *XI*', in K Marx and F Engels, *The German Ideology*, edited by CJ Arthur (London, Lawrence and Wishar, 1977).

[36] GWF Hegel, *Elements of the Philosophy of Right* (Cambridge, Cambridge University Press, 1991) 23.

decision, and systems theory can be regarded as one way of exploring the themes which that problematic generates.[37] And therefore—it is important to note in this specific context—the theory is impersonal in its focus.

Luhmann's concept of world society is developed (as usual) in terms of a distinction: the distinction between social and interaction systems. And it is this distinction which connects with particular force to the question of race equality and human rights.

We can accept that these ideas—the mishmash of equal respect and race equality and human rights—run fairly well at the level of global communication. They mean a lot at that level and conferences can now be convened to discuss them.[38] At this level one can talk about the human rights records of governments and exhort nation-states to do more to tackle racism.[39] One can insist (in society) that more should be done to build a 'culture' of human rights and one can set up bodies to monitor and 'audit' progress and report the results, ie continue communication on these themes. But to the extent that these themes are to be activated in some form of social practice, we need to look to how they do or can perform in organisations. A separate and much more difficult question in some ways is how what happens in society and in organisations can connect with what happens in the setting of interaction systems.

ORGANISATION

The early stages of UK race relations legislation can be seen from a systems-theory perspective as focused on organisation-building. This at any rate was their principal effect. The aim of the legislation was supposedly the enshrinement of the principle of non-discrimination, the programme here being that race should not be used as a distinction. The law was to eliminate 'prejudice' and its overt expression, in a context of some racial disturbances and tightening immigration laws. More restricted immigration was needed in order to keep the lid on relations between the native population and those immigrants who were 'already here'. Correspondingly, the law aimed at improving race relations by requiring a range of decision-makers to be blind to race in contexts like employment. The philosophy spread—slowly—through the public sector. So in due course university admissions forms became race-neutral although applicants were requested to indicate race separately so that monitoring of the outcomes could occur through the collection of aggregate data via HESA etc.[40]

There were, to be sure, some behavioural consequences. 'No coloureds' or 'No Irish' signs disappeared from advertisements. Decisions were more emphatically couched in the language or rhetoric of 'merit'. It is rather difficult to tell,

[37] R Boudon, *The Unintended Consequences of Social Action* (London, Macmillan, 1982).
[38] For an early example, see C Levi-Strauss, above n 12.
[39] Cf, the recent exchange between the US and China on China's Human Rights record in 2003.
[40] Higher Education Statistical Agency.

however, what was really achieved. Race riots continued to happen from time to time and generated anxieties and sometimes reports.[41] A cynic might say that people simply had to be more circumspect about what they said and did. The logic, however, it is important to note for present purposes, was still the logic of prohibition, of 'thou shalt not'.

But by creating organisations—first the Race Relations Board, then the Commission for Racial Equality, now the planned Equalities and Human Rights Commission—the theme of race was given a home. It became some people's job or even career to communicate about race. And over time, unsurprisingly, this led to a complexification of the problem or rather problems: the problem of race and the problem of race relations.

Racial prejudice, seen in the context of what was blandly termed race relations, transmuted into the concept of racial discrimination, just as 'racialist' suddenly became old-fashioned and was replaced by the buzzier 'racist'. Following American precedents already adopted for the enactment of the Sex Discrimination Act, a concept of indirect discrimination was introduced in 1976. This was still couched in terms of prohibition—but this time intentions were irrelevant (this was now relabeled direct discrimination) and the statistical impact of applying an unjustifiable requirement or condition with unequal effects became discrimination.

Of course, by moving from the sixties' context of race relations as a rather specific problem rooted in (as it then seemed) decolonisation and its aftermath to discrimination encompassing both race and sex, the path was opened to expansion of the theme of discrimination. If race and sex, why not other forms of discrimination—religion (which Northern Ireland, also high on the governmental agenda from the late sixties onwards, had shown to be a problem-area), sexual orientation (unavoidable since the AIDS crisis first surfaced in social communication in the eighties) or age (especially relevant now that anxieties about pensions and their funding have increased)? Or disability? What about people of reassigned genders? In other words, how to 'build' a society without any unacceptable discrimination? The short point here is that governments don't build societies. They can build organisations to have 'ownership' of problems that should irritate and disturb society. In a sense, building and funding these organisations is a way, the only way, of 'tackling' the problem while at the same time these organisations serve as a way of identifying or constructing the problem (through investigations, through commissioning research, through publicity).

The core lever here for the new organisations thus created was the concept of indirect discrimination. This introduced the general idea of unintended consequences into what had now been redefined, rather abstractly, as the field of discrimination. With the enactment of the Human Rights Act 1998, the

[41] For example, the Scarman Report into the Brixton riots.

scene was set for stopping the proliferation of organisations—should each new anti-discrimination set of rules have its own organisation or should everything all be brought together under one roof? Should discrimination go generic in other words and be folded together with human rights? For funding and organisational reasons, the latter option seemed preferable.[42] And so the different equalities will have to fight it out for airtime inside one organisation—whose personnel strategy will inevitably be a logistical nightmare, and whose strategic goals will almost inevitably be conflictual and require the packaging of an ad agency.

I have already referred to the fact that, conceptually, a partial result of indirect discrimination has been the emergence of the idea of institutional racism. No-one really understands this concept but that does not stop it being useful. In the present context, it might be better termed organisational racism, since here the focus shifts to organisations as such and in general. It shares with indirect discrimination the shift of emphasis away from conscious decisions made by intentionally discriminating decision-makers. It complexifies the problem by broadening the issue from one of applying a precise requirement (insisting that turban-wearing Sikhs discard their turbans and wear helmets or that headscarves are not worn in school) to the vaguer issue of an institutional (ie organisational) 'culture' in which no-one is precisely aware of what they are doing but where the outcomes are clearly discriminatory in terms of career progression, incidence of harassment, job experience and satisfaction etc. As with ~~race~~, 'culture' has to serve as a sponge-like concept for constructing and communicating about a problem whose real nature we do not understand and do not need to in order to proliferate communication about it.[43]

It is in this context that the Race Relations (Amendment) Act 2000 takes shape and makes sense. This Act introduces a new concept—race equality. Inequality had persisted despite the old legislation; the data on outcomes established that. Therefore positive action was needed to tackle inequality and institutional racism. And this required more organisation and the organisation of organisations. Contrary to what is often supposed, the thrust of this new programme is not to admonish society (whose admonishment in a society where people have rights to freedom of expression is not so difficult and not a new preoccupation) nor even to build organisations (though I come to this issue in a moment) but to address the 'attitudes and feelings' and experiences of individuals. In the next section, I will turn to this core aim. For the moment, it should already be clear that this goal is mysterious, except and insofar as 'progress' towards it can be measured in terms of statistical outcomes. If race is ~~race~~, then what can race equality be? In fact, new unstable differences proliferate: race/ethnicity (what is

[42] <http://www.womenandequalityunit.gov.uk/equality/project/CEHR_parliamentary_statement.doc> (accessed 16 December 2003).

[43] On 'culture' cf, N Luhmann, 'The Ecology of Ignorance' in *Observations on Modernity* (Stanford, Stanford University Press, 1998).

African?), race/ethnicity/nationality (Bangladeshi/Indian/Pakistani), 'Chinese' etc . . .[44]

As I have indicated, the devil is not in the detail here but in the animating spirit, except to the extent that someone has to decide on the ethnic categories if monitoring is to be possible, progress or failure within organisations measured, benchmarks and targets to be set, and outcomes assessed and evaluated. This is reflected in the fact that the legislation authorised the issuing of statutory codes of practice which have in turn been followed by sector-specific 'performance guidelines' for, eg, HEIs. The CRE has a concept of an organisation in this context[45] whose emphasis on leadership bears little or no relation to organisational theory or to familiar well-trodden issues about top-down/bottom-up.[46]

In practice, as I have said, this new agenda reduces in practice to the organisation of organisations. Taking race equality seriously primarily means matters of technique. It means establishing committees, gathering and regular monitoring of data, benchmarking and statistics, and the production of many reports to be circulated to committees. It means commissioning surveys on how people 'feel'. It means the dissemination throughout an organisation of models or guidelines as to 'good practice'(which may be externally derived). At the organisational level, it means moving towards the 'exemplary society' with government departments endeavouring to show that they are exemplary in this respect (by publishing data on personnel outcomes as well as vague and vacuous personnel policy statements).[47] And it means reviewing, and where necessary, improving procedures, eg in relation to harassment.[48]

INTERACTION AND PSYCHIC SYSTEMS

But how do we conceptualise race equality and human rights at the level of the interaction systems where they are supposed to operate? And how should this take account of psychic systems?

The issue here is how we understand interaction. In this context the systems-theoretic distinction between psychic and social systems is crucial. This is because both are 'activated' in interaction. And both are crucial to the operations

[44] On these problems of classification for statistical gathering and monitoring purposes, see National Statistics (www.statistics.gov.uk) 'on ethnic classification'.

[45] <http://www.cre.gov.uk/duty/pdfs/pg_fehe.pdf> (accessed 7th April 2004).

[46] I have discussed aspects of this 'leadership' issue elsewhere: see my 'Modernising Justice Inside "UK PLC": Mimesis, De-Differentiation and Colonisation' in J Priban and D Nelken (eds), *Law's New Boundaries: The Consequences of Legal Autopoiesis* (Aldershot, Ashgate, 2001), 218–248.

[47] On the exemplary society, see B Bakken, *The Exemplary Society: Human Improvement, Social Control, and the Dangers of Modernity in China* (Oxford, Oxford University Press, 2000). On careers from a systems-theoretic perspective, see G Corsi, 'The Dark Side of a Career' in D Baecker (ed), *Problems of Form* (Stanford, Stanford University Press, 1999) 171.

[48] The law is particularly complicated here because the RR(A)A 2000 provisions are supplemented by new EU-derived regulations which are not identical. The details of these differences are not relevant here but again flag up the need for organisations to build compliance mechanisms.

of 'mutual respect' and 'feelings' (including self-respect) which provide the furniture or armoury of equality legislation. One could approach these issues through the route of the issue/concept of human nature.

In communication one can 'share' experiences (but how to tell what is attributable to communication and what to experience?) but one cannot observe experiences, only receive and transmit communications about them (so they may be true or untrue, authentic or inauthentic). One can't share perspectives. One can imagine the perspective of the other and communicate about that imagining and the other may accept or reject the communication. If the other says 'You can't know how it feels unless . . .' s/he is right; you can't know, you can just imagine and imagining suffering (eg) is not the same as feeling it.[49] The project of 'perspective sharing' is something of an illusion.[50]

Observers observe. Systems theory is solipsistic not communitarian. But this solipsism is at the level of the psychic system not the social system which by definition brings everyone 'together' in the world of communication. Observers observe observers and communicate their observations to other observers. And communication is helped by theories, taxonomies, hierarchies, as well as random modes of authorisation and credentialisation—exam results, citation scores, journal prestige, publishing houses and their reputations and so on. Other things being equal, more and more communication is possible. In this sense there are more and more human rights world-wide: more talk, more organisations, more regime criticism. The bad state of the world is a good theme for communication. Communication is easy.

Things are more difficult in interaction systems. The message here is that in this realm you live as you die, alone. *Ego* observes *alter* who observes *ego* and so on—and all interaction, however intimate, is time-limited. I send signals, you send signals, but neither party 'really' knows what the other thinks. And what does it mean anyway? Do you know what you yourself think? Do people know what they think?

In time-limited interaction, psychic systems exchange words—with varying degrees of meaningfulness—and other communicative signals (like body language or the observation of 'colour' and other physiognomic aspects)—themselves, one might say, pre-coded or freighted with 'meaning' as constituted in social communication. 'Meaning' is not inherent to things as they are; indeed the idea that things inherently possess meaning is nonsensical in systems-theoretic terms. Increasingly, perhaps, meaning in this context depends on or refers to meanings circulating more generally in society. In this sense 'race' can become a serious theme in interaction even if it is not really clear what it means. Indeed, it has meaning precisely because it has no meaning. Vagueness is tolerable in interaction because interaction is time-limited—unlike society, it ends.

[49] L Boltanski, *Distant Suffering: Morality, Media and Politics* (Cambridge, Cambridge University Press, 1999).

[50] From a systems-theoretic position this is one of the central flaws in Habermas's neo-Kantianism.

So being 'in favour' of or 'passionate' about human rights is easy—it means everything and nothing most of the time. It is not clear that Luhmann had any theory about human nature. However, there is no reason to suppose that he would not have endorsed or followed with interest emerging work in evolutionary psychology.[51] What is clear is that to build a theory of society on the basis of human nature was, to Luhmann, absurd. A 'sociological enlightenment' required different tools and a different starting point than 'man'. Humans come into the Luhmannian optic with all their limitations, defects and weaknesses. This is not a redemptive vision. 'Hope' is not high on the agenda.

WHY THE SOCIAL/PSYCHIC SYSTEM DISTINCTION IS IMPORTANT: A HABERMASIAN EXCURSUS

Already in the early Christian tradition we have the problem of establishing the truth in one's relation to self—the perils of self-deception well described by Augustine.[52] The role of external agencies—God, Satan—as mediating this relation to self does not perhaps, in a general sense, alter or affect its structure but does affect its meaning and the nature of the technologies thought appropriate to help confront and resolve the problem of the truth 'within' or of the self. In this sense, Freud radically influences the modern formulation of the problem but does not alter its structure. Whether the relation of the 'I' to the 'me' or however we should put it is unique to the West or to Judaeo-Christian societies I doubt,[53] but the way the problem has been worked through and is worked through today no doubt has much about it that is culturally specific.

If this is already a problem, then the relation to others, the 'I and Thou' of Martin Buber,[54] is also difficult in terms of knowing the truth of the other. How can I understand what it is to 'be' someone else if I'm only half-aware of what it is to 'be' me? It would seem that our ability to understand others rests largely on our capacities to understand ourselves, and the limits inherent in the latter hardly seem to fall away in the former. So we are endlessly confronted with the difficulty, and in some cases what we see as the impossibility, of understanding others ('I simply can't imagine how she feels/ why he behaves like that'), and

[51] See N Luhmann, *Social Systems* (Stanford, Stanford University Press) chapter 12. To ignore the question of 'hardwiring' of humans seems more and more pointless—see H Plotkin, *Evolution in Mind: An Introduction to Evolutionary Psychology* (Cambridge, Mass, Harvard University Press, 1998); S Pinker, *The Blank Slate: The Modern Denial of Human Nature* (Harmondsworth, Penguin, 2002); JL Elman *et al*, *Rethinking Innateness: A Connectionist Perspective on Development* (Cambridge, Mass, MIT Press, 1998). And so to regard humans as systems seems not a criticism (humans are subjects after all!) but quite sensible.

[52] M Foucault, *L'herméneutique du sujet* (Paris, Gallimard Le Seuil, 2001); Augustine, *Confessions* (Harmondsworth, Penguin, 1961).

[53] J Goody, *The East in the West* (Cambridge, Cambridge University Press, 1996); however see DJ Munro, *The Concept of Man in Early China* (Stanford, CA, Stanford University Press, 1969) comparing positive and normative ideas of equality in Confucianism and in Western thought.

[54] M Buber, *I and Thou* (New York, Scribner, 2000).

with the difficulty of communicating to others ('I simply can't describe how it feels/words fail me'). In the end of course, we can't share experiences; we can only talk about them and sometimes words fail. There is no Habermasian common world.

There may be a link here to the problem of not being able to help yourself behaving in a certain way in a certain kind of situation, even though in reflection afterwards and/or in forward planning, you ratiocinate a different form of behaviour ('I must keep/wish I had kept my mouth shut').

When it comes to differences like race or gender or sexual orientation, do we really move to a different problem from the one I'm suggesting is inscribed in the 'human condition'? Not just necessarily in modern thought,[55] we attribute certain differences and then postulate consequences which flow from them, whose incommunicability across the boundaries thus drawn we take to be in some way decisive or fundamental for the possibility of meaningful or successful or 'domination-free' communication. A man cannot know the desire for a child or what it means/feels to carry it or give birth to it; a man is thus at one remove from nurture; etc. Gay men and straight men cannot understand each other's desire; but the gay man can, additionally, point to a cruel history of oppression for his desire, and therefore, in certain modern settings, claim certain privileges, including his unique competence to explain and decipher his desire, over the heterosexual. White men cannot get inside a black man's skin and whites cannot inhabit the black universe.

The project of mutual understanding necessarily means that all we can do is exploit the resources of language and discourse—especially the use of analogy—to try to communicate about our experiences, in the course of which, no doubt, there would be many occasions when someone would say 'But you don't understand'—to which there is always a dual response: 'Try to explain again' coupled with 'Listen again and with sympathy'. Attributing differences which are then supposed to function in an *a priori* manner as barriers to communication (or, correlatively, as markers constituting micro-communities of discourse) can be seen as a way of refusing to try to do what is intrinsically possible in the situation. None of this is to say much at all! But then post-metaphysical thinking cannot say very much apart from the fact that it cannot say very much;[56] as a theory it must be both empty and open. The most we can ask is that it makes some kind of historical/sociological sense and the problem with this 'sense' is that it again requires resort to an 'us' who are already in communication and potential agreement with each other or to monadic psychic systems that cannot know for certain what other similarly isolated psychic systems think or feel and therefore have no access to what makes sense to others.

All this concerns ability (in principle) to communicate. Willingness to communicate raises related but different issues.

[55] F Hartog, *The Mirror of Herodotus: The Representation of the Other in the Writing of History* (Berkeley, CA, University of California Press, 1988).

[56] J Habermas, *Postmetaphysical Thinking: Philosophical Essays* (Oxford, Polity, 1992).

Can those who assert religious beliefs on a dogmatic basis ('It's true because God said so') be regarded as willing to communicate? I'm not sure that they can even if those who hold these beliefs claim that their beliefs are open to discussion or that they are at least willing to participate in discussions. 'Respecting' religious beliefs in a post-metaphysical age—which UK law now requires—seems somewhat dishonest: the most that liberalism can allow is that possession of these beliefs should be tolerated as long as these beliefs are not brought into discussions with those who don't hold them. Religion means, in effect, that there's nothing to discuss. Not infrequently, that seems to be the whole point of it (eg the psychic unburdening of the convert to something dogmatic and authoritarian like Catholicism). But now, as part of the broader project of making people good, respect for all religions and 'beliefs' is enjoined. The structure of the problem is similar to that of race/culture (and of course overlaps with it as well.)

The idea of the willingness to communicate and reach mutual understanding seems to me to be rooted in a one-sided understanding of the conditions of the lifeworld. Truth-seeking and deceit are equiprimordial.[57] So is hate as well as love. One understands all this if one understands the structural ambivalence of the mother-child relation, instead of imagining it one-sidedly as Habermas tends to do. Rational discussion abstracts and recodes this but does not resolve it nor can offer a lasting compromise.

So in some situations people may be motivated to reach agreement but in others not; they may seek to win in a discussion or not; and they may try to tell the truth or lie or equivocate in a discussion. It just depends. The felt need to be seen to conform, or the need for approval, often shapes what is said and how it is said in a discussion. 'Empirical' factors like idleness (the enemy for ever of the labour of the notion!) and disinterest are surely far too important to sideline as incidental to a theory of society. Boredom really does so often determine what many people do or do not do. So does exhaustion, or, more generally, finitude.

Does the problem of cultural difference make any difference? First of all it is another instance of boundary attribution. It is something we choose to allow to function as a barrier, or even more precisely these are barriers we make and treat as if they are natural. This modern making of cultural difference is shadowed by the growth in treating culture reflexively, and the logic of this is to make differences less different. As with race, gender or sexual orientation there are all sorts of reasons, not just strategic ones, which generate responses along the lines of 'You must understand that in China we have always . . .'; 'Only a Jew can really understand the Holocaust' and so on (and on).[58] I increasingly think these are

[57] See WT Murphy, 'The Habermas Effect: Critical Theory and Academic Law' (1989) 42 *Current Legal Problems* 135 reprinted in R Cotterrell (ed), *Sociological Perspectives on Law*, Vol I: *Classical Foundations* (London, Ashgate, 2001) 383–413.

[58] No-one can know what has 'always' happened. There is no 'always' just pasts which operate in the present and 'move with the times'. On the Holocaust see especially P Novick, *The Holocaust and Collective Memory* ((London, Bloomsbury, 2000).

bogus though commonplace. But in any case even if we believe that our language is just one game among many, how can this be anything more than a matter of belief? Whether the anthropologist is 'native' or 'western', is not his/her work of culture precisely an attempt to explain 'it' to (and I would also say fabricate it for) us? And are not these 'profound' differences in reality effects of genres—literary, film, scholarly—our genres? Even if then there are profound differences, the only ones we can understand are the ones we understand (or think we do). And reflexively or self-critically we now know that the anthropologist can be more inventive than the native, or the native can be inventive for the benefit of the anthropologist.[59]

There is also the question of future generations. It is improbable that humans have the capacity to think seriously beyond the present and the future which is present in that present. One or two generations—children and grandchildren—have traditionally provided some kind of horizon for measuring this present future and this is embedded in the most fundamental device for the purposive coordination of society which is the rules of inheritance. Cryogenics and cloning may come to offer a sci-fi dissolution of this limited time-frame and elongate the present future. Beyond that, we can allow future generations in as virtual present discussants to speak for their interests, however we try to institutionalise that.[60] (In a partly pre-institutional sense, that is what Greenpeace and Friends of the Earth and other groups are trying to do.) But what often gets muddled up here is the distinction between the worlded nature of postmetaphysical thinking and the viability of transposing our traditional language of trusteeship and responsibility from this world to the world of the future and of its inhabitants. This is necessarily an abstract problem (the cultural allegiances of Greenpeace etc often obscure this) and I suspect it can only be formulated technocratically, ie through calculations, statistics, measurements, computer simulations, and, in the end, probabilistically. And at this level the problem is that it's difficult to do these calculations for ourselves and it's difficult to choose between alternative calculations and so it's difficult to have open-ended discussions about what we should do faced with an agenda assembled in this way.[61]

In response to all this, Luhmann's position is blunt:

> [Habermas's] theory sides with the human to join the latter in battle against enemy forces. But isn't this human merely an invention of this theory, merely a veiling of this theory's self-reference? If he or she were meant as an empirical object (with the name of subject), the theory would have to declare who, then, is meant, for obviously it cannot send five billion humans, who at the same time are living and acting, on a discursive search for good grounds. Not only the length of this process of searching, and the conditions of 'bounded rationality', but already the sheer simultaneity of

[59] Cf, the *Writing Cultures* debate literature.

[60] J Habermas, *The Future of Human Nature* (Oxford, Polity, 2003).

[61] Cf, the debate around B Lomborg, *The Skeptical Environmentalist: Measuring the Real State of the World* (Cambridge, Cambridge University Press, 2001).

behaviour would doom such a project. One cannot idealise sociality without taking account of time.[62]

In other words, the opacity of the problem cannot be redeemed through communicative rationality, because that solution has no possible foundation in actual communicative situations. It is not just that there is no escape from the distinction between social and psychic systems; it is also the presumption at least that proposals which ignore or bury this problem are doomed to fail. There can, of course, be no proof of this. But why prefer hope to skepticism or circumspection in a world with many possibilities, many of which are 'sub-optimal'?

CONCLUSION

One could perhaps describe the race equality agenda as a therapeutic or palliative one at the (national) societal level (and equally this can be regarded as a sub-dimension of a larger pan-European project). The aim is at once to cure or 'ease' pathologies and to build a 'strong' and healthy societal organism. The assumption is that diversity is to be cherished and that diversity is itself productive. A diverse society is better than a non-diverse, culturally homogenous one. Parekh has some intelligent arguments to support this position (in reality, a more sophisticated position).[63] However, who believes this?

I believe it. But I have personal reasons for believing it. That is, in any self-description which I would put into communication, I would offer a selective biography which would explain, if that was demanded, why I 'personally' prefer to work in a university with students from all over the world (multiethnic, multinational) compared with one where most of the students are from Hertfordshire or Surrey, and most of my colleagues would agree—that is—they would nod assent in an interaction system, although what they really think I do not know. I don't know if they know. One doesn't critically test through 'introspection' whether one believes all the things one assents to in communication. In addition, work is work. Where I live is another matter. What I want or need from where I live is for the most part a quiet environment because I work from home a lot. Certain cultural practices in my immediate environment (neighbours) might not be consistent with that. I may need to make neighbour-related predictions in deciding where to live (along with affordability, space requirements etc). Prejudice is pervasive. Without it 'personal' decisions cannot be made.[64]

[62] N Luhmann, *Theories of Distinction: Redescribing the Descriptions of Modernity* (Stanford, Stanford University Press, 2002) 193.

[63] B Parekh, *Rethinking Multiculturalism: Cultural Diversity and Political Theory* (Basingstoke, Palgrave, 2000).

[64] TC Schelling, *Micromotives and Macrobehaviour* (New York, WW Norton, 1978) chapter 4.

In identity politics one observes using, as in all observation, distinctions. But is one allowed to observe race (to use race as a distinction) in this context where racial discrimination is the enemy and where there is a strong impetus to link this to the human rights agenda? These are already difficult questions.

More difficult still is how to make sense of political and legal systems which take as one of their (perhaps shared) projects the goal of making 'people' good. In systems theory terms this requires manipulation of the psychic system. But is this possible? Presumably it is, up to a point. Otherwise, other things being equal, advertising and PR would not exist. What can be said in social communication can be controlled in various ways. Societies committed to 'freedom of expression' can nonetheless be censorious. It is probably unnecessary to provide examples. There are and will be things which always must not be said. However, even the unsaid, the proscribed, still circulates in social communication—even as the unsaid. Psychoanalysis understood this well in the concept of the repressed, but was unable to differentiate psychic and social systems, and used findings based on interaction to generalise about social systems—which was mistaken.

And so we reach the core paradox: one of the things that must not be said, about which we must keep silent, is race. But there is a difference between keeping silent about this theme and talking about it or 'celebrating' it. If a theme or topic like this is put into social communication and institutionalised into legal and governmental regimes then the differences between society, organisation and interaction and social and psychic systems become important.

It is not the purpose of this chapter to be normative or prescriptive. It is rather to question the assumptions of prescriptivism itself. To develop a policy of celebrating 'difference', of proliferating distinctions, seems an unlikely recipe for success if the objective is greater equality. It might be more appropriate to make fewer distinctions, to embrace what biologists are already telling us are the outcomes of their observations, and let race equality evolve by ceasing to use 'race' as such a freighted theme in society, in organisations or in interaction. We need, in other words, to address the paradox: anti-discrimination regimes (an end to distinctions!) proliferate the use/visibility of distinctions including in the area of 'forbidden' categories—race, sexual orientation, age etc—'celebrations of difference' (of course). The thematisation and valorisation of diversity—what quickly becomes identity politics—amounts to a construction of identity which resides in difference. And we also need—a bigger question—to think carefully about the idea that law can make people good.[65]

From a systems-theoretic perspective, it is not the artificiality or constructedness of these distinctions which is of significance. These dimensions are obvious. What is significant—and, it must be added, somewhat opaque in normative or policy terms—is the problem of the paradox of race/~~race.~~ The proliferation of racial distinctions that we have witnessed in recent years—in large measure as

[65] I hope to expand elsewhere on this question.

the direct result of legislative measures and the attempts at classification and monitoring that have accompanied them—make the problem seem even more opaque. To the extent that psychic systems are focused or shaped by social communication, however vague or diffuse the themes that circulate in it are, we are in the process of creating through Europe a more rather than less racist society. Ideas like tolerance fail to address the central problem.[66]

Were society to acknowledge or accept that discrimination was not a problem then the paradox could be overcome—matters could be left in a state of indeterminacy or oscillation between these impossible poles of the distinction. We could retreat to the old world—which now seems like a world of make-believe—in which we liked to think and say that we were blind to distinctions. But in a world very conscious of distinctions and very active in distinction-making, such a plan or proposal seems absurd. So how do we live in a world in which we proliferate distinctions between human beings and at the same time deny their validity, and are not even very sure, despite the litany of human rights, what a human being is anyway, or where the boundary between the human and the non-human should be drawn, and on what basis?

[66] This was the weakness of an earlier paper of mine—'One of Us? Politics, Difference and Affirmative Action' (1995) *Current Legal Theory, XIII* Special Issue 2: *The Rhetoric of Reconstruction. Architectural Moves beyond Interpretation* (ed J Broekman, D Kennedy, J Lenoble) 21.

4

Niklas Luhmann's Political Theory: Politics after Metaphysics?

CHRIS THORNHILL

THE SOCIOLOGICAL RECONSTRUCTION OF ENLIGHTENMENT AND THE END OF METAPHYSICS.

BY GIVING THE title *Sociological Enlightenment* to his inaugural lecture and to the six-volume collection of his miscellaneous essays, Luhmann implicitly announced that he wished his work, in its entirety, to be viewed as a reconstruction of the legacy of the Enlightenment, both in its sociological-methodological and political-theoretical implications. This decision demonstrates a clear and concerted intellectual strategy, and it reflects Luhmann's intention to place his work at the very heart of the key theoretical debates in modern philosophy, sociology and political theory. From Nietzsche to Derrida, the most influential recent philosophical views have, in different ways, defined themselves as part of a continuing critique of the universalist, normative and rationalist programmes of the Enlightenment. From Weber to Habermas, similarly, the most dominant perspectives in modern sociology and political theory also revolve around a critique or theoretical transformation of the socio-ethical and explanatory principles of the Enlightenment. Luhmann is therefore quite clear about the centrality and weight, in sociology, philosophy and political theory, of the debates in which he engages in defining his own work as *sociological Enlightenment*. Indeed, in entering these debates he makes a strong (though always implicit) claim for the conceptual core of his sociology. This claim is, no less, that his own work is a (if not *the*) defining perspective in post-Enlightenment sociology and political thought, that it both exposes the fallacies and resurrects the miscarried potentials of the Enlightenment, and that his work accomplishes a reconstruction of the Enlightenment more effectively than those who came before him and those with whom he participates in discussion.

In Luhmann's terms, sociological Enlightenment is a methodological approach to the analysis of society which incorporates a far-reaching change of paradigm against the Enlightenment as it was originally conceived, and which aims to question and transform the rationalist and anthropocentric fabric of theories deriving from the first Enlightenment. This is not to say, as Habermas has suggested, that Luhmann is a resolutely anti-Enlightenment thinker, or that his work reflects a discrete sympathy for pre-modern socio-political forms. On the contrary, he agrees with many principles of the first Enlightenment, especially with its assertion that modern society is marked by processes of evolution, positivisation and rationalisation which might, in their totality, be viewed as progressive and emancipatory. Like the first Enlightenment, his sociology is committed to explaining human evolution, and to examining the development of society away from static, religious and traditional conceptions of its own essence and necessary structure towards a condition in which it can freely provide positive terms for its own internal consistency. At this level, Luhmann is clearly a progressive theorist, who sees an increment of social autonomy and plurality as an essential characteristic of modern society. Moreover, more fundamentally, he clearly concurs with the first Enlightenment in its hostility to immutable, essentialist or metaphysical accounts of social reality, and in its rejection of all suggestions that social reality is determined by immutable theological or ontological conditions, existing independently of the local or passing events of social evolution. In fact, his claim that the formation of meaning and validity in modern society are entirely positive—that is, that they are entirely self-generating, and are not bound by definite or unchanging structure—manifestly echoes the main conviction of the Enlightenment: namely, that all inquiries into the necessary moral or political order of society must dispense with religiously or metaphysically founded constructs. In this regard, as discussed below, Luhmann's sociology chimes in with the great theoretical ambitions of Enlightenment, and it might be seen both to continue with and intensify the original anti-metaphysical insistence on human autonomy and self-determination which marked the original Enlightenment. Above all, in this respect Luhmann's interest is directed towards the key Enlightenment concept of *rationality*. Like thinkers in the tradition of Enlightenment theory, his primary objective is to account for the function of rationality in modern society, and for the ways in which processes of rationalisation determine the shape of modern society and free it from unifying structural and metaphysical principles.

Despite this, however, Luhmann also underlines the critical and dialectical nature of his coupling of sociology and Enlightenment, and he places himself in direct methodological opposition to certain preconditions of the first Enlightenment. For Luhmann, the Enlightenment has the key weakness that it believes that all questions about society can be resolved 'through the use of reason', and it views reason as the defining attribute of the human being—both as the arbiter and gauge of all 'human conditions' and as the determinant of social improvement and progress.[1] The Enlightenment is, therefore, obsessively preoccupied with questions relating to the 'essence (the nature) of the human being', and it lacks the theoretical instruments which might enable it to

[1] N Luhmann, 'Soziologische Aufklärung' (1967) 18 *Soziale Welt* 97.

comprehend 'the social as such', as a complex of relations independent of particular human beings and their attributes:[2] the Enlightenment only understands society by deducing its content and character from an idealised or essentialised projection of original human attributes, so that all social facts are viewed as an expression or amalgamation of characteristics that all people are supposed to possess. For these reasons, from a sociological perspective, the Enlightenment only ever offers the most reductive and schematically anthropological account of social events and transformations, and it construes social occurrences as the corollaries of primary human orientations, behavioural emphases, and rationally steered choices or normative prescriptions. Sociology, by contrast, is far better equipped to grasp the plural, simultaneous and multi-causal character of social development. Sociology 'looks for a hold less in immutable laws of universal-human reason than in ascertainable facts and the social conditions of behaviour',[3] and it is able to view the factors determining society, and the evolution that it experiences, as unpredictable, intensely variable and sporadically emergent. Most importantly, sociology looks for the causes of social events in society itself, not in any primary anthropological or rationalised substructure which it might impute to society.

This juxtaposition of sociology and Enlightenment provides the key for understanding the aims of Luhmann's work. Although the Enlightenment, he concedes, has its own claim to validity in its original attempt to construe the progressive and rationalising dynamics determining social conditions, it also suffers from the great flaw that it associates such rationalisation with the specific operations of individual human beings, whose atomised faculties of 'reason' are viewed as the causal and prescriptive centres of all social reality.[4] From a sociological point of view, therefore, clearly Enlightenment misunderstands society; however, it also misunderstands rationality itself. It incorrectly identifies the origin of rationality by locating it in the faculties of the isolated human mind. Then, extrapolating from all factual social process, it naively imputes to rationality the ability to establish binding theoretical insights, truths or *laws*, and to organise and control social existence through the application of these insights. Against such standard views, Luhmann argues that the rationality which triggers social change, even that which brings social improvement or 'progress', is not the reflexive rationality of concrete people, but the internal

[2] N Luhmann, *Die Politik der Gesellschaft* (Frankfurt am Main, Suhrkamp, 2000) 12.

[3] N Luhmann, 'Soziologische Aufklärung', above n 1 at 97.

[4] In an important article on these themes, Dirk Baecker emphasises Luhmann's hostility to the 'lazy rationalism of the 18th century', and he examines his proposed concept of 'self-critical reason' as a counter-term to this. Like this discussion, Baecker also stresses Luhmann's sense that sociology also has a potential for Enlightenment, insofar as sociology 'observes society in a manner different from the way society in its different milieus observes itself'. Yet Baecker does not fully account either for ways in which Luhmann's concept of sociological Enlightenment perceives itself as a rectification of the original intentions of Enlightenment, or for the philosophical foundations of his attack on Enlightenment rationalism. See: D Baecker, 'Gypsy Reason: Niklas Luhmann's Sociological Enlightenment' (1999) 6 *Cybernetics and Human Knowing* 5.

rationality of the *systems of society*. This rationality becomes manifest and effective as systems reduce and develop complexity in the process of their self-stabilisation. It is for this reason, on Luhmann's account, that Enlightenment needs sociology: that Enlightenment needs to be a *sociological Enlightenment*. Sociology, in Luhmann's view, categorically denies that 'the individual human being can, by reflecting on his or her own rationality, find things common to all people, obtain consensus, or even truth'.[5] Sociology, therefore, is always inclined to view rationality as a systemic attribute, and to detach processes of rationalisation from simple or personalised causes. Sociology, in consequence, is a corrective counterweight to the naivety and simplicity of the Enlightenment. The key theoretical shortcoming of Enlightenment, he argues, resides in its claim that people, not the systems of society, are at the origin of social evolution. In reality, it is systems themselves, not integral people, which stimulate and perpetuate the processes of societal rationalisation: systems, consequently, are the genuine 'medium of Enlightenment',[6] and this medium can only be understood *sociologically*.

Underlying Luhmann's proposed fusion of Enlightenment and sociology is, therefore, an attempt to refract our view of society and its systems through a multi-paradigmatic methodology, which is capable of accepting that there exist a number of quite different types of rationality and social causality, and which shifts the examination of society away from its normative or ideal focus on human endowments. Nonetheless, Luhmann still argues that sociology and Enlightenment are not finally 'heterogeneous, incomparable or incompatible attitudes of mind'.[7] On the contrary, he maintains that the fundamental role of sociology is to elaborate the original insights of Enlightenment, to refine the methodological means by which these are obtained, and so to integrate these insights into a perspective on society which fundamentally differs from the mono-centric outlook of classical Enlightenment theory.[8] Sociology can only accomplish this, however, if it examines the facts of social development and evolution under the aspect of 'latent functions',[9] not as rationally ordained processes, originating from some manifest human source. Luhmann thus sees the unity of sociology and Enlightenment in a method of functional analysis which rejects rationalised or external 'laws of causality' as the hypothetical basis of inquiry, which scrutinises social developments and realities as components in the overarching evolution and self-rationalisation of function systems, and which is willing to acknowledge extreme diversity in the accounts which function systems provide for themselves of their own rationality and legitimacy.[10]

[5] N Luhmann, 'Soziologische Aufklärung', above n 1 at 98.
[6] *Ibid*, 109.
[7] *Ibid*, 98.
[8] *Ibid*, 103.
[9] *Ibid*, 103.
[10] *Ibid*, 108.

This conception of sociological Enlightenment follows the first Enlightenment in accepting that there are certain characteristics (i.e increasing complexity, increasing rationality, functional differentiation, increasing autonomy, legal positivisation), which mark modern society out against earlier periods of history, in which societies were more traditionally organised or more rigidly stratified. Indeed, in his insistence on rational differentiation and plural autonomy as the adequate conditions of modern society Luhmann's thought is clearly pledged to the Enlightenment, and to the socio-political reality envisioned by Enlightenment; Luhmann, quite evidently, has no sympathy at all for obviously pre-Enlightenment modes of hierarchically structured or centred social organisation. At the same time, however, the sociological Enlightenment is expressly *sociological* in that it rejects all explanations of the complex reality of modern society which link the emergence and the increasing complexity of social systems to self-identical and enduring causes, which are in some way *outside* the systems in which evolution occurs.[11] Most especially, the Enlightenment postulation of human rationality as a factor affecting social evolution and offering ethical standards, norms or laws which might be held against the complex and emerging realities in which social evolution takes place is, for Luhmann, a rather desperate and reductive analysis of social development. This analysis only manages to make sense of the world by positing the most crudely abstracted schemes of causality.

For Luhmann, in short, the only meaningful rationality is 'system-rationality': rationalisation is the autopoietic self-reflection of a social system as it reacts to the complexity of its environments and generates adequate levels of internal complexity. Such rationalisation, however, is in many respects indifferent to the individual human being, and it cannot be refracted into principles or laws designed to serve the needs of particular human beings.[12] 'A system acts rationally,' Luhmann explains, 'to the extent that it can absorb complexity and can solve the internal problems thrown up by this [. . .] to the extent that in an extremely complex world it can preserve a higher, more intelligible world, which excludes other possibilities.'[13] Rationality, conceived in this way, is not a specific human attribute, located in one consciousness or in the dialogical interstice between one person's consciousness and that of another person. Certainly, it is not an endowment which might allow particular people to acquire immutable insights into social conditions, and it is not a deductive faculty providing exemplary theoretical postulates or criteria for assessing the worth of social events or for legislating how events might be changed. Instead, rationality is simply the internal reality of an effectively functioning autopoietic social system, and a system obtains and enacts its rationality insofar as it fulfils its functions of self-differentiation, complexity-reduction and complexity-maintenance. Rationality

[11] *Ibid*, 120.
[12] *Ibid*, 114.
[13] N Luhmann, 'Politische Planung' (1966) 17 *Jahrbuch für Sozialwissenschaft* 283.

and practical reality, consequently, are always functionally identical in the self-processing operations of a social system. Systemic rationality is not manifest in a fixed and invariably demonstrable series of postulates or norms: it is simply the evolving reality of an operative social system, and it is always already realised—'as an occurrence'—at each moment in the system's self-perpetuation.[14] As an account of the character and role of rationality in society, therefore, *sociological Enlightenment* is always construed as something profoundly different from a *human Enlightenment*, or, more especially, from a *humanist Enlightenment*. It renounces all belief in the 'common possession of reason' by all human beings, and it abandons all claims that humanity might have 'foreseeable purposes' or be oriented towards determinate shared objectives.[15] Indeed, Luhmann claims that 'classical conceptions' regarding the 'correctness and rationality of individual decisions' are wholly inadequate to the functional complexity of modern society, and they serve only to place prior limits on society's potential for complexity,[16] and thus on its potential for rationality and rationalisation.

It is worth repeating, nonetheless, that Luhmann's paradigm does not utterly renounce the theoretical plan behind the original Enlightenment. In stressing the need for multi-rational and multi-perspectival approaches to social reality, Luhmann does not simply negate the belief of Enlightenment that reason is a dynamically transformative force in the emergence of modern society, creating conditions of greater independence, autonomy and self-reliance. On the contrary, one key theoretical implication of the sociological Enlightenment is that the first Enlightenment, which focused on single aspects of human reason and human autonomy, is not actually Enlightenment at all. This Enlightenment, Luhmann suggests, sought to provide a firm ground for human autonomy and self-determination by identifying human reason as the centre of social evolution, and so by imagining that reason can act as a universal theoretical measure, guide and cause of all social events. In so doing, this Enlightenment endeavoured most particularly to overcome metaphysical accounts of human reality: ie accounts of social being which see the validity of human reason and action as determined by prior, transcendent, or ontological principles. However, the rationalist Enlightenment is—for Luhmann—in fact still caught up in the pre-Enlightenment metaphysical view of the world, which attributed the order and structure of the universe to a prime mover or a sequence of primary causes. Indeed, it is precisely in its conception of reason, through which the Enlightenment hoped to escape classical metaphysics, that the first Enlightenment remains incarcerated in metaphysical constructs. The rational Enlightenment, he explains, fails to understand social modernity because it clings to a counter-factual image of a society centred on, and interpretable by, simple, monadic or universal forms of human reason. The rational Enlightenment thus reconstructs first metaphysics, or 'ontological

[14] N Luhmann, *Die Wirtschaft der Gesellschaft* (Frankfurt am Main, Suhrkamp, 1988) 278.
[15] *Ibid*, 293.
[16] N Luhmann, 'Soziologische Aufklärung', above n 1 at 114.

metaphysics', as a secondary metaphysics—that is, as a 'metaphysics of consciousness', a 'metaphysics of reason', [17] or as a 'subject-metaphysics'—which places the faculties of the atomised human being at the causal centre of the social world.[18] Through this reconstruction, the Enlightenment concludes simplistically that the use of 'one's own reason' will always serve to 'find true being',[19] and that true being can be distilled as a set of standards and causes existing independently of all factual reality. This inevitably results in a simplification of social complexity and of the 'unlimited possibility' borne by the evolutionary dynamics of modern social reality.[20] Such Enlightenment merely reproduces those same metaphysical assumptions which it criticises, and it crudely replicates essentialist ontological claims that the universe is organised to comply with some single underlying plan or with some abiding universal regulatory structure. It is only sociological Enlightenment which is able truly to account for the great plurality and diversity of the rationalising processes in society, and so to recognise the 'conditions and chances of a real Enlightenment'.[21]

For Luhmann, therefore, the imputation of rational, causal or moral criteria separate from social reality is in fact only the most rudimentary, underdeveloped expression of Enlightenment. Genuinely post-metaphysical Enlightenment would be prepared to accept the existence of socially suspended, infinitely complex and changing forms of reason, and it would construe social evolution as following extremely variable and fluctuating rational imperatives. Above all, real (*sociological*) Enlightenment must necessarily reject the quasi-metaphysical fictions that the social world has an essential or perennial structure, originating in the human being itself, and that this can somehow be causally divined in the medium of human rationality, or morally prescribed in the medium of human *law*. In fact, perhaps the greatest conceptual weakness of the Enlightenment—especially in its political implications—is that it detaches *law*, as a rational or universal order of norms, from factual social reality, and that it then burdens law with the expectation that it might prescribe conditions of rational adequacy and justification to the factual social reality from which it originated. The most striking misconception at the heart of the Enlightenment is thus that it sees law as a transmitter of rational human values, capable of recognising necessary social conditions and of effecting measurable levels of social progress, and it sees the deduction and political implementation of law as the consummate activity or entelechy of human reason. This, for Luhmann, clearly indicates that Enlightenment has not adequately disentangled itself from the originally metaphysical or theological conviction that some invariable juridical order inheres

[17] *Ibid*, 106.

[18] N Luhmann, *Social Systems*, J Bednarz Junr and D Baecker (trans), (Stanford CA, Stanford University Press, 1995) 101.

[19] N Luhmann, 'Soziologische Aufklärung', 106.

[20] *Ibid*, 107.

[21] *Ibid*, 123.

in the universe, and that human thinking is charged with responsibility for interpreting and enforcing this order.

MODERN POLITICAL THEORY AS METAPHYSICS.

In his attempt to cut away the metaphysical and anthropological foundations of post-Enlightenment social and political thought, Luhmann also squares up to the central political conclusion of the Enlightenment. This is expressed in the rational-legal concept of political *legitimacy*, which argues that the proper use of rationality will lead to the deduction and prescription of universalisable laws which provide a gauge for assessing whether organs of governmental authority do or do not possess the attribute of legitimacy. As a consequence of his anti-metaphysical turn, Luhmann asserts that the conceptual mainstays of modern liberal political theory—the belief that the human being, defined as a rational legal subject, gives foundation to the political system, and the belief that the human being is endowed with specific rational faculties of law-giving and law-deduction, which allow it to hold a mirror of adequacy (legitimacy) to the political systems which it inhabits—are fictitious and simplifying metaphysical constructs, which form the root of the errors of political analysis arising from the Enlightenment.

Underlying Luhmann's work, therefore, is a rejection (or at least radical refiguration) of the classical belief, underscoring the entire tradition of post-Enlightenment reflection on the democratic legal state, that *legitimacy* is the public or objective corollary of *legality*, or that law can provide reasonably stable terms for enshrining and legitimising the deployment of power. For Luhmann, the argument in the Enlightenment that the conditions of political legitimacy depend on the invariable, or at least quantifiable, encasing of order in rationally sanctioned law offers only a most reductively formulaic conception of the legitimate polity, and it only conceives of political freedom and autonomy on the basis of a metaphysically reduced construction of what such freedom and autonomy might in fact be. Legitimacy in the political system, Luhmann in fact argues, is merely the 'formula of contingency' for politics.[22] The political system does not obtain and utilise legitimacy by conforming to externally deduced norms or obligations. Rather, it secures legitimacy by conferring upon itself a differentiated and contingent form, which allows it to establish a level of predictability *in its own communications*, and so to gain acceptance for itself and, more broadly, to establish its political processes through society as valid and plausible sequences of operations. Legitimacy in the political system is thus a formula in which the political system can consistently and persuasively talk about itself to itself, and then provide itself with a coherent account of what it does and why it does it. Having established its legitimacy internally, the

[22] N Luhmann, 'Soziologische Aufklärung', 125.

political system is then able to create a core of self-referring communications by means of which its operations become externally meaningful, plausible, and so likely to be met with some degree of compliance. As the *formula of contingency*, in short, legitimacy is the realised *self-reference* of the differentiated autopoietic political system, and the legitimate political system is a political system which has woven a convincing web of legitimacy out of its own, utterly contingent, operations.[23]

For a political system to be legitimate does therefore emphatically not mean that it conforms to standard or consensually accepted definitions of what legitimacy might be; it merely means that the system proposes itself in its differentiated contingency as a plausible reality. All motivations for acceptance of political decisions are then based on that fragile contingent foundation. Importantly, this theory of legitimacy makes no substantive or legal claims about the necessary character of government or about the necessary content of policies and laws. For Luhmann, government is legitimate wherever, and for whatever reason, it can motivate citizens to recognise and follow laws, and wherever it can introduce autonomously validated 'laws' (or policies which ultimately assume the form of law), which are then *accepted as legitimate*. The processes through which laws are accepted as legitimate can be manifold and highly diverse. The key moment in the generation of acceptance and legitimacy, however, is not that the political system explains its regulations by appealing to the personal motives or to the rationally motivated consensus of its addressees. On the contrary, the political system legitimises itself by institutionalising rule-bound procedures which are able to stimulate a 'generalised trust in the system' and so to create conditions in which compliance can be secured and demonstrated.[24] Political government is legitimate, therefore, wherever it can ensure that 'the legitimacy of pure legality finds recognition'.[25] On Luhmann's account, in fact, legitimacy *precedes* the law, and law has no directly constitutive role in the production of legitimacy. In principle, this model of legitimacy allows for an extremely high degree of relativity in the definition of political legitimacy and legitimate law, and political systems can be accepted as legitimate in many different ways and for many different reasons. In fact, if a political system can explain its operations in a satisfyingly plausible and consistent manner, 'legitimate legal validity can be claimed for any content'.[26]

In his reconstruction of this central post-Enlightenment category of legitimacy, Luhmann quite clearly indicates that the theoretical methods, and indeed the store of concepts, around which post-Enlightenment political thought is organised are based in a fundamentally misguided mode of questioning. Indeed,

[23] N Luhmann, 'Die Unbeliebtheit der Parteien' (1992) 37 *Die politische Meinung* 11.

[24] N Luhmann, *Legitimation durch Verfahren* (Frankfurt a M, Suhrkamp, 1983) 34, 193.

[25] N Luhmann, 'Soziologie des politischen Systems', in N Luhmann, *Soziologische Aufklärung*, vol I: *Aufsätze zur Theorie sozialer Systeme* (Cologne and Opladen, Westdeutscher Verlag, 1970) 154–177; 167.

[26] N Luhmann, *Die Politik der Gesellschaft*, above n 2 at 180.

if we define the most essential concern of modern political theory as an attempt to draw up a set of prior conditions, grounded in rational conceptions of human rights, needs, well-being or reason, against which the legitimacy of the political order can be assessed, the political-theoretical implication of Luhmann's work is quite straightforward. Modern political theory, he indicates, asks the wrong questions, and it even asks these wrong questions in the wrong way. Contemporary political theory, archaically fixated on rational or essential-anthropological models of the legitimate order, clings to counter-factual images of a society centred on and serving abstractly determinable human interests, and subject, via the medium of law, to steering by theoretically synthesised (rational) reflections of these interests. Modern political theory, in short, still craves the perennial simplicity and the facile certitude of metaphysics. By dimly hoping that the political system can give public representation to the laws of human reason, modern political theory merely replaces the original metaphysical conceptions of the ideal polity with an anthropologically recast, yet still fundamentally metaphysical, perspective on legitimacy, and on the relation between politics and law.

In this respect, it is illuminating to place Luhmann's work briefly beside that of his major rivals in modern political thought, and so to illustrate ways in which he poses a quite fundamental challenge to established and widely admired perspectives of contemporary political-theoretical orthodoxy. In certain points, the attempt to reconstruct and refine the Enlightenment, so that human rationality might finally declare itself an entirely free-standing reflexive faculty, stripped of all attachment to metaphysical essences and constructs, is an enterprise which connects Luhmann (however surprisingly and paradoxically) with the main recent proponents of normative political theory. Indeed, in his methodological perspective on the Enlightenment, there are important critical parallels between himself and the two great normative political theorists of the last three or four decades: Habermas and Rawls. For all the otherwise almost innumerable differences between them, Habermas, Rawls and Luhmann are linked by the fact that each of them seeks to account for rationality, and for rationality's role in society, by divesting it of the quasi-metaphysical or transcendental foundations which it has inherited from the Kantian Enlightenment, and by reflecting the outcomes of reason as insights produced in complete independence and autonomy, without any recourse to prior certainties and without any circumscription by ontological or external criteria of truthfulness. In this respect, therefore, Habermas, Rawls and Luhmann are all thinkers who seek to extend the Enlightenment beyond its original assumptions, and who wish to make good the promise in the Enlightenment that reason might become fully self-sufficient and self-legislating. Furthermore, Habermas, Rawls and Luhmann all also concur in identifying the post-transcendental use of reason as the source of legitimacy in the modern political system. All, in fact, might be seen diversely to radicalise the original demand of the Enlightenment—and especially of the Kantian Enlightenment: that is, namely, that rationality should be fully autonomous, that rationality and autonomy are in fact coterminous, and that rationality, autonomously generating its own foundations and preconditions, is the sole ground of legitimate political order. Across their great methodological and ideological conflicts, thus, Habermas, Rawls and Luhmann are all united in the endeavour to give a conclusively secular and irreducibly autonomous description of rationality's character and scope, and so to conceive legal validity and political legitimacy as the expressions of an exclusively post-metaphysical rationality.

Luhmann's treatment of the Enlightenment legacy, as discussed above, revolves around the reinterpretation of rationality as an attribute of systems, not of persons, and around the claim that political legitimacy is obtained where a political system plausibly rationalises itself in its contingency, free of all reference to transcendent or immutable laws—or, indeed, to external consensus. Habermas, by contrast, is naturally still far more of a Kantian than Luhmann. However, he too seeks to detranscendentalise human rationality and to detach our understanding of rationality from the universalistic constructs of the Enlightenment. He attempts to accomplish this, firstly, by differentiating between instrumental and communicative rationality, and so by arguing that rationality is oriented towards distinct validity claims in different modes of human practice. On these grounds, he emphatically states that rationality is not directed towards the deduction of one single truth, and that it claims truthful validity in different ways for different purposes. Secondly, then, in accounting for the universalistic aspect of rationality as *communicative reason* he again implies that the highest validity claims of rationality should be viewed in resolutely post-transcendental terms: not, that is, as functions of a monadic model of consciousness, nor bound by formal-universal standards of truth measurement, but as functions of independent and contextually embedded consensus-finding, obtaining validity only where all prior principles or claims are suspended.[27] He therefore concludes, in the spirit of Enlightenment, that human rationality, as communicative reason, can indeed arrive at universalisable principles or agreements, and it can ultimately channel these, as binding laws, into a framework of legitimate legality for the political order. This can only be accomplished only, however, on the basis of a thorough-going demystification of the faculty of reason, through which reason is examined both in its socio-functional contextuality and in its non-transcendental interpersonal structure. In direct analogy to this, Rawls also seeks both to alter and redeem the objectives of the Enlightenment by setting out his theoretical stall against all reliance on transcendental claims in his examination of the practical functions of rationality—especially in the deduction of binding laws. In the early phase of his trajectory he argues that the normative standards of fairness and justice which form the basis of legitimate laws can be derived through the use of

[27] J Habermas, *Postmetaphysical Thinking*, WM Hohengarten (trans), (Cambridge, Polity Press, 1992) 10–27.

rationality in a constructivist or hypothetical situation, in which rationality is occluded against all transcendental principles and all factual information.[28] Then, in his later works, he asserts that the historical structure and daily fabric of reasonable societies always contain practically given and overlapping moral principles which provide a generalisable foundation for law and for legitimacy for government.[29] For all the diversity of their approaches, these three thinkers are thus joined—however paradoxically—in their intention to demonstrate how rationality can freely obtain securities in the everyday processes and activities of social and political life, how it can articulate these securities without recourse to transcendental supplements or first principles, and how legitimacy in politics and law gives expression to the temporal securities of such autonomously defined rationality. All respond to the Enlightenment by denying the existence of immutable or absolutely prior principles of right, but all still seek to show how rationality, once truly emancipated from metaphysics, can generate independent premises for legitimate politics and valid law.

Concern with the problem of metaphysics, or with the incompleteness of the rejection of metaphysics in the first Enlightenment, is therefore clearly not unique to Luhmann, and this marks a point of open or implicit dialogue between himself and more mainstream political theorists. It is at least arguable, however, that Habermas and Rawls, like all normative theorists, are both unsuccessful in their attempt to escape the metaphysical conceptions of rationality which they hope to supersede, and that neither successfully accounts for legitimacy in politics and law as a genuinely post-metaphysical reality. Both these thinkers remain lastly in the paradigm of the Kantian Enlightenment, and they arrive at a non-metaphysical account of rationality, and of rationality's role in founding legitimate law and legitimate power, only by virtue of a rather surreptitious sleight of theoretical abstraction. Both argue that human rationality alone produces the laws which constitute legitimate politics; to construct this argument, however, both presuppose that human beings are innately rational, that rationality invariably manifests itself in the establishment of laws, and that all rational people and their rational laws are always likely to be rational in much the same way. At the heart of this claim, then, is the rather circular or tautological conviction that people produce rational laws because, as people, they are naturally rational, and rational people are naturally inclined to produce rational laws. These people can then assess the value of their laws because they are rational, and the rationality which produces rational laws is always the same as that which assesses the value of the laws. In short, therefore, the possibility that members of a society might institute universally acceptable laws, and a universally acceptable polity, is always and invariably embedded in the innate constitution of the (rational) human being, and the obtaining of universally acceptable laws requires, in essence, nothing more than a disclosure and reali-

[28] J Rawls, *A Theory of Justice* (Oxford, Oxford University Press, 1973) 136.
[29] J Rawls, *Political Liberalism* (New York, Columbia University Press, 1993) 175.

sation, in the medium of law, of the founding emphases which are imputed to human reason and human character. Habermas and Rawls thus both elaborate their models of legitimacy only by translating the first metaphysical belief in substantial order into an invariable account of natural human orientation, and of reason's capacity (even in dialogical or proceduralist configuration) for abstracting generalisable norms from social facticity. For all their communicative (Habermas) or constructivist (Rawls) refiguring of the Enlightenment legacy, both finally adhere to a categorical model of inalienable rational human faculties as the natural cause and chief legislative arbiter of all acceptable social reality, and underlying their theories is always an (albeit residual) essentialist typology of positive human attributes, tendencies and needs. It is on this fixed doctrine of rational human nature that they found their views on political ethics, and that they define the conditions of legitimacy in all social, political and legal institutions.

Luhmann's legal and political response to the problems of metaphysics, autonomy and rationality in the Enlightenment is certainly less morally attractive than that of Habermas and Rawls, and also far less serviceable as a selective stimulant for critical discourse. His argument is that if we are to be serious about the claim that the characteristics of social reality are not determined by external laws and cannot be justified by perpetually inviolable principles, then we must also be very wary of deriving our view of the necessary nature of social reality from the postulate of an innate human constitution or an innate set of human emphases, which simply internalises and takes as its own the ethical-juridical order originally imputed to the world by metaphysics. Instead of this, we must accept that social systems evolve in ways which are not subject to prior control or determination, and that foundational or essentialist explanations for the evolution of social systems are usually nothing other than the self-explanatory constructs produced by these systems by and for themselves. Substantive determinations of legal validity and political legitimacy, most especially, are always likely to be unreliable and badly adjusted to the infinite complexity of modern societal evolution. Easy refuge in the solace offered by rational humanism is for Luhmann therefore not an acceptable option for theory which is serious about what post-metaphysical rational autonomy and legitimacy truly mean. It is not sufficient, he implies, for theory simply to assume that dilemmas regarding law and legitimacy can be reduced to ultimately soluble questions about moral principles, human needs, or agreements on right and wrong. It is certainly not sufficient to presuppose that legal and political questions can be adequately resolved through reference to an ideal or rationalised model of genuine human nature or genuine human interests. In fact, where theory endorses categorical concepts of legitimacy or validity on the ground of imputed ideas of nature, reason or need, this merely indicates that the theory has curtailed its inquiry into the contingent and intensely variable conditions of autonomy, rationality and legitimacy in modern society, and has simply settled for a convenient substructure on which to base its prescriptions.

On these grounds, the uncompromising stringency of Luhmann's perspective on the legacy of Enlightenment produces insights which necessarily undermine and disconcert his critics and interlocutors in more orthodox lines of political thought. His reflections on the role of rationality parallel those of his neo-Kantian contemporaries, mirroring their quest for a new Enlightenment, with a truly autonomous description of rationality and legitimacy. However, he is prepared to draw more consistent, though far less placatory, conclusions from this undertaking. This leads him to refuse all constructs of human reason and agency which are statically defined, or which repose on residually foundational assumptions about what it means to be a human being, or on universalised ideas about how social reality might best conform to the ideal nature of this human being. It also leads him to oppose all models of legality and legitimacy premised in such assumptions. His critique of normative political thought thus replicates his broader critique of the first Enlightenment, and it asserts again that such theory has not mustered the courage to examine the conditions of political freedom, plurality and independence in categories liberated from the legacy of metaphysics, and it resolves its questions merely by insinuating an enduring and self-identical stratum of right and unity (the human being) in all social events. Such theory thus seeks, even against its own express intentions, to stabilise the entirety of social reality around highly selective, temporally petrified, and often tautological theoretical conceptions of right human essence and right human need.

Luhmann's relativising and pluralising account of rationality's role in politics and law casts, in sum, an intensely unnerving light on other rationalising views on metaphysics, and it challenges these to provide a self-critical and self-reflecting account of the origins of the founding principles on which they base their claims. How, Luhmann might ask, does Habermas *know* that human beings are anthropologically oriented towards the communicative-rational production of generalisable norms, that human beings possess determinate needs and attributes which legitimate political systems must represent, and that such human beings can always be located as the legislative source of authentic legitimacy? How, similarly, did Rawls *know* that human societies (or those societies which we are happy to deem 'reasonable') disclose overlapping points of consensus on questions of right and justice which allow us to outline certain verifiably rational conditions of morality, legitimacy and fairness for all societies? We can suggest, in any case, that more recognised lines of political thought might productively follow the example of Luhmann's theoretical rigour, and should at least allow themselves to be disconcerted by his de-centred and contingent vision of social and political reality after the end of all metaphysical traces. At the very least, we might say that theory must be quite serious in its attempts to imagine a social reality beyond metaphysical principles, and it ought to engage closely with Luhmann's implication that the critique of metaphysics, especially in its resonance for law and politics, should not be obstructed by constructs of human reason, interest or character, before its full implications have been drawn out.

NON-NORMATIVE NORMATIVITY

Despite his opposition to normative political thought, however, one unusual aspect of Luhmann's reflections on politics is that, at first glance at least, they appear to sit rather uneasily with the resolutely descriptive methodology that he employs in his more general sociology. It is quite clear that Luhmann does not view his sociology as conforming to any prescriptive conception of political theory and political philosophy.[30] Quite manifestly, in fact, his anti-metaphysical definition of legitimacy as a formula for the contingency of the political system indicates that legitimate political order cannot be conceived as according with any invariable principles and that no one method of imagining or technique for upholding legitimacy can assume definite priority over others. Despite this anti-normative position, however, he also, on occasions, quite clearly intimates that in complex societies certain types of political system are more likely to enjoy legitimacy than others, and that certain types of political system are at particular risk of *de-legitimisation*. For this reason, although he never endorses one categorical and exclusive model of good or preferable political order, Luhmann's political writings can be seen to offer a broad and flexible blueprint for determining what political systems might do (and what they might avoid doing) in order successfully to preserve themselves in a reality of plausible contingency (ie maintain their legitimacy).

Above all, Luhmann indicates that one characteristic of the functionally differentiated reality of modern society is that it tends to be *democratic*, and that social differentiation creates broad-ranging societal conditions of liberty, pluralism and autonomy, which are usually construed as the features and pre-conditions of political democracy. This is not meant to suggest that Luhmann promotes differentiation and systemic rationalisation as an ideal-type of socio-political order or as a fixed measure for calibrating the quality of a given society. However, the claim can be discerned in his work that advanced differentiation is the most adequate condition of modern social life, and that the systems of modern society obtain their greatest stability through their ability to communicate with other systems as different from themselves. Systems that do not do this are unlikely to regulate their own communications effectively, and they run the risk of ultimately falling behind the essentially modern social reality of differentiation, plurality and variety. In consequence, a political system is unlikely to make its contingency plausible (legitimate) if it fails to reflect and respond to the plural and differentiated reality of democratic societies. This might occur, for example, if a political system tends to form unmanageable structural couplings with other systems, if it harnesses its own self-reference to the communications of other systems (to religion, perhaps), if it colonises other systems by overspecifying the medium of power on the regulation of issues (ie medical, economic or aesthetic questions) which, in a differentiated society,

[30] N Luhmann, *Social Systems*, above n 18 at 101.

are not susceptible to collectively binding decisions, or if it inclines towards unsustainably centralised modes of coercion and power-application and so curtails its ability to communicate accurately with other systems. The normative components of this aspect of his thought are rarely absolutely explicit, yet certain underlying political preferences can surely be extrapolated from Luhmann's political sociology. The primary normative implication of his work is that the common features of modern societies are sustained by the high level of differentiation and differentiated communication that mark these societies. Societies determined by a condition of realised differentiation are always likely to have pluralistic and *democratic* political systems. That is—they are likely to support the rule of law, to accept a general societal condition of widespread pluralism and autonomy, to resist unquestionable or dogmatically orthodox justifications for the exercise of power, and to maintain optional liberties for all social agents. Conversely, then, societies that experience or stimulate processes of *de-differentiation*, perhaps through a *re-centration* of society on the political system or a simplification of the complex fabric of sub-systemic interdependence and communication, are always likely to see the end, or at least the erosion, of conditions normally seen as characterising democracy.

Parallel to his general account of legitimacy as a formula of political contingency, therefore, Luhmann indicates that a fully evolved and differentiated political system is likely to obtain legitimacy in the form of democratic legitimacy. At different junctures in his work, in fact, he even sets out quite detailed characterisations of democratic political systems, and he identifies certain necessary (or at least probable) technical and institutional preconditions of democratic rule, and describes how a political system might maintain itself as a legitimate democracy in a differentiated democratic society. The features that Luhmann views as probable characteristics of a democratic—and thus plausibly legitimised—political system are set out below.

First, Luhmann argues that the democratic political system is a system which differentiates itself internally into the three distinct subsystems of *politics*, *administration* and *public*. In this, he mirrors more conventional doctrines of the separation of powers. This differentiation allows the political system to support processes of democratic self-checking or self-observation between its internal resources, and it tends to prevent the excessive centration of power at one or other point in the communications of the system. In the triadically differentiated political system, *politics* provides resources of symbolic legitimacy whilst permitting *administration* to transmit decisions in the medium of law. *Public* comprises the addressees of law, and it communicates with *politics* via public opinion, elections, or through formalised or semi-formalised shows of dissent. Democracy, Luhmann argues, is the 'title' for a political system organised around this triadic differentiation.[31]

[31] N Luhmann, 'State and Politics: Towards a Semantics of the Self-Description of Political Systems', in *Political Theory in the Welfare State*, J Bednarz Jnr (trans), (Berlin and New York, de Gruyter, 1990) 125.

Second, Luhmann argues that a democratic system is one where the exercise of power is limited, or *second-coded*, by *law*, and where power is communicated through society in legally sanctioned form. In such a system, power is not applied vertically in the form of a prerogative or fiat, but is disseminated as law: all policies formulated as politics can only be activated insofar as they can be transformed into generalisable legal media, and through this transformation power itself is subsumed to the 'scheme lawful/unlawful'.[32] Paradoxically, Luhmann comes close here to endorsing a model of the *Rechtsstaat*, as he suggests that the second-coding of power by law obstructs excessive centration and mandatory or hierarchical application of power, and that the ceding of power to law helps uphold broad societal conditions of differentiation and systemic autonomy.[33] For all his opposition to the classical Enlightenment, therefore, he also endorses, albeit in a fundamentally new vocabulary, the major political objective and accomplishment of the rationalist-humanist doctrines of the Enlightenment.

Third, Luhmann claims that the democratic political system contains two or more political parties and other mechanisms for the self-testing of power and for maintaining variety and flexibility in its own operations. Parties, he explains, create options in government and they allow the political system to communicate with itself about its resources and about the optimal strategies and methods for the application of power. Above all, however, political parties give manifest form to the coding *government/opposition*, which allows politics to determine what does and what does not qualify as politics, and what can and what cannot be implemented as collectively binding decisions in the medium of power. By specifying its operations on a party which is in *government*, the political system restricts its functions to relatively circumscribed acts of decision-making: only *government* has 'political power which can be applied in the form of law'.[34] However, by admitting the existence of other parties, in *opposition*, the political system also creates flexibility for itself to rehearse new policies and new variations in the communication of power.

Fourth, Luhmann asserts that that the democratic political system implements further semantic means (laws of state, catalogues of Basic Rights, constitutions, formal devolutions of competence, etc) by which it can reflect the necessary distinctions between its internal sub-systems, and protect itself from conflation with other arenas of social communication. Gert Verschraegen has treated this issue extensively elsewhere in this volume, and I do not wish to repeat his arguments. Here, it is simply important to note that Luhmann views the democratic-constitutional organisation of the state both as a formula

[32] N Luhmann, 'Widerstandsrecht und politische Gewalt' (1984) 5 *Zeitschrift für Rechtssoziologie* 40.

[33] He consequently admits a 'reciprocal and parasitical relationship between law and politics'. (N Luhmann, *Law as a Social System*, KA Ziegert, (trans), F Kastner, R Nobles, D Schiff, and R Ziegert, (eds), Oxford University Press, Oxford, 2004) 371.

[34] N Luhmann, *Die Politik der Gesellschaft*, above n 2 at 20.

through which the political system differentiates itself internally, and prevents excessive power being vested at any given point in its communications, and as a formula through which the political system shows itself to be adequate to wider conditions of societal differentiation, and reflects the fact that entire areas of social communication cannot be regulated by the application of power. The constitution is, therefore, a mechanism for obviating de-differentiation, and the rights enshrined in constitutions have the function that they serve 'the preservation of the differentiation which constitutes the total order'.[35]

Fifth, Luhmann indicates that the democratic political system is a system which recognises its legitimacy as a precarious resource which can easily be eroded wherever it undertakes performances (ie in the name of welfare or regulation) in areas of society not easily regulated by collectively binding decisions, wherever it ties its operations to categorical principles or moral imperatives, or wherever it opens itself excessively to demands for broad-based social participation or organised co-determination. As discussed, systems which he sees as unlikely to maintain legitimacy are those which fail to define themselves in adequacy to the overarching condition of societal differentiation, tie their legitimacy to expansive regulatory activities outside the system of politics, and so obstruct their communications with other systems. An obvious example of this, Luhmann claims, might be a totalitarian regime, such as Germany under the National Socialists or the pre-1989 Soviet Union, or other authoritarian one-party states, such as Spain under Franco. These are the most extreme examples of highly de-differentiated political systems, in which politics colonises the economy, the arts, the legal system, the education system, and often religion and medicine as well. The example of such *delegitimisation through de-differentiation* to which Luhmann devotes the greatest polemical energy, however, is that of the post-Keynesian welfare states which, to a greater or lesser degree, featured in all Western European societies through the 1970s and early 1980s. Luhmann sees the welfare state as a neglectful 'self-overtaxing of the political system'.[36] In the welfare state, he explains, the political system makes itself accountable for regulatory objectives which it cannot conceivably fulfil, and it specifies its resources on planning and mandatory organisation. In so doing, it tends to undermine the social freedoms that democracy guarantees throughout society, it damages the fragile differentiations and functions of self-checking which constitute the internal structure of democracy, and it allows its legitimacy ceaselessly to be called into question because of its evident inability to accomplish the regulatory tasks that it ascribes to itself. Despite his claim that legitimacy is nothing more than plausibly reflected contingency, therefore,

[35] N Luhmann, *Grundrechte als Institution* (Berlin, Duncker und Humblot, 1965) 183.

[36] N Luhmann, 'Staat und Politik: zur Semantik der Selbstbeschreibung politischer Systeme', in U Bermbach (ed), *Politische Theoriengeschichte: Probleme einer Teildisziplin der politischen Wissenschaft* (Opladen, Westdeutscher Verlag, 1984) 99–125; 115. The English translation of this article, which I have used elsewhere, distorts the sense of this section, so I refer readers to the original German version.

Luhmann still indicates that the plausible reflection of contingency is improbable in political systems which wilfully expose themselves to the risk of de-differentiation.

Sixth, Luhmann also suggests that democratic political systems usually develop mechanisms of sub-systemic conflict-resolution (normally associated with neo-corporate politics) which allow sub-political problems to be addressed at points of communication which do not overtax the highest legitimatory resources of politics. He expressly endorses the 'organised representation of interests' as an alternative to participatory or welfarist models of democracy,[37] and he clearly views corporate governance as containing a broad set of strategies which allow the political system to consider social issues and problems without triggering a full structural coupling between politics and economy.

On this account, in short, Luhmann views some sort of democracy as the necessary and perhaps even ideal mode of governance in the modern political system, and in modern society more generally. Indeed, it is not too controversial to identify in his thought an endorsement of a quite specific conception of democracy. He supports a model of democracy which restricts political power through law, which protects the autonomy and independence of legislature (*administration*) and executive (*politics*), which rejects the theoretical association of welfare and democracy characteristic of social democracy, which limits public participation in political decision-making but is quite sympathetic to neo-corporate ideas, and which identifies the universal societal condition of socio-economic pluralism as both the foundation and the outcome of the democratic use of power.[38] Luhmann's favoured model of democracy, as set out here, might be placed on an evolutionary continuum with the model of the constitutionally circumscribed legal state which was widespread in the nineteenth century. In the context of more recent debate, his views can in some (but not all) respects be compared with the neo-liberal political conceptions which found expression in the anti-welfarist theories of democracy of the late 1970s and early 1980s.

A POST-METAPHYSICAL DEMOCRACY?

The great paradox in Luhmann's political thought, consequently, is that he endorses the *practical reality* of democratic society, or even of some kind of democratic liberalism (including social plurality, legally enshrined democratic legitimacy, private autonomy free of political coercion), but his sociology dismantles the usual *theoretical centre* of democracy and democratic liberalism

[37] N Luhmann, 'Participation and Legitimation: The Ideas and the Experiences', in *Political Theory in the Welfare State*, above n 31 at 226.

[38] For a different reading of Luhmann's vision of the effectively self-legitimising political system which raises some of the same points as my account, see K von Beyme, 'Der Staat des politischen Systems im Werk Niklas Luhmanns, in K-U Hellmann and R Schmalz-Bruns (eds), *Theorie der Politik: Niklas Luhmanns Politische Soziologie* (Frankfurt am Main, Suhrkamp, 2002) 131–148.

(that is, the rational human being, endowed with powers of legal deduction and prescription). On one hand, Luhmann extends the theoretical principles of anti-Enlightenment social theory, and his critique of humanist rationalism revolves around a quite fundamental opposition to the postulation of the rational human being as a prior source of political order. Yet at the same time he is also sympathetic to the fully positivised and post-traditional social reality usually associated with the consequences of Enlightenment, and he obviously rejects all political conceptions which promote manifestly pre-Enlightenment models of power, authority and state-control.

For all the dialectical finesse of his perspective on the Enlightenment, however, it is still necessary critically to inquire into the model of legitimacy and legality which Luhmann outlines, and it is crucial to consider whether his concept of sociological Enlightenment does indeed, as he claims, open a theoretical horizon which marks an advance both on the classical Enlightenment and on the classical counter-Enlightenment. For all his attempts to reflect the origins of legitimacy and legality in the disembedded reality of post-rational, post-humanist systemic contingency, Luhmann does not simply elude all accountability for the great questions of modern political theory—or indeed for the great questions of the Enlightenment, and of its offshoot in liberalism. His theory must, therefore, still be questioned, first, on the extent to which it plausibly provides an account of democratic society, and, second, on whether his conception of law as a positive medium which (among other functions) communicates contingent decisions does truly explain legitimacy in politics as a meaningfully democratic condition.

In addressing these issues, it might be noted, first and foremost, that democracies are normally (and not without good reason) defined as political systems that accept and promote the *external conditioning* of political power at two crucial procedural points: first, through law and legislation, and, second, through politicians, delegates and other members of representative political organisations. On the first point, however, Luhmann argues that the political system is at base a decision-making apparatus, which certainly cannot be conceived without law, yet which, lastly, only has a secondary relation to law. Owing to the processes of evolution, differentiation, positivisation, and, not lastly, pacification, which mark the democratic conditions of political modernity, the modern political apparatus certainly now deploys power in very varied and flexible ways, and the recursive communication of power through all the three sub-systems of politics (*politics*, *administration*, and *public*) ensures that power is always checked or self-checked at the intersections between these sub-systems. As a result of this, power gradually allows itself to be second-coded by law (in a process close to that usually taken to characterise a democratic *Rechtsstaat*), and power is thus disseminated through society in the generalised medium of law, not through vertical or prerogative application.[39] Despite this,

[39] For a more detailed discussion of this, see Jean Clam's essay in this collection.

however, Luhmann is also always clear that the second-coding of power by law in the democratic legal state does not imply that law can ever actually *constitute* power, or that the legitimacy of power hinges upon its accountability to substantively determined and prescribed standards. For all his sporadic closeness to the legal-state perspective, in fact, Luhmann often accentuates his conviction that power is *before the law*, that power always possesses a certain primacy over law, and that law is primarily useful to power because it transmits in generalised form decisions which politics struggles to communicate in the pure form of power. Above all, therefore, the founding or defining principles of a political order can never be instituted in the form of laws, which then set enduring norms to which the state is accountable. Politics can never 'presuppose' any pre-existing legal or principled 'foundations' for 'its decisions'; instead, it must ceaselessly, *ex nihilo*, 'create' the contingent parameters of its own legitimacy, and so establish on its own the legal order which supports its decisions.[40] In essence, therefore, the political system is legitimate wherever it can propose itself as legitimate, and wherever it finds plausible legal forms for communicating its decisions and its power through society. It arrives at this goal because it activates complex democratic processes of symbolisation, transmission, second-coding, proceduralisation, adjustment and complexity-management, not because of what its laws actually mean or contain. Where law is recognised as legitimate, Luhmann concludes, 'in a central question of human co-existence'—that is, in the constitutively democratic processes through which public power is forced to justify itself—'arbitrariness becomes an institution'.[41] Democracy, in short, has the arbitrariness of law as its key variable, and law is never more than a formal variable in the communication of power.

On the second point, then, in his historical reconstruction of the evolution of the modern political system, Luhmann stresses that the first and original component of the political system was the administration. In its primary function, he claims, the pre-modern political system was an administrative organ for addressing problems by means of *decisions*. Only later did the political system assume its modern triadically differentiated form, as *politics*, *administration*, and *public*, and the emergence of 'party-based politics' (*politics* proper) as an arena of personal or symbolic consensus-production was only a secondary (or even tertiary) evolutionary phenomenon. This became necessary, first, when the administration began to engender levels of complexity which could not be processed without public compliance,[42] and then when, owing to its internal complexity, it began to require freedom and latitude to order its relation with its environment through the transmission of power as positive law—instead of through substantive claims to legitimacy or through the hierarchical application of power. The development of 'a particular sphere of politics' concerning itself

[40] N Luhmann, 'Komplexität und Demokratie' (1969) 10 *Politische Vierteljahresschrift* 317.

[41] N Luhmann, 'Soziologie des politischen Systems', above n 25 at 167.

[42] *Ibid*, 163.

'with the forming of political support for various programmes and decisions' was thus the result of an evolutionary process in which 'the decision-making criteria and programmes of the bureaucracy' became 'variable' and law was positivised.[43] The internal differentiation of the political system into the form of democracy only occurred, in other words, because the *administration* required resources of legitimacy which it could not on its own produce. Politics then developed contingent criteria of legitimacy—for example, 'election victories, maximisation of votes or maximisation of posts'—which, in turn, created a contingent context of probability or plausibility in which the administration was able to continue with its own primary obligation, which is to 'make consistent decisions',[44] and to apply these as law. Here too, therefore, Luhmann sees the defining hallmarks of a democracy, and especially those points in democratic systems where politics opens itself for external communication, as nothing but variable attributes of the political system, whose chief purpose is simply to facilitate the dissemination of power. Politics, he thus concludes, is originally and primarily the transmission of administrative power, and no substantive or specific character attaches to the symbolic resources of legitimacy produced in and as democratic politics. These are simply options and fictions which are triggered by the administration for its own functions, and which give the administration freedom to continue its work relatively untroubled by broader thematic questions or by matters of principle.

On Luhmann's account, therefore, the systemic and institutional structure of modern democracies results, from the fact that—at certain junctures in its evolution—the administration has required greater internal differentiation in order to communicate power, that it has sought to unburden itself of the direct political function of producing legitimacy, and then that it has needed complex and variable media (laws) in order to communicate power. These processes have then led to the partial separation of executive and legislative functions in the political system, and stimulate the processes of legal second-coding and self-testing usually associated with legal states or at least with constitutionally organised democracies. The emergence of democracy and of democratic techniques for obtaining legitimacy are, in short, always events of evolution occurring within the political executive itself and stimulated by the functional exigencies of the executive. Luhmann's particular model of democracy can therefore be characterised as *executive democracy*—as a type of democracy in which the deployment of law in the communication and the application of power, the need for public consensus concerning this application, and the separation of institutions in the political system to observe and obstruct misapplications of power, are developments which come into being merely to make the primary administrative application of political power *more effective*. Democracy, he argues, cannot derive substance from any source outside the

[43] N Luhmann, 'Soziologie des politischen Systems', above n 25 at 164.
[44] *Ibid*, 164.

political system, and it cannot channel extra-political principles into politics (as law, perhaps). Democracy is simply a self-reflexive condition of politics itself, in which the political system maximises its own ability to address its own constantly escalating complexity and to transmit power without overburdening one particular point in its communications.

It is in the legal facet of his political theory that the practical implications of Luhmann's deconstruction of legal rationalism and legal subjectivity in the Enlightenment become clearest. In its implications for the law, Luhmann's account of the political system offers only a very limited theory of the positive-democratic or liberal-democratic legal state, close in its implications to the early-positivist doctrine of the 'normative force of the factical' set out by Georg Jellinek,[45] and later reconstructed for rather different political reasons by Carl Schmitt. Crucially, Luhmann's theory neither places the restriction of arbitrary power under the independent authority of laws, nor does it bestow countervailing power on institutions (eg parliaments, chambers of review, regional legislatures, councils etc), which possess free-standing legislative power. The restriction of power in fact occurs only because power needs to restrict itself in order to be communicated through society, in legally acceptable form. Laws might have the capacity formally to check power, as the legal system inevitably communicates its own autonomous terms when it assimilates directives from politics: administrative rulings do not finally become law until they are communicated in the legal system. Yet, most importantly, law, as an autopoietic system, cannot determine the character or shape the content of power; nor are the legislative (administrative) functions of politics able to alter power or place any fundamental external constraints on power. Indeed, Luhmann is quite clear about the limitations of law (and laws) in relation to power. In modern societies, he explains, power is always coded by law, and 'the use of power is tied to a prior decision (*Vorentscheidung*) as whether it lawful or non-lawful'. However, this second-coding of power is 'in itself not a limitation of power, but merely its formal condition'.[46] Laws, consequently, might operate as the universalised form of power, but they also remain subordinate to power.

Luhmann clearly sees himself as an eminently modern theorist, for whom the legitimacy of the political system reflects the complex plurality of its relations to other systemic environments, and for whom the democratic reciprocity of power and law is of central theoretical importance in the self-maintenance of the democratically legitimised political system. 'Effective power,' he states simply, must in modern societies always be communicated as 'lawful power.'[47] Nonetheless, his administrative theory of legislation and democracy can only quantify whether law is valid by assessing the degree to which it helps unburden the political system. Democratic legislation, in practice, might be seen most

[45] G Jellinek, *Allgemeine Staatslehre* (Berlin, Häring, 1900) 308.
[46] N Luhmann, 'Widerstandsrecht und politische Gewalt', above n 32 at 41.
[47] *Ibid*, 40.

accurately as the gradual reflexive adjustment, usually via slight alterations to administrative norms, of the sub-systems of politics and administration to their own internal and external environments, which include the *public*. The purpose of such legislation is always, rather alarmingly for those to whom it is addressed, to secure 'an almost motiveless, unthinking acceptance of binding decisions'.[48] Indeed, Luhman is quite clear that under political systems which effectively underwrite the positive conditions of their own plausibility, legitimacy can no longer be viewed as a 'consensually founded legal relation' and administrative decisions are 'to a large extent independent of the consensus of those affected by them'.[49]

CONCLUSION

In one guise or another the history of Western democracy and Western liberalism, from Kant through to Habermas and Rawls, might be seen to rely on the postulation of an autonomous human quality of *legislative reason*, by means of which human beings obtain the entitlement to deduce and insist on their own laws. This is expressed theoretically in the complex philosophical history of the rational-legal subject, and it is manifest practically in the core liberal-institutional conception of the democratic legal state, which stipulates that the legislative body should be separated from the executive and that the executive should be formally and substantively answerable to the laws produced, through processes approaching consensus, in the legislature. Luhmann, by contrast, argues that democracy emerges as a contingent reality, generated from the increasing internal complexity of the political system, and its primary function is to manage and alleviate the political system: it is to this end that it needs laws. In this change of paradigm, the origin of democracy is the political system itself, and the mode of rationality which influences the shaping of politics and law as democracy is not that of the human being: it is the rationality which the political system itself contains, enacts and variably reproduces.

In this model of democracy, Luhmann dramatically raises the stakes in the critique of metaphysical heteronomy, which accompanies the Enlightenment from its inception to the present. Arguably the greatest contribution of Luhmann's work to modern political reflection is its ceaseless insistence that rival theories of rationality, autonomy and legitimacy do not theorise rationality, autonomy and legitimacy at all, but merely serve to instantiate new figures in the political legacy of European metaphysics. Underscoring the entirety of his political thought is the assertion that all political theory should reconsider the vocabularies and objectives which it employed and formulated during its first endeavour to supplant the earlier doctrines of metaphysics and theology.

48 N Luhmann, 'Soziologie des politischen Systems', above n 25 at 159.
49 N Luhmann, *Legitimation durch Verfahren*, above n 24, 167, 209.

Political theory, he demands in short, should strain itself to imagine politics, legality, legitimacy and democracy *without metaphysics*—as occurrences of an absolutely plural and contingent political reality, lacking all self-identical substructure in rationalised constructs of right, interest and nature.

Perhaps, however, the importance of Luhmann's contribution to political theory does not entirely overshadow the more questionable political implications of his sociology. On an immediate level, these might be seen to reside in the minimalism of his theory of the democratic relation between law and power, in his implicit attachment to nineteenth century models of administrative positivism and limited legal-statism, and, most obviously, in the obvious appeal of some of his ideas to quite standard versions of reactionary theory (especially neo-liberalism). More fundamentally, however, the question might also be raised whether his refusal to centre political order on the legislative promptings of human rationality, and in his resultant rejection of the priority of law over power, Luhmann does not, at least by implication, fall backwards, behind the Enlightenment, into a political world in which the sources of order are obscured from human thinking and closed to all human prescription or participation, and in which human actions are regulated by principles for which human reason does not account. If this is indeed the case, the world outlined by Luhmann's political thought would be rather like the primary metaphysical reality which the secondary metaphysical dialectic of the Enlightenment first aspired to overcome.

5

Systems Theory and the Paradox of Human Rights

GERT VERSCHRAEGEN

INTRODUCTION

HUMAN RIGHTS ARE not commonly accepted as a field of study in sociology,[1] despite their great societal and symbolic importance. In our world society the thirty articles of the United Nations Declaration of Human rights are increasingly seen as the building blocks of a universal moral code. At the same time, human rights play an important role in world politics, for they provide the most important basis of legitimisation for the politics of 'the international community'; nearly every state has already accepted, at least on paper, the Universal Declaration. Nevertheless, as one pundit put it, 'sociology has neglected the empirical issue of human rights and has not developed any general theory of social rights as an institution'.[2]

Despite this, this article will argue that Luhmann's systems theory offers a sophisticated theoretical model for describing the place and function of human rights in contemporary world society. By making use of the theoretical vocabulary of systems theory, it will reconstruct the historical and sociological processes that make visible why human rights emerge as a central feature of modern society, and will also explain their basic paradoxes. But before I start, I should inform the reader that this article, keen to make use of the above-mentioned theoretical potential, reformulates systems theory with a view to the particular features of human rights. This is because, rather surprisingly, there is not much to be found in Luhmann's writing that explicitly addresses questions of human rights and international law.[3] Like most sociologists, it was only quite

[1] The social sciences, particularly sociology, have until recently largely neglected human rights. Before the 1980s almost all work on human rights was done by lawyers, and most articles were published in law journals. For more information, see M Freeman, *Human Rights: An Interdisciplinary Approach* (Cambridge, Polity Press, 2002) 77 ff.

[2] BS Turner, 'Outline of a Theory of Human Rights' (1993) 27 *Sociology* 489.

[3] As far as I know, only one of Luhmann's numerous articles explicitly addresses the issue of human rights: N Luhmann 'Das Paradox der Menschenrechte und drei Formen seiner Entfaltung' in N Luhmann, *Soziologische Aufklärung*, vol 6: *Die Soziologie und der Mensch* (Opladen, Westdeutscher Verlag, 1995) 229–236.

recently that he focused on the global dimensions of law and politics. Luhmann also trained as a state lawyer, and, as such, was more concerned with the working of domestic (national) civil rights. That is the reason why many of the main themes of human rights are treated in terms of constitutional or fundamental civil rights in an older book by Luhmann, *Grundrechte als Institution* [Fundamental Rights as an Institution] (1965).[4] Not surprisingly, I will take this book as a starting point for my analysis.[5] My reading of *Grundrechte als Institution*, however, will be expanded to include more recent works by Luhmann, such as *Das Recht der Gesellschaft* [Law as a Social System] (1993),[6] *Die Gesellschaft der Gesellschaft* [Society's Society] (1997) and *Die Politik der Gesellschaft* [The Politics of Society].[7]

Since most of the main themes of human rights are treated in terms of constitutional rights, I shall begin with an overview of the evolution and the function of these rights. The constitution will thus be used as the framework for the protection and implementation of basic rights. Only in the second part of the essay shall I treat the emergence of human rights as a separate paradigm. My basic hypothesis here will be that the central paradox of human rights in contemporary world society consists precisely in the fact that the vast body of international and regional human rights law, developed after the Second World War, is still dependent upon the willingness of states effectively to constitutionalise human rights.

FUNDAMENTAL RIGHTS AS AN INSTITUTION

Obviously, Luhmann's sociological conceptualisation of fundamental rights differs from the current philosophical, political or juridical approach.

[4] *Grundrechte als Institution* (Berlin, Duncker & Humblot, 1965) is one of the least known works by Luhmann. Within sociology the book has barely received any attention. This can be partly explained by the fact that *Grundrechte als Institution* has not been translated into English (or French). A more general aversion to systems theory in the post-Parsonian age was probably also responsible for the striking lack of interest in a systems-theoretical approach to fundamental rights. In the field of ethics, the philosophy of law and legal studies' however, the book found some response from German-, Dutch- and French-speaking authors. See F De Wachter *et al*, 'Ethiek en mensenrechten' in (1987) 49 *Tijdschrift voor Filosofie* 579; W Brugger, 'Menschenrechte im modernen Staat' in (1989) 114 *Archiv des öffentlichen Rechts* 114 (1989) 537; J Clam, *Droit et Société chez Niklas Luhmann: La Contingence des Normes* (Paris, PUF, 1997) 81–103; CB Graber and G Teubner, 'Art and Money: Constitutional Rights in the Private Sphere?' (1998) 18 *Oxford Journal of Legal Studies*, 61.

[5] My reading of *Grundrechte als Institution* is based upon G Verschraegen, 'Human Rights and Modern Society: A Sociological Analysis from the Perspective of Systems Theory' (2002) 29 *Journal of Law and Society* 258.

[6] Recently translated into English as N Luhmann, *Law as a Social System*, KA Ziegert (trans), (Oxford, Oxford University Press, 2004).

[7] N Luhmann, *Das Recht der Gesellschaft* (Frankfurt a/Main, Suhrkamp, 1993) 110–117, 135, 233 ff, 452–495, 513–516, 571–586; N Luhmann, *Die Gesellschaft der Gesellschaft* (Frankfurt a/Main, Suhrkamp, 1997) 145–171, 618–634, 967 ff, 992 ff, 1021–1022, 1026, 1075–1076; N Luhmann, *Die Politik der Gesellschaft* (Frankfurt a/Main, Suhrkamp, 2000) 189–197, 220–227, 352–358, 423 ff.

Sociological systems theory phrases the issue of basic rights neither as an ethical question of finding fundamental principles for rights, nor as a question of consolidating and implementing basic rights law. As a sociologist, Luhmann is interested instead in linking human rights to specific societal structures; human rights are thus not considered in an ethical or juridical way, but seen *as a social institution with a specific function*.[8] As Luhmann explains

> The core concepts of fundamental rights law, such as 'liberty', 'property', 'freedom of speech and expression', 'equality' and the corresponding articles symbolise institutionalised expectations and mediate in their implementation in concrete situations. The institutionalisation of fundamental rights is hence a factual event—that is something which even the inclusion of fundamental rights in the constitution should not make us forget—an event which function (and thus not only: intended normative meaning) has to be examined.[9]

Constitutional and human rights are not a creation of the law, but are pre-legal as a social institution, as a self-protecting device of society. Naturally, the law positivises, interprets and stabilises them. But this should not obscure the fact that fundamental freedoms and human rights are first and foremost institutionalised expectations which underlie the legal system.[10]

What is then the function of fundamental rights and liberties? In *Grundrechte als Institution*, Luhmann argues that constitutional rights should be seen as mechanisms for protecting and stabilising a functionally differentiated society. By institutionalising fundamental freedoms and human rights, modern society protects its own structure against (ever present) tendencies towards regression or de-differentiation. In other words, fundamental rights ensure that the differentiation between different functional subsystems is maintained. An example of this, for instance, is that when modern society institutionalises religious freedom and freedom of conscience, it also prevents the continuous interference of

[8] It is important to note that in Luhmannian theory the notion of functionalism is completely reformed from previous sociological ideas of what is and what is not functional for society (for instance, Talcott Parsons' structural functionalism). Luhmann's concept of function is not equivalent to the goal or the use of a social system or institution, neither is it compatible with the idea of agencies 'being functional' to society, performing part of the task of the whole. Hence, Luhmann does not mean that fundamental rights carry out a particular task for society or that they came into being for the good of society. Systems theory is not another history of universal progress. The concept of a function in the Luhmannian sense is precisely meant to break down the image of society as an organism and the notion of causality implied thereby, replacing it with a technique of comparing functionally equivalent alternatives. In this perspective, fundamental rights are functional because they increase the structural flexibility of society. They guarantee a high degree of societal differentiation and make it possible for society to become more complex and at the same time increase its stability.

[9] N Luhmann, *Grundrechte*, above n 4, 13. All translations into English are by the author.

[10] Graber and Teubner rightly remark that 'this relation between the social and the legal explains why certain countries that have only a weak legal institutionalisation of constitutional rights nevertheless have them institutionalised socially. And it explains why the legal imposition of constitutional rights has only a limited effect in those countries where social differentiation and its complementary institutions are not present as a social basis for the legal superstructure.' CB Graber and G Teubner, 'Art and Money', above n 4 at 65.

religion and politics. At the same time, Luhmann argues, fundamental rights ensure the protection of individual spheres of action typical of modern society. This is necessary because, with the transition towards functional differentiation, the position of the individual becomes fragile. As a consequence, fundamental freedoms and human rights institutionalise specific mechanisms to increase stability and protection of the individual. By formulating these rights as 'natural' and 'fundamental' rights, to which every citizen has an equal and unconditional claim, each citizen is endowed with entitlements that are morally prior and superior to society and the state.

A brief look at the history of law shows us that rights as unconditional and individual entitlements come about only after a long process of societal evolution, and their relevance is tied to the historical emergence of individual spheres of action which are typical of modern society. In pre-modern societies, individuals, as such, were not rights-bearing entities.[11] On a semantic level this is expressed by the term law (*ius*): in Antiquity and the Middle Ages this term always implied a reference to the objectivity of the social order. *Ius* mostly meant nothing more than the factual legal order itself: that is, the totality of norms, laws and institutions that defined the rights and duties of social groups or the specific roles that persons were expected to assume. The pre-modern is not made up of individual rights, but should be considered as an intricate pattern of specific freedoms, privileges and corresponding duties that one can only obtain on the ground of membership of a specific social group: royal rights and duties, monastic rights, the freedoms of the nobility, city freedoms, and so on.[12]

It is only with the advent of modernity that the individual as such became a bearer of rights: from the end of the Middle Ages on, a subjective conception of rights was gradually introduced.[13] According to Luhmann subjective rights are rights 'that have legal quality, because they are due to a subject and therefore need no further foundation'.[14] The legal ground is, thus, no longer the social order, but the individual itself, here conceived of as a juridical subject. And rights are no longer seen as an objective thing (*res iusta*) but as an attribute of the subject itself: the will-power (*potestas*) or the capacity (*facultas*) to act freely or to have the disposal over something. In the Enlightenment tradition, actually commencing with Hobbes, this subjective right of self-determination is considered as an inalienable attribute of the subject, irrespective of the objective legal order.[15] All individuals are then entitled to subjective rights simply because they

[11] N Luhmann, *Gesellschaftsstruktur und Semantik: Studien zur Wissenssoziologie der modernen Gesellschaft* in 4 Volumes (Frankfurt a/Main, Suhrkamp, 1981) *II*: 48 ff.

[12] H Bielefeldt, 'Die Menschenrechte als Chance in der pluralistischen Weltgesellschaft' (1988) 21 *Zeitschrift für Rechtspolitik* 428.

[13] A detailed overview of the quite complex historical transition from objective to subjective law can be found in N Luhmann, *Grundrechte*, 48–68; see also N Luhmann, *Ausdifferenzierung des Rechts: Beiträge zur Rechtssoziologie und Rechtstheorie* (Frankfurt a/Main, Suhrkamp, 1981) 360; M Villey, *Leçons d'Histoire de la Philosophie du Droit* (Paris, PUF, 1957).

[14] N Luhmann, *Grundrechte*, above n 4 at 45.

[15] *Ibid*, 57–68.

are a 'subject', that is to say an individual who is no longer defined by his or her social status, but who has the capacity to define himself or herself.

From the point of view of social systems theory, the introduction of subjective rights can be linked to a specific structural societal transformation (please note the word 'can': there is no sociologism). More particularly, it is possible to relate the concept of subjective rights to the transition from a stratified to a functionally differentiated society with the help of the sociological principle of *inclusion*. Inclusion is the social mechanism by which social systems take human beings into account, ie constitute human beings as accountable actors, as persons.[16] We shall see that the form of inclusion changes with the transition to modern society and that this has far-reaching consequences for the semantics of law.

In segmental as well as hierarchical societies objective law suffices to regulate social interaction, and subjective rights are not necessary. This is because the individual here has a fixed social position; he or she is comprehensively embedded in social contexts. The relationship between society and individual is determined by this 'total inclusion': individuality and social position are identical.[17] Belonging to a tribe, family, corporation, or estate encompasses all the aspects of an individual. Dual membership is not possible: one can belong to one estate only, therefore social hybrids are considered to be monsters. This overall inclusion has the advantage of delivering a stable and protected position for the individual. Precisely because the individual is defined in all spheres of life by his or her fixed social position, he or she is at the same time included in and protected by a network of social bonds, which constitute a sort of buffer against the power of the sovereign, the church, and so on. The disadvantage of overall inclusion however is that social exclusion equals death. The unattached individual during the Middle Ages was one condemned either to excommunication or to exile (and thus: close to death). To exist one had to belong to an association—a household, manor, monastery or guild. There was no security except through group protection and no freedom that did not recognise the constant obligations of a corporate life. One lived and died in the identifiable style of one's class and one's corporation.

The central thesis of systems theory is that, with the formation of a functionally differentiated society, this order had to be abandoned.[18] Social differentiation

[16] See N Luhmann, *Die Gesellschaft der Gesellschaft*, above n 7, 618–634.

[17] N Luhmann, *Gesellschaftsstruktur und Semantik: Studien zur Wissenssoziologie der modernen Gesellschaft*, in 4 vols (Frankfurt a/Main, Suhrkamp, 1989) *III* 149; R Laermans and G Verschraegen, 'Modernity and Individuality: a Sociological Analysis from the Point of View of Systems Theory' in A Van Harskamp and AW Musschenga (eds), *The Many Faces of Individualism* (Leuven, Peeters, 2001) 111–127.

[18] For a general outline of this evolution see N Luhmann, *Gesellschaftsstruktur und Semantik III*, above n 17, 154 ff.; R Laermans and G Verschraegen, 'Modernity and Individuality', above n 17, 121ff.; see also N Luhmann, 'The Individuality of the Individual: Historical Meanings and Contemporary Problems' in TC Heller, M Sosna and DE Wellbery (eds), *Reconstructing Individualism: Autonomy, Individuality and the Self* (Stanford, Stanford University Press, 1986) 313–325.

can no longer be based on dividing 'whole persons' into distinct groups, *it is no longer groups of people that are differentiated, but types of communication.* It is obviously impossible to distribute people over systems for religion, the economy, science, education and politics, so that every individual lives in one and only one of them. On this, Luhmann writes:

> What previously seemed normal is now impossible. The singular person can no longer belong to one and only one societal subsystem. He can engage himself professionally in the economic system, in the juridical system, in politics, in the educational system, and so on, and in a certain way social status follows the professionally delineated paths of success; but he cannot live in only one functional subsystem.[19]

Societal inclusion thus becomes a heterogeneous, even hybrid matter. Rules of access replace the old order, in which persons were divided into distinct groups. As an individual, a person lives outside the function systems. But every individual has to have access to every function system if and insofar as his or her mode of living requires the use of the functions of society. Everyone should be able to enjoy legal status and the protection of the law, everyone should be educated in schools, everyone should be able to acquire and spend money, and so on.

According to Luhmann this new form of partial and 'multi-functional' inclusion can be connected with the introduction of subjective rights. To ensure the multiple and partial inclusion, individuals should be freed from strong all-inclusive social groups and become entitled to rights and claims to participate in the economy, politics, law, education, religion, etc. In Luhmann's words:

> The inclusion of the population in society has to take a new form and this wish is framed in the form of subjective rights, because it is not realised yet. On the level of symbolism, this figure then has a double meaning: firstly that it concerns *subjective* rights (and not simply the reflexive right of an objective order), it symbolises that individuals now have to be conceived of as more personalised and more independent from social positions. Secondly, that this figure concerns subjective *rights* (and not duties), symbolises that inclusion of everyone in all function systems is not completely successful (. . .) corresponding to this a terminology of rights, not of duties, and a terminology of claims, not of responsibilities is created.[20]

Consequently, subjective rights can be understood as a sort of compensation for the loss of total inclusion and a fixed social position. The societal function of individual rights is precisely to preclude the coercive definition of personal identity through group membership and to assure inclusion in the different function systems. In order to prevent the individual from being summoned and deprived of his rights by family, social stratum, the church or the (absolute) state, the rights are being claimed as natural (and later on, human) rights, indefeasible rights which are attached to the (juridical) subject or the human being as such.

[19] N Luhmann, *Gesellschaftsstruktur und Semantik, III*, above n 17 at 158.
[20] N Luhmann, *Gesellschaftsstruktur und Semantik, II*, above n 17, 84–85.

The introduction of individual rights is thus closely connected with the differentiation of law and morality. By opening up the space for pursuing personal preferences, individual rights release the entitled person from moral precepts and other prescriptions in a carefully circumscribed manner. Within the boundaries of what is legally permitted no one is legally obliged publicly to justify his or her action. With the introduction of individual liberties, modern law—in contrast to traditional legal orders—validates the principle that whatever is not explicitly prohibited is permitted. (As explained below, legal orders without individual rights honour exactly the opposite principle: everything that is not explicitly allowed is forbidden).

Freedom and equality, the central concepts of all fundamental rights declarations, symbolise the legal order that emerges together with the new, modern form of inclusion.[21] The *fundamental freedoms* indicate that society in general and different social groups in particular have to leave it up to the individual when and why he or she wants to participate in the different function systems of society. Fundamental freedoms guarantee that the individual can decide which political party he or she votes for, which profession he or she exercises, which newspaper he or she reads, and so on. For example, freedom of religion is concerned with protecting individual religious liberty from the state and from all sorts of religious groups. The *rights of equality* symbolise that the individual as a juridical subject is equal to all other individuals, precisely because one's social position is not being taken into consideration. Before the law, we are first and foremost equal citizens, equally entitled to a range of rights and protections. In this sense, one could argue that equality of rights, and not liberty, is the fundamental ground for the declarations of fundamental rights. Freedoms existed just as well in the legal order of stratified societies, but not for everyone and not to the same degree. We shall go more into detail about the specific role of the fundamental freedoms on the one hand, and the rights of equality on the other hand later on. First, however, a brief look at the general societal function of human rights is necessary for the understanding of Luhmann's ideas.

FUNDAMENTAL RIGHTS AS A SELF-LIMITATION OF THE POLITICAL SYSTEM

According to Luhmann, fundamental freedoms and human rights constitute a 'multifunctional' institution in the sense that it not only attempts to protect the freedom and interests of the individual, but at the same time wants to strengthen the functionally differentiated structure of modern society.[22] How is this 'multifunctional' protection of both individual and social interests to be understood?

[21] N Luhmann, 'Der Gleichheitssatz als Form und Norm', (1991) 77 *Archiv für Rechts- und Sozialphilosophie* 435; G Verschraegen 'De maatschappelijke evolutie van de moraal', (2000) 21 *Tijdschrift voor Sociologie* 229.

[22] N Luhmann, *Grundrechte*, above n 4, 79–80.

As already stated, pre-modern societies do not require human rights, precisely because the individual here was completely defined by social position and protected by a network of social bonds. In modern society however, the situation of the individual is much more problematic: personality no longer coincides with fixed roles and stereotypes, but has to be built up by diverse and partial participation in different subsystems. The individual can only transitorily, under certain determinate circumstances, belong to the functionally differentiated subsystems of society—as an opponent in a lawsuit, a voter at the election polls, as a pupil, for instance. This transitoriness turns every biography into an individually temporalised sequence, punctuated by individual temporal place-values.[23] Every individual's history of inclusions is different. First, he or she must be excluded entirely from society as an individual or a person. Luhmann therefore speaks about modern individuality as 'exclusion individuality'.[24] The exclusion from society in turn allows him or her to re-enter situationally under specified conditions: one must have money at one's disposal, pass exams, keep to the conventions of litigation, etc. Luhmann's thesis is that this fundamental exclusion entails a dramatic increase in both individual freedoms and risks. The individual no longer has recourse to clear-cut social identities, but has to decide how to build up a personality and how to communicate it to others. At the same time, the individual person becomes dependent for his well-being upon conditions and decisions made elsewhere—in the education system, in politics, in firms or the labour market. 'Under such structural societal conditions and such burdening of behaviour, the individual personality needs special protection (not in the least in its freedom of being impersonal)', Luhmann writes.[25] The more vulnerable the position of the individual, the more society has to develop protection mechanisms for the individual's self-presentation and mobility. The central thesis of *Grundrechte als Institution* is that precisely such mechanisms are institutionalised by human rights law.

Firstly, human rights ensure that the individual has access to different function systems. By equipping individuals with rights and claims to participation in politics, economy, law, education, . . . it becomes acceptable, and even expected, that individuals decide for themselves upon voting behaviour, the choice of a profession, intimate relations, etc. In a comparative (historical and regional) perspective this is not obvious at all. Our experience with political totalitarianism, for instance, shows that fundamental rights and freedoms are required to guarantee the individual that his or her participation in the mass media, a political party or church will not entail political reprimands or repression. A person will only express or publish his or her opinion if he or she does not have to fear

[23] See G Corsi, 'Die Dunkle Seite der Karriere' in D Baecker (ed), *Probleme der Form* (Frankfurt a/Main, Suhrkamp, 1993) 252–265; R Laermans and G Verschraegen, 'Modernity and Individuality', above n 17, 125–126.

[24] N Luhmann, *Gesellschaftsstruktur und Semantik*, 158 ff.; Laermans & Verschraegen, 'Modernity and Individuality', above n 17, 123 ff.

[25] N Luhmann, *Grundrechte*, above n 4, 51.

it will harm him or her; someone will only dare to vote freely if he or she knows he or she is protected by private ballot and hence does not have to justify his or her vote within other social roles.[26] By encouraging the individual to participate freely in different function systems and by preventing one subsystem or social group from completely controlling him or her, human rights strengthen and protect the high degree of individual mobility and communicative openness upon which modern society is built.[27] Thus, by protecting the individual, the social institution of human rights also protects the complex and differentiated order of modern society. Only by giving inalienable rights to the individual can society protect its own level of differentiation and weaken tendencies towards regression or dedifferentiation.

In order not to misunderstand this point, it is important to note that Luhmann's belief in the danger of dedifferentiation is connected with a specific view on the modern social order. Unlike any other social thinker, Luhmann is convinced of the fundamental contingency and vulnerability of the contemporary social order. He asks, 'what makes social order possible?' on the assumption that order is improbable in the face of the general contingency and complexity of modern society. 'What Luhmann emphasises in his work is not the stability of modern societies, but their fragility and improbability and the need to increase, where possible, the conditions for stability'.[28] Modern society is built upon social structures that are, at an evolutionary level, very improbable and therefore need special protection. Without institutionalised mechanisms that enable and fortify the co-existence of highly individualised persons and autonomous function systems, the risk of regression or dedifferentiation is real, Luhmann argues.[29] This is primarily because, owing to its high degree of complexity and its high sensitivity for irritations, a functionally differentiated society and—most particularly—the political subsystem within it—are easily inclined to seek for drastic solutions to problems. In response to increasing contingency, transitoriness and individual mobility, for instance, it is possible to promote and abide by the absolute values of religion, belonging and custom. This constitutes a genuine risk for the dominant structure of modern society. Luhmann has stressed several times that this risk of simplification and dedifferentiation is not a mere theoretical problem. In an interview of his ideas, for example, he says that

> the experience of National Socialism widened our conception of what is possible. Atrocity became politically acceptable, and was even exercised without being legally

[26] N Luhmann, *Legitimation durch Verfahren* (Frankfurt a/Main, Suhrkamp, 1983) 160.

[27] N Luhmann, *Grundrechte*, above n 4 at 23.

[28] M King, A Schütz, 'The Ambitious Modesty of Niklas Luhmann', (1994) 21 *Journal of Law and Society* 270.

[29] N Luhmann here returns to a theme of Parsons. See F J Lechner, 'Fundamentalism and Sociocultural Revitalization: On the Logic of Dedifferentiation' in JC Alexander and P Colomy (eds), *Differentiation Theory and Social Change: Comparative and Historical Pprinciples* (New York, Columbia University Press, 1990) 88–118.

> prevented (. . .) thus, one has to raise the question whether and to what extent this event was being covered by the law, and even more radically, whether it was possible as law.[30]

The subtext of *Grundrechte als Institution* is hence constituted by the traumatic experience of the political totalitarianism of the twentieth century. Luhmann asks whether it is possible to institutionalise protection mechanisms that can prevent such tendencies of dedifferentiation repeating itself. Which mechanisms can modern society invent to block the regressions that jeopardise its own structure?

Contrary to the dominant philosophy of law, Luhmann does not look for answers in any endeavour to revivify natural law:

> After 1945, one looked for security in natural law in order to prevent the return of the 'totalitarian state'. This was not only little convincing, but at the same time a politically dangerous illusion: it distracted from the insight that such security can only be found in the political institutions themselves, and in last instance only in political action itself.[31]

Accordingly, Luhmann's analysis starts from the idea that fundamental freedoms institutionalise a *self-limitation* of the political system. Out of all function systems the political system has the greatest propensity for simplifying the differentiated social order according to its own political goals, as Luhmann argues in 1965—against the background of the Cold War and with the memory of the National Socialist regime still fresh. Without societal protection mechanisms, Luhmann writes, 'the political system tends to subsume all social processes within politics and treat them from a political point of view and this beyond its function of implementing binding decisions'.[32] Now, from the point of view of systems theory it is clear that the political system can only perform its own functional operations (ie making binding decisions) if it is not burdened with all the problems of social life. The political system cannot work effectively if it has to solve problems that can only adequately be resolved in the autopoietic systems of economics, science, art, law, and so on.[33] When the political system nonetheless attempts to solve problems such as choosing investments, deciding on the scientific value of research projects, judging the aesthetic worth of a painting, it not only overtaxes itself, it also seriously disturbs the selectivity of these other function systems.

With the definitive breakthrough of functional differentiation, a new type of self-limitation therefore emerges in the form of the constitution, a structural coupling between politics and law.[34] Constitutional rights emerge as a social

[30] N Luhmann cited in R Stichweh (ed), *Niklas Luhmann. Wirkungen eines Theoretikers* (Bielefeld, Transcript, 1999) 24.

[31] N Luhmann, *Grundrechte*, above n 4 at 41.

[32] *Ibid*, 97.

[33] M King and C Thornhill, *Niklas Luhmann's Theory of Politics and Law* (Basingstoke, Palgrave, 2003) 70–71.

[34] N Luhmann, 'Verfassung als evolutionäre Errungenschaft', (1990) 9 *Rechtshistorisches Journal* 176; See also, N Luhmann, *Die Politik der Gesellschaft*, above n 7, 391–392.

counter-institution, which restricts the colonising tendencies of state politics. Via constitutionally guaranteed rights and freedoms, the political system defines the area of competence of state power and delineates it from all other, non-political social spheres. Only by constitutionally restricting itself can politics perform its own function properly and acknowledge the autonomy of other systems. This internal limitation of political power is even more necessary because the autonomy of all function systems goes together with an increased dependency upon each other. Political power, for instance, is not to be for sale, *precisely because* political decisions are attended by enormous financial stakes and interests. The independence of judiciary has to be guaranteed constitutionally, *precisely because* judicial decisions have a great impact on other function systems. Freedom of the press has to be protected constitutionally, *precisely because* the political dependency upon the mass media is becoming greater and greater, and so on.[35]

In sum, since the American constitution and the French Declaration of 1789, fundamental freedoms have functioned, on one hand, as the internal boundaries between state power and non-political societal spheres, and, on the other, they have acted as boundaries between the state and individual spheres of freedom. By preventing a situation in which the political system absolutises its own perspective, fundamental rights protect both the freedom and interests of the individual and the differentiation between different function systems. One can think, for instance, of religious freedom and freedom of conscience, which prevent interference between politics and religion and which, at the same time, assign the choice and the practice of religion to an individual decision. Other examples are the fundamental right of ownership, which ensures the autonomy of the economic system, and at the same time makes economic operations dependent upon the decision to buy or not to buy; the protection of the freedom of education and research, and so on. One might note here that the division into different fundamental rights reflects the differentiation in different, autonomous, societal spheres.

To conclude this point, I would like to make two additional remarks. Firstly, I would like to stress that Luhmann's conception of the constitution as a self-limitation of the political system does not imply that fundamental rights should be conceived as so-called 'negative rights', which limit the state's interference with freedom of opinion, action and association. In this view, the protection of fundamental rights does not require governmental performance, but only governmental forbearance. The negative conception of, for instance, the freedom of expression assumes or implies that all that is required is the removal of direct official constraints on otherwise articulate, creative, and communicative individuals. From a sociological point of view, however, protection of freedom of expression should be conceived not solely as a mechanism which removes official constraints on issues of public concern debated by political elites, but

[35] N Luhmann, *Die Gesellschaft der Gesellschaft*, above n 7, 776–789.

also as one which enhances material resources and promotes practical opportunities and institutional frameworks for the exercise of this right by all citizens. This implies for example that the government is under a constitutional duty, not only to keep public spaces, streets and parks open for expressive activity, but also to guarantee the institutional conditions for a 'free press', and to make sure that the media system and the economic system, the political system and the press do not coalesce. How meaningful is the protection of individual freedom of expression if there are no constitutional guarantees for the communicative process, for the institution of a 'free press'? Hence, constitutional rights cannot be protected simply by limiting the state's interference in freedom of action and association. Most constitutional rights depend for their existence on positive (and costly) acts by the state, which has the constitutional duty actively to protect and perform.[36]

Secondly, I would also remark that Luhmann's focus on the totalising tendencies in politics—which was understandable in 1965—needs now to be extended to other function systems. The new experience of the twentieth (and the twenty-first) century is that totalising tendencies have their origin not only in politics, but also in other spheres of society.[37] To be sure, the historical role of basic rights has been to protect the precarious results of social differentiation from their politicisation. 'But', Christoph Graber and Gunther Teubner observe:

> this is a historical contingency which depends on the expansive potential of a social system at a given time. Silicon Valley, we submit, carries potentially as many risks for the freedom of science, education, and research (. . .) It is an obsession with phenomena of power that tends to overlook other media of communication as threats to individual and social autonomy. Instead it is the specific communicative medium against which individual and social autonomy needs to be protected, in analogy to the protection against the power medium of the State. Economy and technology are obvious new candidates.'[38]

Today, violations of human rights are experienced not merely as the result of the arbitrary use of state power, but also as a result of the abuse of the economic and technological power of private actors (eg multinationals).[39] In contemporary society, fundamental rights should therefore be directed not only against state action, but also against the intrusions of other expansive social systems, such as economy, mass media, religion, etc. This implies that the classical and narrow liberal view that fundamental rights are constituted exclusively in the triad of individual-power-State should be complemented by a more differentiated view that takes into account other social systems as well.

[36] See S Holmes, CR Sunstein, *The Cost of Rights. Why Liberty Depends on Taxes* (New York/London, Norton, 1999).

[37] Compare CB Graber and G Teubner, 'Art and Money', above n 4, 68 ff.

[38] *Ibid*, 69–70.

[39] See PT Muchlinski, 'Human Rights and Multinationals: Is There a Problem?' (2001) 77 *International Affairs* 31.

FUNDAMENTAL FREEDOMS AND INSTITUTIONALISED INDIVIDUALISM

Fundamental freedoms are primarily protective rights: they protect the individual sphere of freedom from excessive claims from society, not only from political power, but from any social system with totalising tendencies. In this sense, human rights can be understood as negative rights; they guarantee negative freedoms. However, as already indicated, it would be too simplistic to reduce human rights to strictly negative freedoms, for they also require institutional preconditions that enable the individual to participate in society. If individual autonomy is to be a positive, active condition, it requires rights that permit participation and empower one to act in public. The self-determination of individuals cannot be realised by an isolated individual, but is only possible within a broader and differentiated social environment. Luhmann therefore argues that the reduction of basic rights and fundamental freedoms to individual spheres of action does not take into account the fact that freedom in society is realised not only in the individual sphere but in different communicative spheres as well. In this section, I will therefore attempt to show how fundamental freedoms institutionalise not only negative liberties, but also recognise the institutional and social dimensions of personal development. Such rights as freedom of speech, conscience, religion, and association not only protect a sphere of personal autonomy, but they also guarantee the capacity to develop a social identity.

In modern society, fundamental rights are essential to social recognition and to the respect of any human being as a person. Functional differentiation entails that individuals no longer have recourse to clear-cut social identities. While pre-modern societies take the individual for granted as something familiar,[40] modernity has developed a semantics of individuality, according to which the individual is seen as unfamiliar, strange, unpredictable and free.[41] As a result, communicating one's own identity is no longer obvious and fundamental rights and freedoms therefore primarily need to protect the conditions of the possibility of individual self-presentation, Luhmann argues.[42]

How can the conditions of possibility for personal self-presentation be guaranteed? In the first place by the right to life, to physical integrity and to freedom of movement. No one can prevent a person from being present, from speaking, from seeing, from coming and leaving whenever he or she wants to. No one can be subjected to torture or to cruel, inhuman or degrading treatment or punishment. These rights to physical integrity and freedom of movement are the basic rights of communicative self-presentation, which is primarily based upon 'the

[40] Note that they do not consider strangers to be part of society at all.
[41] N Luhmann, *Gesellschaftsstruktur und Semantik III*, above n 17, 158–159.
[42] N Luhmann, *Grundrechte*, above n 4 at 21.

presence, posture and expression of the body'.[43] 'The presentation of self in everyday life'—to use the words of Erving Goffman—is only possible through verbal and non-verbal communications—which have to do with physical presence and appearance, facial expression, gesture and bodily movement. Only by freely employing the body can a person exchange information, convey his appreciation of others present and, at the same time, place himself in the social context they represent. In this sense, the rights to physical integrity and to freedom of movement are not merely biological or physical, they are also inherently social rights, not only because they demand respect for the body of the other, but primarily because they enable an individual to be a 'person', to participate in communication and social intercourse.[44] These rights guarantee that communications can be assigned to a specific person, accountable for his or her own decisions and behaviour, for one can only be regarded as a person if one is looked upon as 'free' to say what one wants to say, to come and leave, to decide on a specific course of action, and so on. Statements obtained through torture for instance cannot be considered as 'personal' communication, for the one who confesses also makes clear that the cause of that statement is not within himself or herself.

Likewise, the right to freedom of thought, conscience and religion, the right to freedom of opinion and expression, the right to freedom of peaceful assembly and association, the right to political participation, work, education, etc aim to guarantee the capacity for the expression of one's own personality and thus for the realisation of one's human dignity. According to Luhmann, fundamental freedoms protect 'the symbolically-expressive dimensions of free action (. . .) and are concerned with the general right to free development of the person'.[45] Social communication and the development of the person, self-determination and sociality are thus indissolubly connected. All these individual rights are at the same time communicative or social rights, they enable the individual to participate in the different communicative subsystems of society and they enable him or her to become a person. They are not rights of the isolated individual, but take into account the specific social environment of modern human beings.[46] For example, the right to freedom of opinion and expression is more

[43] N Luhmann, *Grundrechte*, above n 4 at 21, 79.

[44] *Ibid*, 79–80. This important social or communicative dimension is rarely discussed. The right to freedom of movement and the right to physical integrity are mostly interpreted as rights of the solitary individual. For example, see U Eco, *Vijf morele dilemma's* (Amsterdam, Bert Bakker, 1997), 85 ff.

[45] N Luhmann, *Grundrechte*, above n 4 at 79.

[46] In this sense, so-called cultural rights could also be seen as rights guaranteeing the conditions of possibility of personal individuation and self-presentation. For linguistic and cultural traditions are no less relevant for the formation and maintenance of the personal identity—something always interwoven with cultural symbols and the collective self-representation of different social groups. However, this does not imply that cultural rights should be understood to be 'collective rights'; they are rather individual rights serving the goal of guaranteeing free and equal access to linguistic and cultural forms of communication, traditions and practices, to the extent that these are materials for the formation or maintenance of personal identities. Some of the so-called cultural rights—like the

than a strictly individual, 'possessive' right: is it not merely the right to hold an opinion without interference, but also the right to express an opinion and to be held responsible for it, without, however, having to fear incarceration or loss of income. Press freedom is not the right to write whatever one wants to write; it is rather the right to publish, to take part in the system of the media. As such it guarantees the possibility of the social circulation of information and ideas. The right to work, to free choice of employment also relates to the development of the person with participation in the different subsystems and in the organisations of modern society. On the one hand, one's profession is a very important dimension of individual self-understanding and self-presentation; in modern society one is, to a large extent, what one does.[47] On the other hand, one's profession or work can only acquire that symbolic value if it has been freely chosen.[48] Thus, the right to work and to free choice of employment guarantees free inclusion, free access to various professional roles in the different functional systems. For example, it ensures that familial expectations concerning the choice of profession can be neutralised. Through the human right to free choice of employment, the social expectation that a son has to succeed his father can no longer find general social support.[49] Hence, different individuals can be freely distributed among the various professional roles in modern society. The right to freedom of association also illustrates that the self-determination and self-presentation of the modern individual are only possible if free inclusion in the various organisations of modern society is guaranteed:

> *Because* his choice is free and exit possible, the individual, through the nature and amount of his different memberships, also makes a testimony about himself, (. . .) and at the same time the organisations can—through regulation of those expectations which one has to accept voluntarily if one wants to maintain one's membership—subject one to rather precise prescriptions, that in their detail and differentiation and at the same time in the manner of allowed freedom of movement rise high above everything which could be ensured by coercion.[50]

In short, because fundamental rights enable and legitimise the free choice of the individual, they strengthen the dominant structure of modern society, which is based upon free inclusion and individual mobility. 'Through free choice, a varied and contradictory multitude of norms, roles and institutions can be built up and tried out.'[51] As such, *human rights constitute the unnoticed and elementary condition for participation within modern society.* Human rights enable us,

right to speak your own language or practice your own religion—are in fact essential preconditions for the exercise of individual rights. The right to speak a language of your choice will not mean very much if the language has died out. See J Habermas, 'Intolerance and Discrimination' (2003) 1 *International Journal of Constitutional Law* 10.

[47] N Luhmann, *Grundrechte*, above n 4 at 131.

[48] *Ibid*, 132.

[49] *Ibid*, 134.

[50] *Ibid*, 91.

[51] *Ibid*, 102.

without taking further notice, to take part in the richness of social roles, networks, associations and organisations that make up modern society. The importance and the unnoticed character of this elementary communicative and relational freedom is probably best understood by looking at societies or regions in which fundamental rights are not guaranteed. In such places maintaining functional differentiation becomes very difficult, for individuals cannot be freely included in the various function systems. With every decision, the individual has to reflect on what the people in power will think of the fact that he or she reads this newspaper, exercises such a profession, expresses his or her opinion about the president in public, and so on.

The mechanism whereby authoritarian governments or dictatorships are able to institutionalise such permanent reflection is the massive spread of fear. In rights-abusive regimes (such as Myanmar, former Iraq, Sudan) large-scale control systems exist, in which torture, incarceration and 'disappearance' are organised in a systematic, professional and bureaucratic way. The goal is to scare and intimidate the population in such a manner that everyone will ask themselves whether their actions entail a risk both for themselves and for friends and relatives. People will not only refrain from everything that is forbidden, but will also avoid everything that is not explicitly allowed.[52] As such, the risk of 'politically hostile' activities is kept as small as possible. Consequently, a rich and differentiated context of societal activity or communication is impeded. Individuals are discouraged from taking risks or entering into new relationships; they become distrustful and try to keep the sphere of action that can be attributed to them as small as possible. A situation evolves in which people are necessarily and compulsorily inclined to 'mind their own business'. Since everybody is a potential police spy, one withdraws from public life to the small circle of relatives and friends (but even there, there are clear risks—it is, for instance, better not to talk about politics in the presence of your children. Before you know it, they might start repeating—in all innocence—your opinions in the schoolyard, where there is always somebody working for the secret police). As a consequence, social life retreats to small and relatively undifferentiated enclaves,[53] the simplification or dedifferentiation of society, which we talked about earlier, becomes reality. The boundaries we usually draw between different social spheres are simply erased. What someone does as an artist, as a user

[52] In order to reach this state of absolute restraint, authoritarian regimes introduce an important element of irregularity and uncertainty. 'If everybody would know in advance which kind of actions entail arrest and torture, and which would remain unpunished, then most people would refrain from the first and do the latter carelessly. But the goal of a system of deterrence is precisely to scare people to such a degree that they will freely refrain from things which are otherwise very hard to track and hard to be prevented by the regime. Even a police state is not able to continuous surveillance of all people. Because the regime can not fully command all its do's and don'ts, it has to create a negative game of chance in which the civilians themselves have to avoid risks'. A De Swaan, 'Terreur als overheidsdienst' in A De Swaan, *De mens is de mens een zorg* (Amsterdam, Meulenhoff, 1982) 116–130, 124.

[53] N Luhmann, *Grundrechte*, above n 4 at 69; DA Bell, 'Een Communitaristische Kritiek op het Autoritarisme', *Krisis*. (1995) 45 *Tijdschrift voor Filosofie* 40.

of the media, as a believer, and so on, can have serious consequences for his legal status, income, health, etc. Consequently, the relatively flexible and differentiated mechanisms of inclusion within modern society cannot be maintained. Access to politics, law, education, medical treatment and so on cannot be regulated by functionally specific mechanisms of inclusion any longer but become dependent upon the nepotism of local functionaries, access to the small network of friends of the regime, and so on.

EQUALITY AND HUMAN RIGHTS

Fundamental rights are not only formulated as freedom-related rights but also as equal rights. Modern legal orders are based on the principle of the equal inclusion of all citizens. In fact, so-called equal rights have only been gradually extended to oppressed and excluded groups. Workers, women and gays have been recognised as 'citizens' with a claim to fully equal treatment only after long political struggles. One of the most important steps in this gradual extension of equal rights has been of course the emergence of the concept of human rights. Human rights of the first generation were declared in the great democratic revolutions towards the end of the eighteenth century in the United States and France. Here, for the first time, there emerged a clear written declaration of rights to which every individual, every human being by nature, ie regardless of all social attributes, was entitled. In practice however, these rights were limited to the (male, white, etc) citizens of the respective nation-states. It was only in the course of the twentieth century that the idea of 'human rights' was universalised in the Universal Declaration of Human Rights (adopted by the United Nations on 12 December 1948). Full membership was then no longer based on nationality; it no longer confined itself to Western Europe and North America but instead claimed to represent 'a common standard of achievement for all peoples and all nations'.

If all human beings have human rights simply because they are human, they are held equally by all. The 1948 declaration states clearly that human rights are universal rights. 'Everyone is entitled to all the rights and freedoms set forth in this Declaration, without distinction of any kind, such as race, colour, sex, language, religion, political or other opinion, national or social origin, property, birth or other status' (Article 2). As I indicated before, this equality of rights symbolises that the individual as a juridical subject is equal to all other human beings, precisely because one's social position is not being taken into consideration. The new form of inclusion in modern society requires that everyone has equal access to the different function systems in the sense that no general institutionalised social discriminations can exist which prevent access. Rich people as well as poor people, men as well as women, Belgians as well as Egyptians, have the right to marry and found a family, the right to own property, the right to free education, and so on. Within the different function systems only specific differences or 'inequalities' can determine the way and degree of inclusion. Thus, everyone has the right to free access to the education system, the economic system, and so on, but the way in which inclusion in a specific system takes place, can only be decided within those systems themselves, via, for instance, differences or 'inequalities' in learning capacity, inequalities in states of health, and so on.[54]

From a sociological perspective, the right of 'equality', at least in the modern sense of the word,[55] is consequently neither expression of a 'natural' equality (all human beings *are* equal), nor expression of a value, ie something to be pursued (all human beings *shall* be treated equally). In the light of its function within modern society, the principle of equality should rather be conceived as a principle of *selective indifference*: only relevant features or inequalities have to be reckoned with in the process of inclusion, all other features or inequalities should not be taken into consideration. And once again: what can count as relevant and non-relevant inequalities, can only be determined by the subsystem in question. Within the medical subsystem only inequalities in the state of health are to be seen as meaningful, in the economic system, only inequalities in the means of existence are to be reckoned with, and so on.

It is also possible to formulate the principle of equality in terms of role differentiation. Equal treatment then implies that only *functionally specific* role expectations and requirements should be taken into account. So, consumers should be treated *as* consumers, voters *as* voters, students *as* students, and so on—normally, other roles cannot be taken into consideration. Concerning this, Luhmann writes:

> It is constitutionally prohibited to favour or injure someone in a certain role combination because he or she also assumes other roles—unless specific grounds make such a combination meaningful. An entrepreneur should therefore not be subsidised because he is an adherent of a particular religion; one should not let a student pass because his or her parents belong to the city's nobility; but a fine may be higher because the driver is rich (since the fine is related to income). Every orientation towards an unclear, structurally not relevant, but rather accidental because mere personal role combination is a violation of the principle of equality.[56]

Decisions that imply an unequal treatment can therefore be justified only if they indicate specific grounds for the unequal treatment. In this way the princi-

[54] See R Stichweh, 'Inklusion in Funktionssysteme der modernen Gesellschaft' in R Mayntz (ed), *Differenzierung und Verselbständigung: zur Entwicklung gesellschaftlicher Teilsystme* (Frankfurt a/Main, Suhrkamp, 1988) 261–293.

[55] The idea of equality is widely spread in pre-modern societies as well. In the advanced civilisations of antiquity and Christianity for instance one believes that all human beings are equal before God. This idea, however, does not endanger or disrupt the stratified social order. Human beings are only equal in so far as they are being compared with animals or with God. For a general outline of the semantic evolution of the idea of equality, see N Luhmann, 'Der Gleichheitssatz', above n 21 435 ff; S Holmes, 'Differenzierung und Arbeitsteilung im Denken des Liberalismus' in N Luhmann (ed), *Soziale Differenzierung: zur Geschichte einer Idee* (Opladen, Westdeutscher Verlag, 1985) 9–41.

[56] N Luhmann, *Grundrechte*, above n 4 at 179.

ple of equality guarantees that *functional differentiation is also maintained between different roles*. The right to equal treatment ensures that inclusion takes place only in functionally specific ways, unless certain 'structurally relevant' role combinations can be taken into consideration.

In principle, inclusion in a function system is related only to functionally and role- specific inequalities. Only differences in the health situation of the patients can count in deciding who gets a kidney for transplantation; only differences in the family situation can be taken into consideration when deciding who shall be allowed to adopt children; only inequalities in test scores, school grades, and so on, should be considered meaningful in deciding who is admitted to selective colleges, schools, etc. What matters is that equal cases (that is, equal in a medical, familial or educational perspective) are treated equally and unequal cases (medically, educationally etc) unequally, according to their degree of inequality.[57] To treat unequal individuals equally (for instance, giving all students the same grade) would clearly be unjust. Every function system therefore uses specific criteria and procedures (for instance, examinations, genetic screening, and so on) to sort out equal and unequal cases.[58]

To conclude, it might be said that the rights of equality guarantee that individuals can only be included in the different function systems of modern society according to specific and consistent criteria and procedures. For only in this way can it be guaranteed that non-relevant social features such as colour, sex, language, religion, political or other opinion, and so on, are not taken into consideration. In Luhmann's own words:

> Finally, based on this analysis, we can relate the right to equality to the area of general norms of human rights, or even take it as a paradigm example for human rights. . . . Human rights correspond exactly to the structurally induced open-ended character of modern society. If individuals are to attain access to all functional systems in their respectively different ways and if, at the same time, their inclusion is internally controlled in these functional systems by deciding what is seen as equal and what is not, with the help of functional criteria—if all this is part and parcel of the structural imperatives of modern society, *it is impossible to say in advance who has to say what or who has to contribute what* . . . Functionally, human rights are designed to keep the future open for the diverse autopoietic reproductions of respective systems. No distribution, no classification, and above all no political sorting of people can limit the future. For people belong to the environment of the system and the future at any given point develops unpredictably and only through the autopoiesis and structural drift of society.[59]

[57] *Ibid*, 110–117.

[58] See J Elster, *Local Justice: How Institutions Allocate Scarce Goods and Necessary Burdens* (New York, Russel Sage, 1992).

[59] N Luhmann, *Law as a Social System*, above n 6, 135–6.

TWO FORMS OF EXCLUSION AND SYMBOLIC CONSTITUTIONALISATION IN PERIPHERAL MODERNITY

In short, human rights reflect the fact that the individual in modern society is constituted by exclusion. A society that institutionalises human rights can, paradoxically enough, no longer be conceived of in humanistic terms. Modern society has to admit that the modern individual no longer lives within but outside society, ie belongs to the environment of social systems. At the same time however, human rights provide a solution for the structural inclusion-problem that is connected with this primary exclusion: by guaranteeing that each individual gets access to various social systems under specific conditions (pass exams, fall in love, have a disease, have money at one's disposal, etc) individuals can re-enter society and thus build up an individual career and a personal identity. From this first, primary form of exclusion, one should however distinguish a second form of exclusion: the impossibility of re-entering various social systems. Exclusion in this second sense means that one cannot obtain access to different social systems, because the omission from one function system (eg extreme poverty) leads to exclusion from other function systems as well (eg formal education, legal protection, stable family relations).

This second problem of exclusion also seems to be deeply connected with the protection and implementation of equal fundamental rights. If large groups of the population have few enforceable rights, the factual exclusion from one function system will lead very easily to omission from other function systems as well. For example, if one is largely excluded from access to judicial protection, it can become difficult to enforce one's right of access to the labour market, consumption, education, medical care, etc. Admittedly, the boundaries between inclusion and exclusion are fluid and shifting and to a certain extent defined by culturally specific levels of legitimate expectations. In contemporary welfare states, where 'welfare' has become an indeterminate principle—a project with unlimited scope and no end—one tries to prevent exclusion as much as possible by endowing the whole population with subjective civil and social rights and by intervening politically in the conditions of access or by compensating for exclusion. In welfare states, exclusion and inclusion thereby become a permanent problem for the political system. The second problem of exclusion, however, takes on a different dimension in many regions of world society, where social exclusion has become a generalised phenomenon, notwithstanding basic constitutional protection of the equal rights of all citizens.

Marcelo Neves has called this 'symbolic constitutionalisation', ie the adoption of 'Western' constitutional models by countries with completely different traditions. As indicated, we assume that modern states institutionalise a *self-limitation* of the political system by way of constitutional rights. Yet, the constitution is modelled on specific societal conditions that cannot simply be imported wholesale as a fully functioning system. Paradoxically enough, a constitution can only be institutionalised if functional differentiation is already entrenched, such that the differentiation of the legal system and the political system, the economic system and the political system, the religious and the political system, re-enforce each other and stabilise their boundaries. This presupposes a far-reaching neutralisation of stratification, at least for the inclusion in different function systems. For world society these conditions are realised on the global level, as the different function systems and symbolically generalised media of communication (money, legality, power) know no internal boundaries. Yet, for different regions on this planet these conditions are realised only to a very limited extent. Although all regions are exposed to the effects of world society, and especially to the world economy, a lot of regions have only partially taken over the preconditions of functional differentiation.[60] The survival of hierarchical inclusion structures and (consequently) large-scale social exclusion, severe problems of corruption, poor legitimacy of public institutions and often also lack of material resources, preclude a proper functioning of the constitution and even effect the very principle of functional differentiation. According to Neves, the typical problem of the countries of 'peripheral modernity' is that the constitution is only 'symbolically' realised and not put into practice. It is true that, in order to be recognised and accepted as a 'state', these countries adopt the 'world model' of the constitution,[61] but in practice, 'the political takes precedence over the legal so that one can hardly speak of operative autonomy or functional differentiation of both systems'.[62] Under such conditions, the constitution does not function as a structural coupling of law and politics, but is used as an instrument of the ruling elite, that 'puts aside the binary code legal/illegal and the corresponding criteria, and act, as well as orient their expectations, in accordance with the direct pressures of the economy, power, family relationships, and so on'.[63]

As indicated, this symbolic constitutionalisation is closely related with the generalised problem of social exclusion within the peripheral countries. If the constitution is used as an instrument of the ruling elite, only a minority of 'over-integrated' individuals 'has access to the products and benefits of social systems, without being simultaneously dependent on their constraints and rules', while a growing number of 'under-integrated' people are largely excluded from the access to political power, the labour market, judicial protection, consumption, education, medical care, etc. Both inclusion and exclusion, therefore, are highly integrated (ie positions in different systems are dependent upon each other). Instead of loosely integrated, differentiated inclusion mechanisms, the various

[60] See M Neves, *Verfassung und Positivität des Rechts in der peripheren Moderne: Eine theoretische Betrachtung und eine Interpretation des Falls Brasilien* (Berlin, Duncker & Humblot, 1992).

[61] See JW Meyer, J Boli, G Thomas and F Ramirez, 'World Society and the Nation-State', (1997) 103 *American Journal of Sociology* 144.

[62] M Neves, 'From the Autopoiesis to the Allopoiesis of Law', (2001) 28 *Journal of Law and Society* 260.

[63] *Ibid*, 260.

societal positions are correlated with each other to a high degree. Inclusion in the various societal spheres is thus only possible if one comes from the right family, has the required political connections, capital, etc. On the other side of the social spectrum, the factual exclusion from one function system makes access to other function systems rather difficult, if not impossible: 'no job, no income, no ID, no stable love relationships, no access to juridical agreements and judicial protection, no possibility to distinguish between electoral campaigns and carnival, high illiteracy, medical under-treatment and malnutrition'.[64] Precisely this '*Abweichungsverstärkung*', this *cumulative effect of exclusion*, is a direct consequence of functional differentiation in peripheral societies. If the required social background conditions (neutralisation of stratification, constitutional democracy, etc) are not present, the structure of society (functional differentiation) causes highly integrated exclusion-effects: 'People who don't have an address cannot enrol in a school (India). People who cannot read or write, hardly have a chance on the labour market, and one even discusses (Brazil) whether they should be excluded from voting or not. When one can only find a home in the illegally occupied land of the *favelas*[65] one cannot enjoy legal protection; but also the landowner cannot safeguard his rights, because forced clearance of the land would cause too much unrest.'[66]

THE PARADOX OF HUMAN RIGHTS

From the point of view of systems theory, the globalisation of human rights goes together with the entrenchment of functional differentiation and the emergence of 'World Society'. Since the different function systems and symbolically generalised media of communication (money, legality, power) do not confine themselves to Western Europe and North America but instead spread all over the world, constitutional rights that guarantee equal access to different subsystems should be universalised as well.[67] Human rights are thus proclaimed in general terms as belonging to all human beings, irrespective of citizenship and other social attributes. However, as we already indicated, the universal aspiration to human rights does not prevent them from being highly dependent for their protection and implementation upon states being willing and able effectively to constitutionalise human rights. Although human rights should be independent from the state (for they are intended precisely to protect the individual from the state) their realisation is strongly associated with citizenship of a specific country. In this section, I shall call this the paradox of human rights and try to explain where it originates.

[64] N Luhmann, *Die Gesellschaft der Gesellschaft*, above n 7, 630.

[65] A *favela* is a South American shantytown or slum, mostly placed on former public or private areas around big cities.

[66] N Luhmann, *Die Gesellschaft der Gesellschaft*, above n 7, 631.

[67] *Ibid*, 145–171; N Luhmann, 'Globalization or World Society: How to Conceive of Modern Society', (1997) 7 *International Review of Sociology* 67.

The paradox of human rights seems to go back to the seventeenth century theories of 'natural rights' (to Locke, Grotius, *et al*). Here, for the first time, we witness the emergence of the idea of individual, subjective rights, to which all human beings were entitled, simply because they derived from their nature, and not from the government or its laws (on the contrary: the legitimacy of the government rested on the respect that it accorded to these rights). The modern conception of human rights is a reformulation of this idea: human rights derive from human nature and are thus inalienable, independent from the state.[68] As early as the end of the eighteenth century, however, the concept of natural rights was opposed because it confounds the consequences of legal systems, which give individuals certain well-defined rights, with pre-legal principles that cannot really give one a justiciable right. Marx and Bentham, for example, insisted that rights cannot really *precede* (rather than follow) the institution of the state. How can natural (and later, human) rights have any real legal status except through entitlements that are sanctioned by the state (or another political body with ultimate legal authority)?[69]

In consequence, it became clear that natural and human rights were founded upon a paradox: individual rights to life, liberty and property are found in the state of nature and are thus independent of the state; at the same time however rights claims have to be recognised and enforced by a state in order to be effective. Concerning this, Luhmann remarks that natural rights can be conceived of as 'rights before the law, rights not depending on the recognition of others (for example, the right to preserve and to move one's own body, the old *potestas in se ipsum*)—that is, rights before the distinction of right and wrong.'[70] As such, a natural or human right is a paradoxical right, a right answering the third question: how can we rightly (or wrongly) differentiate between the right and the wrong? The problem with this answer to the third question is quite clear: how can there be rights without complementary obligations? Taken as aspiring legal entities, pre-legal moral claims can hardly be seen as giving justiciable rights in courts and other institutions of enforcement.

In his only article on human rights, Luhmann formulates this paradox as 'the need to positivise pre-positive law'.[71] Being human cannot be renounced or forfeited, and human rights can hence not be taken away by human decisions. But how can one respect this pre-legal moral claim? The solution can only lie in 'the positivation of these pre-positive rights'. This happened first in the purely declaratory texts of the great democratic revolutions, like the American Bill of Rights and the French Declaration, which simply stated that every individual has inalienable rights. 'But soon it became common and also necessary, in order

[68] N Luhmann, 'Paradox der Menschenrechte', above n 3, 229–231.

[69] See J Waldron (ed), *Nonsense Upon Stilts: Bentham, Burke and Marx on the Rights of Man* (London, Methuen, 1987).

[70] N Luhmann, 'The Third Question: The Creative Use of Paradoxes in Law and Legal History', (1988) 15 *Journal of Law and Society* 153, 158.

[71] N Luhmann, 'Paradox der Menschenrechte', above n 3 at 233.

to curb systematic criticism, to include these texts in the constitution, to endow them with the stability of constitutional rights and to give them a normal legal status.' Traditionally, human rights are indeed enacted in national constitutions and laws for domestic application by the judicial and executive organs of the state. Prior to the emergence of the concept of universal human rights, the state was taken to have exclusive 'territorial jurisdiction' in defining and implementing individual, constitutional rights. However, learning from the historical insight and experience that the state cannot be trusted adequately to protect the rights of all persons and groups within its territorial jurisdiction, the modern concept of human rights emerged as a means of ensuring certain minimum standards everywhere. Some of these minimum standards, like the prohibition of genocide, slavery and torture, have evolved as customary international law binding on all states.[72] But as a general rule, standards for human rights are articulated in international treaties that are binding only on states that have ratified them.[73] Hence, the most important paradox of human rights in contemporary world society is the following: notwithstanding the vast body of international and regional human rights law developed after the Second World War, international protection of human rights is still dependent on the active cooperation of states in limiting their freedom of action. Since there is no international sovereign (and in the foreseeable future will never be) that has sufficient power to enforce protections of rights, the protection and implementation of both customary and treaty-based human rights is dependent on the action of the state through its own legislative, judicial, and executive organs.[74]

This 'paradox of self-regulation' is the necessary consequence of the principle of state sovereignty on which the present international political system is still premised.[75] 'How can one achieve international supervision of domestic human rights protection without violating national sovereignty as the expression of the right to self-determination, which is itself a collective human right under the first Article of the 1966 Covenants?'[76] Traditional international law recognises

[72] Some human rights norms can be found in certain principles of what is known as customary international law, like the prohibition of genocide, war crimes and crimes against humanity. These norms are binding on all states, regardless of their ratification of treaties on those matters. Some human rights scholars argue that certain aspects of the Universal Declaration have become binding as customary international law as well. For example, the prohibition of torture is generally accepted as binding on all states as a principle of customary international law, regardless of their ratification of the specific treaties on the subject.

[73] For example, the Universal Declaration of Human Rights of 1948 is not binding as such because, according to the UN Charter, resolutions of the General Assembly are merely recommendations to member states of the organisation.

[74] The paradox of self-regulation by the state of its own behavior is, of course, also true of domestic constitutional and legal protection of states. The crucial difference is that human rights are a matter of international concern, rather than the exclusive internal affair of states. Human rights seek to influence domestic situations in favor of upholding international standards. In other words, the paradox is sharper for the human rights paradigm.

[75] N Luhmann describes this as the segmentary differentiation of the world political system into territorially defined states. See Luhmann, *Die Politik der Gesellschaft*, above n 7 at 221 ff.

[76] A An-Na'im, 'Human Rights' in JR Blau (ed), *The Blackwell Companion to Sociology* (Oxford, Blackwell, 2000) 86–99, 89.

states and organisations of states (the EU, for example) as its only subjects. In other words, the only entities that have the capacity to acquire rights and obligations under traditional international law are states and organisations of states. Although recent developments support the view that individuals may also acquire some rights and obligations under international law, such rights and obligations have thus far been exclusively enforced through the medium of states.

As more and more countries adopted the 'world model' of the constitution, the protection of human rights became highly dependent upon the nation-state and its willingness to constitutionalise (not only symbolically) and implement human rights. As indicated, in many cases, the adoption of a 'Western' state model, meaning the tradition of a constitutional democracy, simply fails. Many of the countries of the Third World—which is primarily characterised by the fact that the state has never succeeded in establishing an effective monopoly over violence—could best be characterised as weak or 'failed' states. On this issue, Luhmann writes:

> One can doubt whether the inherited definitions of the state can still be applied in this situation. Nevertheless all territories are forced to take over the segmentary differentiation of the political system. There are no regions that participate in politics (and there are no regions that can prevent such participation), without taking the form of a 'sovereign' state. That this state of affairs is not guarantee for stability any more, becomes more and more the central problem of the new international order (as one calls it optimistically). A state has to be more than a simple 'address' in international communication. Political effectiveness and internal jurisdiction are necessary conditions.[77]

Most of the weak or 'failed' states exercise only a kind of negative sovereignty, since they do not have the full jurisdiction within their own territory. Nevertheless, in some cases, they make a public display of their sovereignty, invoking the right to 'non-intervention in internal affairs' when the so-called international community demands that they comply with their international obligations in matters of human rights. What the international community can and may do about a state that persistently disregards its international obligations is still not very clear: 'suited forms of intervention still have to be developed'.[78]

[77] N Luhmann, *Die Politik der Gesellschaft*, above n 7 at 225.
[78] *Ibid*, 226.

6

The Problem of Power in Luhmann's Systems Theory

SAMANTHA ASHENDEN

POLITICAL THEORY, FROM Hobbes to Habermas, has been dominated by conceptions of power predicated on the model of sovereignty. Such theory has been centrally concerned with questions of legitimacy, often at the expense of close examination of how power operates.[1] More specifically, in modern scholarship the dominance of normative questions—questions concerning who should have power and the proper boundaries of power—has assumed both that a close relationship exists between law and politics and that political power operates as a centralised source of coercion in relation to a separate sphere of society. Such premises have occluded the possibility of close attention to what power does, its forms and its effects. Luhmann's work promises the possibility of moving beyond this problematic of sovereignty and legitimacy in a way that challenges the state/society dualism that is the premise both of a great deal of social and political theory and of liberal constitutional practice. His work enables one to begin to rethink questions of the organisation of political power, legitimacy and resistance, in a manner that sheds light on intractable problems in the governance of complex systems.

In particular, against the assumption that law and politics are interconnected, Luhmann posits their autonomy from one another in modern society. This is framed explicitly as a challenge to the traditional problematic of sovereignty, and it enables Luhmann to reconceptualise power. In contrast to most sociological theories, Luhmann's work posits the specifically political character of power. But, by contrast with much political theory, his account of power does not sustain a clear state/society dualism. Against both limitedly political views of power and radical conceptions that see power in all social relations, Luhmann makes an argument for the specifically political character of power whilst at the same time giving us a way of conceptualising the functioning of power beyond the political system. This gives his sociology a profoundly anti-dualistic flavour, one that aids it in moving beyond the distinction between state and society and accompanying questions of legitimacy and curtailment of

[1] B Hindess, *Discourses of Power: From Hobbes to Foucault* (Oxford, Blackwell, 1996).

power that animate much political theory and political sociology. The necessity of such a move is made clear by a number of ongoing problems of modern governance that cannot adequately be analysed whilst upholding conventional conceptions of a state/society distinction, and which do not admit of liberal constitutional solutions.

This paper outlines some basic aspects of Luhmann's conception of power, and explores how this opens up new ways of conceptualising social and political questions. It then turns to critical examination of some of the assumptions and theoretical devices that underpin Luhmann's account, concluding that whilst Luhmann's work enables one to conceptualise power beyond a dualistic model of state versus society, nonetheless the theoretical presupposition of the radical autonomy, or autopoiesis, of systems in modern society implies that his work is animated by the ideal of eliminating power from systems other than politics. As such, the conventional state/society dualism of political theory and political sociology is transformed in Luhmann's work into a division between discourses in modernity.

THE PROBLEM OF SOVEREIGNTY

Luhmann describes sociological theories of power as an 'undeveloped country'.[2] His account begins with a reflection on the limits of existing conceptions, two of which are particularly worthy of mention. The first conception of power from which Luhmann distances himself is that found in accounts premised on anthropological assumptions, where power is construed as anything that limits the realisation of a dignified human life (as, for example, in accounts derived from Marx's early work). For Luhmann, such analyses are too broad to designate clearly specifiable paths for empirical research and suffer analytical limitations insofar as they are premised on existing assumptions about the character of the society under analysis. One might also say that they are based on contested philosophical anthropologies as witnessed, for example, in battles over the concept of 'real interests'.[3] The second conception of power from which Luhmann distances himself emanates from rather different premises. This conception is predicated on a classical political theoretical account of power as sovereignty and is instantiated in contemporary discussion in accounts of power that stress the need to delimit its operation, for example through constitutional formulae. This second conception of power dominates political theoretical and practical constitutional discussion today, and Luhmann's treatment of it deserves closer attention.

[2] N Luhmann, 'Machtkreislauf und Recht in Demokratien', (1981) 2 *Zeitschrift für Rectssoziologie* 159.

[3] See T Benton, '"Objective" interests and the sociology of power', (1981) 15 *Sociology* 161; B Hindess, '"Interests" in Political Analysis' in J Law (ed), *Power, Action and Belief: A New Sociology of Knowledge?* (London, Routledge and Kegan Paul, 1986).

We can look at this more closely by specifying the problem to which Luhmann addresses himself with his distinctive conception of power. That problem is the tendency, in the Western political tradition, to see what he describes as a 'unified politico-legal system'.[4] Luhmann points out that this conception of a unified system is evoked by the concept of the state, something that is at the same time legal and political.[5] He notes that the conception of sovereignty and sovereign power that has underpinned the state since its consolidation in early modern Europe has combined two distinct ideas of political power:

> first, the idea of a *generalised* capacity to secure obedience to commands; secondly, the idea of legal force, which reflected the fact that power presented itself and was enforced in the form of law, that is, in a form which was always already *specified*.[6]

As such, the concept of sovereignty combines law and politics in one formulation. Weber's work perhaps provides the best-known social-theoretical expression of this formulation, as the following quotation makes clear:

> Law exists when there is a probability that an order will be upheld by a specific staff of men who will use physical or psychical compulsion with the intention of obtaining conformity with the order, or of inflicting sanctions for the infringement of it. The structure of every legal order directly influences the distribution of power, economic or otherwise, within its respective community. This is true of all legal orders and not only that of the state. In general, we understand by 'power' the chance of a man or of a number of men to realise their own will in a communal action even against the resistance of others who are participating in the action.[7]

It is worth picking apart this statement since we can begin to mark out the distinctiveness of Luhmann's conception of power by comparing it with that provided by Weber. In the above quotation Weber conceptualises power as a hierarchical relation, 'power over', as the ability to control others, events and resources in order to achieved desired results despite opposition. He refers to economic as well as political and other forms of power, and conceives a direct relation between power and law. Moreover, within Weber's broad sociological conception of power the central question is distribution. This provides the basis for many standard sociological accounts of power today. By contrast, for Luhmann power is not necessarily a matter of coercion or domination, but rather flows from the options available within the political system and channels collectively binding decisions. As against the centrality accorded to issues of distribution in standard sociological theories, including Weber's, for Luhmann the central question is not how to distribute power but which

[4] N Luhmann, *Law as a Social System*, KA Ziegert (trans), F Kastner, R Nobles, D Schiff, R Ziegert (eds), (Oxford, Oxford University Press, 2004) 357.

[5] *Ibid*, 357.

[6] *Ibid*, 359.

[7] M Weber, 'Power' in HH Gerth and C Wright Mills (eds), *From Max Weber: Essays in Sociology* 2nd edition (London, Routledge, 1991) 180.

method of organisation will generate power.[8] Finally, where from Marx and Weber sociological theory has worked with broad conceptions of power, for Luhmann power is strictly a code of the political system; the legal system or the economic system might borrow power but power is proper to politics.[9]

Luhmann thus offers a conception of power that is significantly more restrictive than those commonly found within social theory. Against the tendency to conceive law and politics as closely related Luhmann stresses the autonomy of each system, and emphasises that in modern society power is specific to the political system. He states that the possibility of reference to a unity of law and politics passed with the demise of natural law arguments, but that the concept of the *Rechtsstaat* has concealed this and kept alive the idea of a single legal-political system.[10] Where traditional conceptions of sovereignty and sovereign power combine law and politics, therefore, Luhmann emphasises that the state comprises two separate systems of law and politics, and that these are operatively closed and have different functions; with this closure of the systems of law and politics, power is reserved to the political system (as we shall see, this does not mean that law and politics bear no relation to one another in the discussion of structural coupling below.

THE FUNCTIONAL DIFFERENTIATION OF LAW AND POLITICS AND THE SEPARATION OF POLITICAL POWER

Luhmann's analysis of power contains two important sets of observations. First, he notes that power in the political system is recursive such that power checks and controls its own application; in this sense counter-flowing power is a precondition of effective power in the political system. However, Luhmann notes that effective power may also be blocked by counter-flowing power, for example where organised chains of power create possibilities for obstruction. Thus, increases in power do not necessarily mean increased freedom of action for the power holder,[11] and effective power in modern society may be insufficient for system needs. Secondly, he is concerned with what he considers may be a greater problem still: 'societal power which arises and remains *outside* any connection

[8] N Luhmann, *Trust and Power* (Chichester, John Wiley and Sons, 1979) 179–80.

[9] It would be interesting to develop more sustained comparison of Weber and Luhmann. Though they stand opposed to one another with respect to their conceptions of power there are some striking similarities in their overarching concerns. In particular, while Luhmann is critical of Weber's amalgamation of the concepts of domination and administration, against this taking pains to distinguish between bureaucracy and administration and to stress that organised systems are not just the 'lengthened arm of the power holder' (*Trust and Power*, 175, above n 8), nevertheless Luhmann's treatment of bureaucracy as an effect of attempts by the political system to regulate phenomena not properly its own would bear interesting comparison with Weber's discussion of bureaucracy as 'congealed spirit' (M Weber, *Political Writings*, P Lassman and R Speirs (eds), (Cambridge, CUP, 1994) 158.

[10] N Luhmann, *Law as a Social System* above n 4, 364, 380.

[11] N Luhmann, *Trust and Power*, above n 8, 146.

with the political system'; he mentions power within the family, the power of priests, power in the economy, and power exercised in the education system with regard to the allocation of status, stating that all of these forms of power 'raise the question of *the limits to which power can be politicised*.'[12] In order further to examine these observations it is necessary briefly to outline Luhmann's account of the process of differentiation through which politics is separated out as a functionally specific system from which power flows as a generalised medium of communication.

Basic to Luhmann's general social theory is a thesis concerning the functional differentiation of society into autonomous systems of communication.[13] The functional mode of differentiation characteristic of modernity is preceded, on Luhmann's account, by segmented societies which were differentiated into subsystems on the basis of descent, settlement, and so on. Luhmann describes this as the pattern of differentiation of archaic or pre-civilised societies. Segmented societies gave way to stratified, traditional societies, organised hierarchically through inequalities in wealth and power. Such societies were ordered through designations of social rank, with power operative through the categories 'above and below' or 'superior and inferior'. According to Luhmann, by the end of the eighteenth century differentiation by stratification had given way to functional differentiation as the development of a money economy undermined the unity of economic and political systems.[14] Thus:

> Modern society, unlike all earlier societies, is a functionally differentiated system.
>
> [. . .] Society can no longer be grasped from a single dominant viewpoint. Instead, its dynamic is clarified through the fact that functional systems for politics, the economy, science, law, education, religion, family, etc have become relatively autonomous and now mutually furnish environments for one another.[15]

In this latter form of society power has been reserved to the political system; it issues from the organisation of the political system and has a role in controlling or shaping the form and direction of systems.[16]

Luhmann states that, as a result of functional differentiation, modern society is composed of multiple separate autonomous function systems; society is radically decentred. Within modern society a system distinguishes itself from its environment through codes and programmes that enable it to distinguish between internal and external. In their most abstract form, system codes are simply binary distinctions, 'this and not that',[17] that denote the difference between internal and external. This enables a system to reduce complexity by

[12] *Ibid*, 168.
[13] N Luhmann, *The Differentiation of Society* (New York, Columbia University Press, 1982).
[14] N Luhmann, *Law as a Social System* above n 4, 387.
[15] N Luhmann, *The Differentiation of Society*, above n 13, *xii*.
[16] N Luhmann, 'Machtkreislauf und Recht in Demokratien', above n 2, 159–60.
[17] N Luhmann, 'Widerstandsrecht und politische Gewalt', (1984) 1 *Zeitschrift für Rectssoziologie* 44.

ignoring all that is not meaningful to its specific code. So, for example, the legal system encodes phenomena law/non-law and legal/illegal, while the political system operates through the binaries government/opposition and government/governed. Such codes enable systems to draw boundaries between themselves and their environments, and order the phenomena to be dealt with by the system.

Luhmann characterises modern function systems such as law and politics as self-referential, as systems that constitute themselves reflexively through developing their own codes and programmes. This specification of the self-referentiality of systems has led Luhmann to adapt from biology the concept of autopoiesis. 'Autopoiesis' refers to the 'autonomy and historical individuality of all social systems'.[18] An autopoietic system is one that 'defines the elements that are allowed to operate within a network of operations, by the network of its *own* operations';[19] that is, it constructs its own environment and its own identity within that environment. An autopoietic system thus regards itself as operationally closed. Such systems are functionally differentiated and autonomous, that is their functions cannot be replaced by other systems without problematic de-differentiation. At the same time, however, these autonomous systems may be mutually dependent and co-evolve as subsystems of the social system. They do not interpenetrate, they cannot as they fulfil different functions; however, they can 'observe' and react to one another, they may 'irritate' one another, and they may become 'structurally coupled'.[20]

The concept 'structural coupling' denotes a specific relation between a system and its environment. Luhmann suggests that two systems are structurally coupled where each presupposes features of the other as an ongoing part of its environment:

> coupling mechanisms are called structural couplings if a system presupposes certain features of its environment on an ongoing basis and relies on them structurally—for example, the fact that money is accepted, or that it could be anticipated, that people can find out what the time is.[21]

Such couplings 'trigger irritations'; they simultaneously reduce and facilitate influences of the environment on the system such that, for example, increased complexity in the political system can irritate further complexity in the legal system and vice versa. Luhmann is quite clear that structural coupling does not imply that two systems synchronise with one another, but rather that they co-evolve.[22] According to Luhmann, autopoiesis and structural coupling are preconditions for the evolution of the systems of law and politics; their separ-

[18] N Luhmann, *Law as a Social System*, above n 4 357.
[19] *Ibid*, 378.
[20] *Ibid*, 382–3.
[21] *Ibid*, 382.
[22] *Ibid*, 383.

ation is necessary to their internal differentiation and to the intensification of their contacts.[23]

Luhmann's account of societal differentiation is thus both an account of the separation of different systems of communication from one another—their closure, and an account of the way that these systems produce internally an image of themselves operating within a self-constructed environment. Increasing internal complexity is a system's response to increased complexity in its environment. He describes the way that law and politics separated from one another, achieving autopoietic closure, such that each system provides an environment for the other. To examine Luhmann's conception of power further we need to specify both the separation of law and politics from each other and the process of the internal differentiation of the political system.

Luhmann describes how, in modern functionally differentiated society, politics and law form distinct, autopoietically constituted systems, where this is demonstrated by their different coding—government/governed, government/opposition and law/non-law, legal/illegal respectively.[24] He states:

> systems reproduce themselves and in so doing decide on their own boundaries. This occurs with the help of their own codes. In the political system, this is achieved by the distinction between superior power (authority) and those subordinate (the governing/the governed) and by the coding of authority by the schema government/opposition. In legal system, coding is based on the quite different kind of distinction between legal and illegal.[25]

Luhmann gives an account of the 'positivisation' of law through several stages beginning in the eighteenth century. He expresses this development as a working out of problems of self-referential autonomy in the context of a legal system adapting to the demands of a complex evolving social environment.[26] Alongside this, societal differentiation produces a demand for a distinct political system that is specialised in the formation and manipulation of power,[27] so that congruent with the development of self-reference in the legal system is self-reference in politics. Turning from the separation of politics and law to the internal differentiation of the system of politics, Luhmann observes that from the French Revolution onwards, changes in the political system are not simply changes in the form of rulership—from monarchy to democracy—but changes in the type of internal differentiation of the political system.[28] He specifies these changes in terms of a transformation from rulership as a hierarchy of above and below, to a three-fold differentiation of public, politics, and administration. These three are related to one another through a 'circular power constellation'.[29] He adds

23 *Ibid*, 265, 375, 380.
24 *Ibid*, 367.
25 *Ibid*, 378.
26 N Luhmann, 'Machtkreislauf und Recht in Demokratien', above n 2, 161–2.
27 N Luhmann, *Trust and Power*, above n 8, 168.
28 N Luhmann, 'Machtkreislauf und Recht in Demokratien', above n 2, 163.
29 *Ibid*, 164.

that the more thoroughly these three forms of participation in the political system are separated from one another and understood in relation to one another, the more strongly a circular process is established, so that the political system constitutes itself as a closed self-referential system. In this way, he posits a process whereby the differentiation and self-constitution of political and legal processes is at the same time the precondition of their mutual dependence. [30]

Luhmann observes, 'the positivisation of law and the democratisation of politics support each other reciprocally'.[31] The 'exchange dependency' of the legal and political systems results from their common basis in control over the physical world: the legal system requires action from the political system in order to deal with changing life conditions and secure behavioural expectations; the political system requires the legal system in order to offload politically problematic issues, dealing with these through reference to given legal norms.[32] The structural connections between the legal and political systems are thus connections between two self-referentially grounded systems of communication that increase their exchange independence and dependence at the same time.[33] The semantic for the structural coupling of law and politics is the state, which since the end of the eighteenth century has been underpinned by the device of the constitution. Luhmann expresses this in the following manner:

> the 'state' eventually emerged as the carrier of the structural coupling between the political system and the legal system—however, only under the special condition that the state was given a constitution which made positive law the instrument of choice for political organisation and, at the same time, made constitutional law a legal instrument for the disciplining of politics.[34]

Luhmann elaborates this by arguing that, with the development of modern conceptions of sovereignty, law becomes a code of political power. He suggests that while in simple societies strength was sufficient to secure the credibility of power, this breaks down with increasing complexity so that legal schematisation becomes necessary.[35] Law codifies power lawful/unlawful, so that effective power becomes lawful power.[36] Thus, while Luhmann maintains that in its pure form power is 'predicated existentially on asymmetry',[37] that is on the possibility of superior force, he nonetheless comments that power achieves general effectiveness insofar as it is not an exercise of force but is second-coded by law. This legal second coding makes possible the circulation of power as a generalised medium. Luhmann explains that the second coding of power by law is not necessarily a limitation of power but a formal condition of power becoming a

30 *Ibid*, 165.
31 N Luhmann, *Law as a Social System*, above n 4, 364.
32 *Ibid*, 371.
33 N Luhmann, 'Machtkreislauf und Recht in Demokratien', above n 2, 166.
34 N Luhmann, *Law as a Social System*, above n 4, 404.
35 N Luhmann, *Trust and Power*, above n 8, 140.
36 N Luhmann, 'Widerstandsrecht und politische Gewalt', above n 17, 40–1.
37 *Ibid*, 40.

generalised medium of communication capable of circulating through society.[38] The power code thus has a 'dual nature': 'strength/weakness and lawful/ unlawful'.[39] We can now specify Luhmann's conception of power more closely.

LUHMANN ON POWER

Luhmann notes that it is difficult to define what power is and is not; instead of attempting to provide a definition, therefore, he turns to a 'reference problem';[40] that reference problem is the reduction of complexity.[41] Luhmann states that power consists in a 'social relation in which action *could always have been different on both sides of the relation*',[42] that is it operates under conditions of 'doubly double contingency'[43] or 'double contingent selectivity'.[44] Thus, power is distinguished by its (re)shaping the possibilities of action of the person subject to it, and by the fact that the person enjoying power could have acted otherwise.[45] In modern, complex, functionally differentiated society contingencies multiply; in such society power, operating as a medium of the political system, institutionalises expectations and enforces collectively binding decisions. In other words power has an 'ordering function'.[46]

Luhmann begins by conceptualising power as a symbolically generalised medium of communication. He notes that generalised media such as money and power are key to the differentiation of systems since these provide abstract, technical, non-linguistic means of co-ordinating action.[47] The abstract and technical character of such media is central to their capacity to transmit selections without continuous reliance on conscious decision-making processes. They thus have a role in reducing complexity whilst taking pressure off the need for consensus.[48] To elaborate, Luhmann suggests that the political system creates power through the selection of particular constellations of alternatives, and that to conceptualise power as structure dependent selection leads to the hypothesis that more complex systems with more alternatives and thus larger

[38] *Ibid*, 41.

[39] N Luhmann, *Trust and Power*, above n 8, 149; also 'Widerstandsrecht und politische Gewalt', above n 17, 41.

[40] N Luhmann, *Trust and Power*, above n 8, 115–16.

[41] N Luhmann, 'Klassische Theorie der Macht: Kritik ihrer Prämissen', (1969) 2 *Zeitschrift für Politik* 151.

[42] N Luhmann, 'Societal Foundations of Power: Increase and Distribution', in J Bednarz Jr (trans), *Political Theory in the Welfare State* (Berlin, Walter de Gruyter, 1990) 155.

[43] *Ibid*, 156.

[44] N Luhmann, *Trust and Power*, above n 8, 111.

[45] In an early essay he suggests that it is debatable whether power has a substantial or relational character, stating that possession can be regarded as substance or as relation: 'Klassische Theorie der Macht', above n 41, 158.

[46] N Luhmann, *Trust and Power* above n 8, 127.

[47] *Ibid*, 131, 154–60.

[48] *Ibid*, 113, 154.

selective activities must be able to activate more power.[49] There is, therefore, a connection between the complexity of the political system, power increase and power distribution,[50] such that to understand how power operates we need to conceive it in terms of the 'reduction of complexity' and 'selectivity of structured systems'.[51] Thus for Luhmann power is, as Clam states, something that 'stimulates and menaces the relative invariance of a system'.[52] It is a product of contingency, augmenting the possibilities of alternatives in society, and is active in shaping selection within contingency.[53]

To address the importance of this, we need to dig a little more deeply into Luhmann's critique of classical conceptions of power. Luhmann isolates a number of features that underpin classical theories of power. He suggests that such theories are unified through the principle of physical superiority, that they understand power as possession of a constant sum, and that they are framed in terms of cause and effect. As regards the first point Luhmann stresses that classical theories have no appropriate conceptualisation of peace, the condition of peace being less the concentration of power than a product of the disappearance of physical force as such means are placed in barracks and reserved for politically legitimate application.[54] Thus, while he subscribes to a broadly Weberian account of the foundation of the state in exclusive control of the legitimate use of violence,[55] Luhmann comments that in differentiated society power is not enforced by force.[56] Secondly, the 'power sum constancy principle' underpins the concern, seen in both classical liberalism and recent discussions of participation, that the growth of the state is equivalent to the loss of individual freedom.[57] This, Luhmann suggests, explains 'attempts by classical theory to domesticate power',[58] attempts that nonetheless founder through failure to comprehend that processes of differentiation open up increased possibilities of power. Thirdly, Luhmann observes that classical models of power are framed in terms of cause and effect. He takes issue with this, pointing out that causal modes of analysis always presuppose anterior causes, and face problems of substitutability of causes.[59] He notes that causal models support unified, hierarchical conceptions of power, and are premised on the assumption that those exercising power know how the future will turn out; that is, such models involve a conception of time that regards the future as already settled with few

[49] N Luhmann, 'Klassische Theorie der Macht', above n 41, 168.
[50] *Ibid*, 166.
[51] *Ibid*, 152.
[52] J Clam, *Droit et Société chez Niklas Luhmann: La contingence des normes* (Paris, PUF, 1997), 185.
[53] *Ibid*, 186, 189.
[54] N Luhmann, 'Klassische Theorie der Macht', above n 41, 157.
[55] N Luhmann, 'Societal Foundations', above n 42, 158.
[56] N Luhmann, 'Klassische Theorie der Macht', above n 41, 157.
[57] *Ibid*, 162–3.
[58] *Ibid*, 164.
[59] *Ibid*, 167.

alternatives.[60] This, he suggests, historically has been underpinned by natural law arguments, but is now being replaced by the idea of variable and adaptive systems whose world is open and whose structure allows a multiplicity of behavioural possibilities.[61] It is to this changed conjuncture that Luhmann addresses his theory of power.

In response to the classical problematic of sovereignty and legitimacy Luhmann takes pains to differentiate force and power. While he states that in a genetic sense power is based on violence, he argues that it is not controlled through violence.[62] In fact he states that in modern society political power is annulled by physical coercion,[63] and that power and force are inversely related:

> Precisely because it is not used and as long as it is not used, the possibility of imposing negative sanctions is a source of power. Power, therefore, comes to an end if the exercise of this possibility can be forced. The exercise of physical violence is not an application of power but an expression of its failure—or, at best, a presentation of the considered possibility *of being able* to apply sanctions repeatedly.[64]

Furthermore, he proposes that power is not a constant sum but rather is augmented by differentiation, a process that also renders power relations diffuse and prevents them from being amenable to centralised control. Finally, in contrast to causal models, Luhmann states that it is systems that make causes possible, not the other way round, and that the task is therefore to analyse which selection of causes within the system steers.[65] He suggests that we move the focus of analysis from a causal model to analyses of power in terms of system dependence, in a way that opens up the possibility of looking at complex connections. This account also suggests that 'the future confronts the present with an overflow of possibilities'.[66]

This distance from classical conceptions of power enables Luhmann to make a number of distinctive observations. In particular, he emphasises three important features of power in modern society: first, power operates increasingly through 'negative sanction'; secondly, complexity requires that power is organised into chain formations; and thirdly, power operates in a manner analogous to money, such that there can be 'inflationary' and 'deflationary' trends in its operation.[67] We will specify these features a little more closely, before examining their impact on understandings of power as legitimate sovereignty.

[60] *Ibid*, 149.

[61] *Ibid*, 153–4.

[62] N Luhmann, *Trust and Power*, above n 8, 151.

[63] *Ibid*, 147.

[64] N Luhmann, 'Societal Foundations', above n 42, 158. There is an interesting comparison to be made here with the work of Hannah Arendt, for whom power consists in our capacity to act together, and for whom violence is the antithesis of power. One might also compare Luhmann's account of the productivity of power with that provided by Michel Foucault, or with Slavoj Zisek's account of violence as the breaking of the symbolic.

[65] N Luhmann, 'Klassische Theorie der Macht', above n 41, 167.

[66] *Ibid*, 152.

[67] N Luhmann, 'Societal Foundations', above n 42, 158.

Luhmann observes that in modern society power increasingly takes the form of 'negative sanction'. By this he does not mean that power takes the form of negative sanctions as these are classically understood, for example as a system of repressive measures designed directly to punish offence.[68] Rather, he develops this as a reflection on the ways in which society and organisations bind their members, where power operates not by compelling action in one specific direction, but by the threat of loss (of status, esteem, monetary reward and so on) if one does not conform. Viewed in this way, the welfare state is an example of a vehicle for the increase of power (and, according to Luhmann, one that is evidence of politics overstepping its proper boundaries): insofar as welfare provisions provide regular forms of assistance that incorporate people into a system of social advantages, then the possibilities of negative sanction in the form of the potential power of withdrawal of such advantages grow. This feature of welfare states is, as Luhmann points out, inadequately captured by conceptions of power that conceive it as a force of centralised repression.[69] Rather, such power operates in a diffuse and productive manner, and is not amenable to centralised control.

The second feature of power that Luhmann highlights is organisation. Luhmann comments that the growth of complexity and functional differentiation of society increases the number of events calling for decision; however, these cannot be borne at one point or controlled by one point and therefore responding to them requires organisation.[70] Thus organisation, rather than rank, is the ground of modern forms of power. Organisation produces chains of power that break old bonds of solidarity founded on distinctions of social rank. For Luhmann, organisation differentiates and distributes power, but it also transforms and multiplies what is distributed. Power resides in the chains found within organisations, which once again have the function of turning positive sanctions into negative ones, as membership of organisations ties members to detailed patterns of behaviour (at pain of the risk or threat of withdrawal of membership). Moreover, the unfolding and blocking of power within organisations is not amenable to centralised control so that limits on decision-making power themselves become sources of counter-flowing power, for example power to obstruct through negative decisions.[71]

Thirdly, and following from the above, Luhmann suggests that power relations in modern society can be analysed in terms analogous to the operation of a money economy. In modern society power, like money, is liquid. Luhmann comments that, 'as with a money economy, there also seems to be a *limitedly meaningful overdraft of resources* in the domain of power that is comparable to

[68] N Luhmann, 'Societal Foundations', above n 42, 157.

[69] *Ibid*, 158–60.

[70] N Luhmann, *Trust and Power*, above n 8, 163.

[71] *Ibid*, 133, 164.

credit.'[72] Though it is important not to push this analogy too far,[73] the similarity with money deepens when we consider that both money and power are effective precisely insofar as we have confidence in them, or uphold their symbolic value. Here, Luhmann points to differences between attribution of power and actual power. He suggests that, seen from the outside, the apex of an organisation is likely to be attributed more power than it actually has, and that this attribution has to be maintained by the organisation in its representation of itself to the outside world. This model suggests that there might be 'structurally conditioned (ie difficult to correct) tendencies in our societal system toward the inflation of power.'[74]

With this account Luhmann provides an alternative conception of the problems of governability of modern societies from those that comprehend such problems as problems of the legitimation of centralised power. He points to structural questions concerning the constitution of political power, its organisation, and its limits. It is to these that we now turn.

SOME IMPLICATIONS OF LUHMANN'S ACCOUNT OF POWER

Luhmann's account overturns the central premises of liberal constitutionalism: that political power can and must be curtailed, and that this is possible through the separation of powers within the state and through the separation of state and society. Rather, Luhmann points out that while what he calls the 'bourgeois theory' of society has wanted a separation and limitation of powers, with a view that in this way power could be controlled and reduced by being bound by law, this in fact multiplies power, though not in centrally controllable forms.[75] As we have seen, Luhmann conceives the second coding of power by law as a necessary feature of the operation of power as a generalised medium of communication.

This observation raises for question of the place of classical questions of legitimacy in modern conditions. It suggests, perhaps, that theories focused on questions of legitimacy operate with a liberal political architecture in what is a post-liberal context and thus miss their target. To elaborate, Luhmann suggests that those accounts which stress legitimacy and believe that this can be delivered or augmented through constitutional limitations (liberalism), or through greater participation in and proceduralisation of the political system (eg Habermas), are still premised on the possibility of centralised decision-making

[72] N Luhmann, 'Societal Foundations', above n 42, 164.

[73] N Luhmann's argument should not be taken to imply that money and power are interchangeable. Luhmann is clear that money as the medium of the economic system has achieved a qualitatively different level of abstraction than has power, so that the analogy between money and power is exactly that, an analogy, and not an homology. Thanks to Chris Thornhill for helping me clarify this.

[74] N Luhmann, 'Societal Foundations', above n 42, 165; also *Trust and Power*, above n 8, 133, 166.

[75] N Luhmann, 'Societal Foundations', 161, 165.

and on the moralistic category of the 'good society',[76] a category whose effectiveness has broken down with the progress of functional differentiation. Instead of maintaining the state/society dualism characteristic of many social and political theories, Luhmann describes modern society as constituted through multiple autopoietically constituted systems. He promotes a view of society as radically decentred, and draws our attention to the ways in which attempts to control power centrally are overburdened by complexity, to the need to comprehend power in terms of the operation of systemic structures, and to the analysis of alternatives produced from these developments.[77]

This brings us to the implications of Luhmann's account for thinking about resistance. Luhmann suggests that as the form of political power has changed, so have the possibilities of resistance to political power. Where classically political theory has attempted to deal with the problem of the arbitrary use of power through specifying rights of resistance (for example, in the works of Hobbes and Locke), Luhmann argues that the constitutionalisation of the state means that the right of resistance has lost its structural preconditions and central direction, so that in modern contexts resistance encourages law.[78] Moreover, since a legal order cannot be targeted at one point, it cannot be defended at one point.[79] That is, against classical conceptions of resistance as resistance against arbitrary power, Luhmann suggests that in modern societies resistance is itself bound up with the augmentation of power.[80]

Thus the problem, according to Luhmann, is not simply the delimitation of power to the political system but also the generation of sufficient politically constituted power for the direction of systems. Although Luhmann observes that power increases with system differentiation he states that this does not imply increased freedom of action for the power holder due to the system dependence of power.[81] This pushes him to examine power as something that is bound into complex organisational chains that can become overburdened and unable to direct systems. In this context Luhmann mentions that power in the political system no longer seems sufficient for system needs. He cites a number of 'critical symptoms' that, he suggests, indicate that techniques of politically constituted power are beginning to fail and that substitutes for this are developing; in reference to the latter Luhmann mentions the 'self-mystification of leaders' and 'intimations of success which impress the masses'.[82] According to Luhmann, therefore, system complexity poses a twofold problem: the possible jeopardising of the political system as politically constituted power begins to fail, and the diffusion of social power and limits to its becoming politicised.[83]

[76] N Luhmann, 'Machtkreislauf und Recht in Demokratien', above n 2, 160.
[77] N Luhmann, 'Klassische Theorie der Macht', above n 41, 166.
[78] N Luhmann, 'Widerstandsrecht und politische Gewalt' above n 17, 41, 42.
[79] *Ibid*, 43.
[80] N Luhmann, *Trust and Power*, above n 8, 179.
[81] *Ibid*, 146.
[82] *Ibid*, 164.
[83] *Ibid*, 169.

But Luhmann's account of power is more ambiguous than it at first appears. First, theorising power as a '*symbolically generalised medium of communication*'[84] we have seen that Luhmann simultaneously stresses that power is the medium of the political system, which as such is restricted to the political system, and that, in a manner analogous to money, power is liquid and capable of circulating throughout society. Secondly, while Luhmann maintains that in its pure form power is predicated on superior force, he is nonetheless keen to stress that power is not an essence;[85] it does not operate 'originally' but only through reference to a symbolic code. We can examine the ambiguities in Luhmann's account by revisiting his attempt analytically to restrict power to the political system, and by further examining his comments on the relationship between power and law.

As noted above, Luhmann states that the differentiation of political power took place through the development of a specialised power code.[86] As such, he theorises power restrictively as the medium of the political system concerned with producing collectively binding decisions, and his concern in relation to this is with the overburdening of politics and with the ways in which the formation of organised chains of power can undermine capacities for the direction of systems. However, the restriction of power to the political system is an analytical move that Luhmann's own theory threatens to undo. On one hand Luhmann holds to a conception of power as all pervasive (at least as a possibility). He states 'Power is a universal factor for societal existence, rooted in the world of living experience.'[87] He also comments that the starting point for legal and political systems is the problem of violence (see above). On the other hand Luhmann argues that, as a result of the process of system differentiation, power has become restricted to the political system. The latter is both an historical and a theoretical claim. The historical claim is premised on a common and uncontroversial view of constitutions as devices emerging at the end of the eighteenth century and promoting the specification and separation of the functions of law and politics.[88] The theoretical claim—that the differentiation, autopoiesis, and structural coupling of the systems of law and politics, and the delimitation of power to the political system is necessary to their evolution—is more contentious.

According to Luhmann the evolution of law and of politics requires that power be reserved to the political system. He states that the evolution of law depends on a parallel evolution of the political system that 'with a kind of primary expropriation of society, withdraws the means of power, of physical force, from society and consolidates its own power on this basis.'[89] This argument for

[84] N Luhmann, 'Societal Foundations', above n 42, 157; also *Trust and Power*, above n 8, 108.
[85] J Clam, *Droit et Société chez Niklas Luhmann*, above n 52, 184.
[86] N Luhmann, *Trust and Power*, above n 8, 168.
[87] *Ibid*, 167.
[88] N Luhmann, *Law as a Social System*, above n 4, 404–408.
[89] *Ibid*, 262.

the restriction of power to the political system is a necessary feature of Luhmann's argument for the autopoietic closure of the systems of law and politics in modern functionally differentiated society since the argument posits that different systems separate themselves through differentiation of codes and specifically that the differentiation of politics occurs through the development of a specialised power code.[90] It is on this basis that Luhmann observes a 'problem' in the continued existence of societal power outside politics.[91] Yet here we run into a key ambiguity in Luhmann's account of power since he argues that power is not self sufficient, but that it refers both to the distinction strength/weakness, and to the binary lawful/unlawful. Therefore, though Luhmann argues that the differentiation of political power takes place through the development of a specialised power code,[92] when we ask 'what is the code of power?' we find Luhmann argues that power is not self-sufficient but that in order to be generalised power is second coded as law.[93] Luhmann states 'Power is not a completely self-sufficient complex';[94] rather, in order to circulate, power is dependent on a legal system that creates legitimacy structurally.[95] Therefore his statement that the power code has a 'dual nature': 'strength/weakness and lawful/unlawful'.[96] What are the implications of this ambiguity?

Luhmann states that his account of the dual coding of power through the designations strength/weakness and lawful/unlawful demonstrates that the formula 'might is right' is too simple, and that a straightforward opposition of legitimacy and violence is misleading.[97] However, it also demonstrates some of the tensions in Luhmann's theoretical framework: is power, for Luhmann, a medium or something with one foot outside modern autopoietically constituted systems in the possibility of violence? As Luhmann comments, even unlawful power is power.[98] And if this is the case, doesn't this threaten the autopoiesis of law and politics?

CONCLUSION

Luhmann's work moves beyond the questions of sovereignty and legitimacy that animate much political theory and political sociology. In particular, as we have seen, his work poses some stark questions to accounts that counterpoise state and society in a dualistic manner, and to those that understand law as

[90] N Luhmann, *Trust and Power*, above n 8, 168.
[91] *Ibid*, 168.
[92] *Ibid*, 168.
[93] *Ibid*, 128, 146, 170–1.
[94] *Ibid*, 146.
[95] *Ibid*, 135, 139. Luhmann describes legitimacy as 'no more than the linking up of contingencies in the realm of power.' *Ibid*, 139.
[96] *Ibid*, 149; also 'Widerstandsrecht und politische Gewalt', above n 17, 41.
[97] N Luhmann, *Trust and Power*, above n 8 149, 152.
[98] *Ibid*, 136.

straightforwardly delimiting of political power. However, at the same time, it contains a number of ambiguities and points of tension. This conclusion outlines three such points.

We can begin by noting that Luhmann's radically decentred view of society is challenged by his discussion of the relation of law and politics. In his analysis of the evolution of these two systems Luhmann makes it clear that he considers politically constituted power necessary for the direction of systems; law might be necessary in order to second code political power, but law itself cannot direct systems. He cites 'Hobbes's problem—how to account for the ubiquity of physical force', and states that 'law has to start from the condition of peace already secured' if it is to be more than the conditioning of such force.[99] Moreover, insofar as Luhmann accepts that the problem of the political system is the problem of sovereignty 'the paradox of the binding of necessarily unbound authority',[100] and that 'every supreme position—God's as well as that of the sovereign state—is premised on an *unformulable* rule',[101] then this political problem is prior to law. There is a sense, then, in which Luhmann's discussion recreates the problematic of the classical conception of sovereignty that he does so much to try to escape. At the very least, his radically decentred view of society runs up against the logically prior position of politics and power.

Our consideration of Luhmann's discussion of the relation of law and politics also raises questions concerning the status of the concept of autopoiesis. We can see some of the limiting implications of this in Luhmann's concern with what he calls 'societal power' that remains outside the political system. While one might be pleased at his recognition that power does indeed exist outside the political system, Luhmann's formulation can only construe this as a problem for the political system. His argument suggests that the problem lies in not being able to eliminate power from non-political interactions. Thus, Luhmann recognises that family relations or relations in the education system are, or can be, structured through power, but he seeks the elimination of power from such relations in order that power be restricted to politics. Luhmann's account here functions as a description and as a prescription: the theoretical presupposition of the radical autonomy, or autopoiesis, of systems in modern society means that his work is animated by the ideal of eliminating power from systems other than politics. As such, the classical state/society dualism of political theory and political sociology is transformed in Luhmann's work, into a division between communicative systems in modernity. The result is that Luhmann can only see power that is not politically constituted as a problem, a position that is peculiarly liberal, especially for one who eschews conventional distinctions between state and society and who recognises that legitimacy and violence are not straightforwardly oppositional.

99 N Luhmann, *Law as a Social System*, above n 4, 262.
100 *Ibid*, 408.
101 *Ibid*, 409.

Finally, these considerations raise questions concerning the underlying premises of Luhmann's general social theory. Luhmann builds an account of the evolutionary differentiation of autopoietic systems that encompasses an increased potential for power as contingency flourishes. This provides useful insights into the ways in which power exceeds and escapes the analytical gaze of theories of power that conceive it as premised on centralised means of (legitimate or other) coercion. It pushes us to analyse specific formations of power, and suggests that we need new analytical tools to deal with modern complex societies and the circulation of power and resistance within them. However, Luhmann's account of differentiated autopoietic systems is not simply a description of conditions of action within modern society, but an evaluation. It is an evolutionary account on the basis of which de-differentiation constitutes, if not regression, at least a threat. In this way, Luhmann smuggles normative concerns into an otherwise descriptive and analytical social theory. In this context, one might ask whether societies evolve, or whether they have histories. Luhmann's evolutionary schema raises the question of how one might hold onto the historicity of systems of communication in order that analysis does not become static and uncritical. While he emphasises contingency, Luhmann's account of the differentiation of law and politics threatens to hypostatise these in their modern forms. How is it possible to take seriously the idea of 'contingency' whilst at the same time suggesting that the features of the modern world that Luhmann analyses are necessary?

NOTE

I should like to thank Chris Thornhill and Michael King for their helpful comments on an earlier draft of this argument, Martin Hedemann-Robinson for assistance with translation, and the participants of the workshop on the legal and political sociology of Niklas Luhmann at Onati for lively and thoughtful discussion.

7

What is Modern Power?

JEAN CLAM

THE QUESTION CONCERNING MODERN POWER

THE QUESTION I would like to reflect upon is a very simple one: *How much power still exists in the politics of today?* To what extent is politics still based in power or mediated by power?

The intention of this question is to test out an impression arising from the current experience of politics in societies of the developed world. Politics seems to have lost much of the drastic character which it formerly possessed as the major system of society, responsible for ensuring social cohesion and regulating the production and employment of most of the means of coercion which society can mobilise. It seems that domination (*Herrschaft*) is no longer the formula of politics; that power is no longer what holds human societies as polities together; that the constant correlation and intuitive association of politics with power no longer possesses the firm ground on which it rested throughout human history. Perhaps we are witnessing, though still without full consciousness of its implications, a transformation of politics caused by the emergence of a new type of political communication, in which the weight and the harshness of axial scarcities[1] is decreasing, if not dwindling away. Democracy, law and welfare-statehood, coupled with the impossibility of warfare on a global level, seem now definitively to have an assuaging and humanising impact on politics.

Our societies today are in fact profoundly pacified. Internal conflicts are resolved through the channels of a complex political process that transforms crises into non-crises and non-crises into crises, thus staging a public and institutional treatment of social dissent. This process reduces the complexity of

[1] Under 'axial scarcities' I understand the inflexible rarity of the elementary means of living (food, clothing, shelter) and the correlative rarity of the means of exchange that make their circulation—in such an extremely limited measure—possible. Those scarcities have been lifted with the control post-industrial civilisation has gained over almost unlimited quantities of energy and information. The elementary means of living whose axial scarcity determines the shape of all cultures preceding the late modern one are now given in profusion and critical moments of their exchange and circulation are conditioned by the difficult management of their profusion itself. Whole sectors of our economies work constantly under regimes of overproduction and must cope with the volatility of buyer markets facing permanently excessive supply offers.

conflict by transforming its terms along leading distinctions that confer new principles of relevance and problem definition on its content. These are coupled to observation styles, techniques and procedures directed at the production of workable and balanced transitory solutions. On the whole, the political process enables statements and restatements of social conflicts along strictly political procedures which in themselves can guarantee types of solution achieved at very low levels of polemical energy.

State theory, political science and sociology have produced extremely detailed and precise descriptions of these processes. No one sole aspect of democratic politics seems to have escaped scientific observation within those disciplines. However, most of these observations and theorisations fail to reflect the distance of what they are to what they are observing. On one hand, these theories show a deficit in their reflection on the contingency of the described processes, the 'accidentality' of their emergence and the equifunctionality of possible alternatives to them that constitute the medium of their own selection and stabilisation. On the other hand, they show a deficit in their reflection on the contingency of the observation itself and of its enclosedness in its own distinctions and discursive constructions. Most descriptions of modern politics are therefore too narrow to offer a view of major transformations which do not remain enclosed in the self-description of the processes in the political system itself.

The facts and relationships we have hinted at, while pointing to the loosening of the close embrace in which power and politics have held each other for so long, are evident. However, to understand this process of loosening we will have to call upon a theory which determines the relationship of power and politics as one of a (symbolically generalised) medium (of communication) to a type of systemic operation (of social communication) taking place in this medium and nowhere else. To understand the nexus between politics and power, the decline of the use of power in politics, and the attenuation of the political substance of politics by law, we will have to mobilise a particular set of theoretical instruments. These derive from a theory of symbolic media of communication, a theory of the differentiation of society into autonomous systems of communication crystallised around non-substitutable social functions, as well as from a theory accounting for the second-coding of politics by the legal code.

These are theoretical elements of Niklas Luhmann's work. My use of them will remain deliberately very intuitive. That means: I do not intend to engage in a discussion of the theory itself, but I would like to try to work with some of its theorems—to apply them directly to the question of modern power, and to try to obtain descriptive accounts of it through them. This is a venture quite opposite to the design most frequently adopted by the Luhmannians, who mostly insist upon the importance of working at the same level of abstraction as Luhmann's theory. My choice is a different one. Under conditions where knowledge of the theory cannot be presupposed, I think it is preferable to work, in an intuitive, and sometimes merely metaphorical manner, with primary aspects of the theoretical elements at hand, rather than attempting to offer one further exposition of them. This has greater justification where a thorough and critical reception of some of those elements can show that they are themselves still incomplete and perfectible, and that their use by Luhmann and his followers still relies heavily on the metaphorical nature and the ambiguity of the concepts which are at stake. This is the case, in particular, with the concept of the medium and the representations of its circulation.[2]

Sociologists might be tempted to formulate my initial question about the possible decline of the intensity of power in politics in the conventional terms of my title: 'What is modern power?' To be sure, all social transformations occurring in our societies can be reconstructed as manifestations of the structural mutation of society, correlated with manifold processes of modernisation. I have nothing against such an approach and I obviously endorse it by giving to my own inquiry the heading which I here quote. However, I would like to accentuate the point that a basic theorem of the sociology of modernity instructs us that the production and the use of power has experienced a tremendous *intensification* in the modern period. This statement, although apparently quite opposite to our descriptive findings, underpins the analysis set out below.

There is no doubt that power, like other central social functions, has been transformed by its entrance into modernity, defined as a new structural universe of social organisation. It is very plausible that the transformation of power occurred in a manner which paralleled that of the media of other social subsystems. We could easily attempt to draw the trajectories of medial transformation in some of the main social systems and to see if some noticeable differences could be discerned between them. However, I believe that it is possible to observe a major difference which distinguishes the evolution of modern power from that of other media, and gives it a specific shape. My main point in the following will be to show that the modernisation of power is a very singular process, and, at a certain point in the later stages of its evolution, exceeds what can be observed in other social functions.

Thus the question concerning modern power is not a question concerning its quiddity. It is, primarily, the question about its contrast with pre-modern power. Secondarily, it is the question about ways in which its late evolution contrasts with that of the other media of modern social communication. There is no need to expand on the first contrast, which would provide subject matter for extensive research and literature. My endeavour will be to bring the second contrast to due sharpness.

[2] See my critical reception of concepts like paradox in: J Clam 'Die Grundparadoxie des Rechts und ihre Ausfaltung. Beitrag zu einer Analytik des Paradoxen' in G Teubner (ed), *Die Rückgabe des zwölften Kamels. Niklas Luhmann in der Diskussion über Gerechtigkeit* (Stuttgart, Lucius & Lucius, 2000) 109–143; as well as in: J Clam, 'The Specific Autopoiesis of Law: between Derivative Autonomy and Generalised Paradox' in J Priban and D Nelken (eds), *Law's New Boundaries: The Consequences of Legal Autopoiesis* (Aldershot UK, Ashgate Publishers, 2001) 45–79.

The theory of social differentiation is, in its origin, a theory of the 'division of social labour',[3] or a theory of the interaction of social actors.[4] In any case, it is a theory of functional interdependence, and in the modern period such interdependence attains a critical level—as a result of which the whole fabric of society is transformed. The paradox of interdependence is that it creates autonomy and enhances the independence of the interdependent. The differentiation of society (*Differenzierung*) thus leads to the perdifferentiation (*Ausdifferenzierung*) of components, which fall out from the whole and assume a self-sustained existence. The movements triggering interdependence and independence are interrelated and mutually reinforcing.[5] Luhmannian theory works through to the end of the perspective that views social evolution as determined solely by differentiation, and, in conclusion, it describes differentiation as the autopoietical autonomisation of social systems, and it shows how this trajectory of autonomising perdifferentiation and of mutual strengthening of interdependence by independence creates a specific and wholly new design of society as a heterarchy of structurally coupled subsystems.[6]

The modern transformation of society can thus be interpreted as the differentiation of its organic, hierarchical and power-centred pre-modern fabric into subsystems built around autonomously operating, heterarchically coupled functions. Pre-modern social structure has a special foundational relationship to power because of its intrinsically hierarchical design. Together with the segmentary and the centre-periphery designs of social structuring, hierarchy is the design that emerged in all high cultures, and all state-building societies.[7] It is the predecessor structure or structural background on which the modern transformation takes place. This transformation leads to the concentration of all power in a political centre and thus enhances in a first move the extent to which politics is mediated by power. At the same time, however, power will tend to be the medium of one system among others, and not the leading system of domination itself. In late modernity, and this is the crucial point, the heterarchical structure of society reaches completion with the unpowering of power, a process which cuts off the links of politics to social centrality and sources of high command. The structure is completed when the co-naturality of politics and domination is definitively broken.

[3] E Durkheim, *De la division du travail social* (Paris, Presses Universitaires de France, 1994) 3rd Edn.

[4] G Simmel, *Soziologie* (München Leipzig, Duncker und Humblot, 1923), 1–31.

[5] On the paradox of the correlated increase of interdependence and dependence by Luhmann, see J Clam, *Droit et société chez Niklas Luhmann: La contingence des normes* (Paris, Presses Universitaires de France, 1997) 116.

[6] On heterarchy, see N Luhmann, *Die Gesellschaft der Gesellschaft* (Frankfurt, Suhrkamp, 1997), 312f and P Fuchs, *Die Erreichbarkeit der Gesellschaft: Zur Konstruktion und Imagination gesellschaftlicher Einheit* (Frankfurt, Suhrkamp, 1992) 58ff and the cited work in general.

[7] On these structural designs of consociation, see N Luhmann, *Die Gesellschaft der Gesellschaft*, above n 6, ch 4, and CR Hallpike, *The Principles of Social Evolution* (Oxford, Clarendon, 1986) throughout.

The modern transformation of society thus has a special impact on the political system, in its quality as mediated through power. Through the later stages of its evolution, the modern transformation of society not only makes political communication paradoxical like all other forms of communication processed in the other social subsystems; in addition, it brings its medium to the point where it ceases to be what it was—something other media do not experience. The phenomenon of power itself changes its structure and its meaning. This happens at the end of modernity and has to do with the *doxic* constitution of late modern social communication—doxic denoting, in my understanding, all aspects pertaining to belief and modes of belief in the context of a given social discourse.

Emerging in the 1970s,[8] sociological and cultural-theoretical descriptions of late modernity as post-modernity have greatly enhanced our understanding of how different, how intense and how profound are the transmutations of concepts as they have descended from their modern configuration to their post-modern one. The contrast that I am trying to reconstruct is partly bound up with that transmutation. However, what is distinctive about the transmutation of power is without parallel in the other systems of social communication.

I would like to show that, however we characterise the *present* state of our societies—be it as modern, or as post-modern, as in continuity with the modern or as in disruption of it—power has undergone a transmutation that has changed its fundamental meaning. This can be shown on two levels:

(a) it can be shown that political power, now definitively disengaged from the distress of life (*Not des Lebens*—to put it with Freud), has lost its constituting enigmatic moments of decision and arbitrariness;[9]
(b) further, it can be shown that political power has lost its constituting moments of being the site, space and core, the contributor, editor and free giver of intense collective and public experience (*Erlebnis*).[10]

[8] See D Harvey, *The Condition of Postmodernity: An Inquiry into the Origins of Cultural Change* (Oxford, Blackwell, 1990) and Z Bauman, *Postmodernity and its Discontents* (Cambridge, Polity Press, 1997).

[9] Such a disengagement has secondarily to do with the decoupling of politics from violence and use of painful physical force (to elicit compliance).

[10] This last point I shall not deal with in the paper. It is the subject of a contribution which still is undergoing work. The idea is that de-politicisation has to do with the loss of the dimension of symbolic exchange based on dosis and antidosis, gift and counter-gift between the top and the basis, between the powerful and the powerless who endow them with and recognise their power prerogatives. The top gives, and the basis expects to be given, a momentum, an intensity of life feeling which cannot stem from another source than power and power mediated politics. What is missing at the place of politics in the late period of modern power is precisely this: the intrinsically political function of hosting and producing the events for an intense feeling of collective public experience. Missing is a political staging of spectacles of transgression and death, bringing to sense the hardness of the penal edges of social life, the earnestness of collective destiny and the sacrificial dimension of community-founding. Thus, one of the major factors of de-politicisation of politics and of un-powering of power is the differentiation, in the late modern period, of politics from its function of mobilising and monopolising collective attention in exchange for gratifications in terms of intensities of psychic—massive psychic, identificatory—enlivenness. Re-politicisation, inversely, is bound to any re-empowering of the political, restoring a measure of symbolic exchange between those wielding, and those subject to, power, by which the differentiation of politics from the media as the

POWER'S TRANSMUTATION

To gain a fuller understanding of this, it is helpful to consider the evolution of modern politics from the onset of its structural change at the beginning of modern times until today. In so doing, we would intuitively, without any special theoretical apparatus, identify a *caesura* between today's society and the end of what we might term the *polemical* age of humanity: this *caesura* is commonly marked by the end of World War II and of the Cold War. Naturally, everybody is aware of a deep change in the history of humanity and in social conditions throughout the globe since then. These changes include the impossibility of war on a large scale—global, world war—and the end of ideological strife. But they also include changes in all subsystems of society. Economy experiences a succession of 'revolutions' of its productive structure; its medium—money—undergoes a process of profound dematerialisation, changing into a pure sign of quantified circulating value. Law accelerates its positivisation and has increasingly to underpin its normative contents with cognitive plausibilities. Science decouples its cognitions from permanent (eternal) truths, from certainty of self-awareness, and from exact knowledge of world processes determined by general and rigorous laws. It works with transitory, currently falsifiable truths within the framework of a plural, ever possible alternative constructability of its objects. Art leaves behind it any reference to nature, mimesis, beauty and meaning. It gives itself themes (its own poiesis), principles of construction (as pure construction—of construction) and intrinsic contingency (non-)rules which prevent the emergence of any lasting artistic Gestalt.[11]

Despite the momentousness of these changes however, they do not, sociologically, constitute a *structural* transformation of society like that which took place with the advent of modern times. The end of the polemic age of humanity does not mark the beginning of a new structure of social ordering. The processes

instance of producing public attention and sensation is being partly lifted. Such a differentiation is reduced every time that the event is drastically produced by politics, ie produced in such a direct way by politics itself that the media's role in the event creation is overwhelmed by it. In a perdifferentiated social setting, the observation of the world by the media creates the event in the sense that it makes the world eventful. The differentiation of a medial system is a correlate of the unease in producing such events in the postpolemic age. Production of the event is the core of the media business and function. It is appreciated as such in society at large because it creates an event where there is none, but only processes, which are what they are because politics cannot any longer be as eventful and as drastic as it was. Re-politicisation of politics brings with it a re-capture of the space of public attention by the political. It restores politics to its drasticity which abolishes its dependence upon the medial eventialising of political processes.

[11] These are very much compressed formulas stemming from the Luhmannian corpus of theory. Singular and precise references to individual texts of that corpus would be artificial. For each of the quoted subsystems I refer to the late *summae* of Luhmann's work; for economy, see N Luhmann, *Die Wirtschaft der Gesellschaft* (Frankfurt, Suhrkamp, 1988), for science, see N Luhmann, *Die Wissenschaft der Gesellschaft* (Frankfurt, Suhrkamp, 1990); for law, see N Luhmann, *Das Recht der Gesellschaft* (Frankfurt, Suhrkamp, 1993); for art, see N Luhmann, *Die Kunst der Gesellschaft* (Frankfurt, Suhrkamp, 1995).

of functional differentiation of social communication bringing perdifferentiated subsystems to a mature form of operative and autopoietic closure still remain ongoing and represent the most decisively determining social processes. In the main systems of society—as well as in all others—there is no change in the pulling dynamic of functional differentiation and its basic structural conversion, in spite of eventually tremendous accelerations and accent displacements of the processes at work.

My thesis, therefore, is that the political system, defined as a power system, cannot be seen as evolving in continuity with its modern transformation and functional restructuring. My argument, in this respect, contains the following components:

a) Power ceases to be power when it loses its connection to will as a self-grounded (arbitrary) will (*Willkür*).[12] Will in this sense is the nonelucidable ground of determination of the powerful. Power is essentially self-enveloping and self-obscuring. It is at its core and source a nocturnal recess that cannot be enlightened. The moment of extreme density at the centre of power is the black hole of decision and will.[13]
b) Politics ceases to be politics based in power and mediated through power as soon as it becomes unrelated to, unsustained by a politicisation of important sectors of social communication. That means in effect: *by contrast, power and politics, as long as they are sustained as such, give to the space in which they operate the shape of a polemic space—as the space of strife and conflict.*
c) The polemic nature (or the polemy) of the political dries up if it is not nourished by emotions and their thymic vibrancy. De-politicisation takes place in a context marked by the accelerated decline of emphatic communication in general.[14]
d) The functional differentiation of society, in its later phases, approached a real polycontexturalisation of social communication. The main effect of this late maturity of modern society is the de-politicisation of society, and the subsequent de-polemisation of politics and un-powering of power (the withdrawal of power from power). The heterarchical structure of society lacking summit and centre is therewith accomplished.

Un-powering power means dislocating the structural arbitrariness of its emanation from unreason and groundlessness.[15] It blunts the hardness of the pain

[12] Coupled with the constant experience of the hard edges of physical constraint as applied to bodies. Bodies are thus always liable to the exaction of suffering by elaborate techniques of forcing compliance. Such techniques of punishment are deterrents of non-compliance. They currently radiate into the space of bodies the terror of harsh carnal retaliations—it is most practical to refer to M Foucault, *Surveiller et punir* (Paris, Gallimard, 1975).

[13] On this, see the pregnant formulations of N Luhmann, *Funktionen und Folgen formaler Organisationen* (Berlin, Duncker Humblot, 1964) 188.

[14] The role of *thymos* has been emphasised by F Fukuyama, *The End of History and the Last Man* (New York, The Free Press, 1992), however in another perspective.

[15] It is an un-nighting of it, a taking away of its self-enveloping, self-enveiling element. To Un-power power is to enlighten the nocturn recess in it.

inducing edges of power. Such an un-powering unfolds as an immersion of politics in a second-medium or second-code (*Zweitmedium, Zweitkodierung*); namely, that of law. The recoding (the doubling of the code) of politics by the legal code is an all-decisive process. In comparison with this, all other contributions to the de-politicisation of social communication stemming from other systems are of limited significance . More precisely, such a recoding stands at the end of the process of un-powering and de-politicising politics: it is the systemic result or the overall systemic expression of the decline of the political as mediated by power.[16]

The main features of the de-politicised figure of politics can be articulated as follows:

a) de-politicised politics is marked by the fact, throughout the political process, that the centre is merely an opinion centre and main basin of political majorities for present day parliaments. Such a centre is the bearer of the largest social consensuses.
b) de-politicised politics are determined by a doxic structure that conditions this type of opinion distribution. It contrasts with the doxic structure of politics made with emphatic beliefs of the non-centre.
c) de-politicised politics has stakes limited to the division and distribution of monetary social products and socialised utilities. Such politics evolves from power-based arbitrariness of will to rational arbitration of public choices restrained by reasonable centre consensuses.
d) de-politicised politics are operated by a professional personnel which lacks, by culture, training and corporate interests, the capacity to bring to prevalence any type of power- mediated politics.

DIFFERENTIATION AND DE-DIFFERENTIATION OF POWER

The question that has to be posed now is the following: *What is the trajectory of power and power-mediated politics leading to these forms of de-politicised politics?* To answer this, we will have to examine the effects of the main evolutionary trajectory of modernisation—which is the restructuring of social communication by functional differentiation and formation of subsystemic autopoieseis—on the power medium of politics. That means that we will have

[16] The tendency within European and American politics is to call upon judiciary instances in order to decide an ever increasing number of social contentions—involving value orientations, ethical standards, assumptions concerning the economic appreciation of contributions which were not to that point discounted as economical. A large number of political questions thus become legal judicial ones eliciting a contamination of the political decision mode through the judicial. Politics is seen as arbitrating claims on the basis of texts, moral and legal representations from a central, wisely moderated position, very similar to that of a judge. It has less and less the character of a wilful decision based on the fact of (a legitimate) being in power and of having power at its disposal. On this problematics of the contamination of the political by the judicial, research and literature is profuse. The discussion runs, in the German field, under the heading *Verrechtlichung*.

to inquire into the relationship of differentiation and democratisation, on the one side, and to the decline of power within politics, on the other. Since the first couple of terms, ie differentiation and democracy, are united by simple and intuitive associations, there is a need to elucidate the link which brings both terms to such a close coupling. Are we justified in assuming a strict coupling between differentiation and democracy? Does a democratic polity result automatically from a restructuring of social communication along lines of functional differentiation of self-referential subsystems?

Due work has been done to show, in the ongoing reception of Niklas Luhmann's theory, how much the emergence of democracy and its establishment as the exclusive political organisation form of functionally differentiated societies is conditioned by adequacy to the specific complexity of such societies rather than by ideological emphasis on proper legitimation of power use. This is one of the salient theses of Chris Thornhill's paper in this book.[17] The more complex modern social communication tends to be, the more democratic 'intelligence' it tends to incorporate. What I term democratic 'intelligence' means a form of organisation and distribution of power that is capable of the highest degrees of fluency, flexibility and handling of innovative disequilibria. The intelligence of democracy is the presence of requisite variety in the political system so that it can host and integrate very high levels of contingency flowing into social communication.

The process of democratisation of European polities undoubtedly ran parallel to that of their functional differentiation. However, while the latter appears, in all social subsystems except the political one, to follow a course of stable unfolding since its beginnings in modern times, the latest stages of differentiation in politics seem to induce a specific transformation of the political. I take such a transformation to be the de-policisation of politics resulting from the paradoxical self-emptying of its medium, ie through what I have called the un-powering of power. This means that modern power unfolds in a two-step advance within the process of functional structuring in modernity. In comparison, all other media of social communication have undergone a continuous transformation, uniformly characterised as an experience of self-intensification. Through their absorption of any scattered elements of their respective subsystems into themselves, these media have tended constantly to increase the exclusivity of their mediation, thus becoming more and more potent within their own range of effectivity. For instance, modern love tends to be still more exclusively, more purely love than it has ever been; modern money tends to capture any other residual or vagrant forms of value exchange and to thus constitute more intensely the sole effective form of money as such; modern art tends to represent all and any reflection of creativity within social communication and to extend the form of the art work to objects whose qualification as art objects can ultimately be reduced to minimal, mentally introduced discontinuity from their further objective environment.

[17] I refer to Chris Thornhill's contribution in this volume.

Modern power shows in the first, and the clearly longer, phase of the differentiation process a similar tendency of self-substitutive intensification. This is the finding of any history of modern power, which has to deal with the monopolisation of power and its legitimation by reference to a doctrine of sovereignty closely inspired by the (political) theology of omnipotence. From the beginning of modern times until the end of polemical age of politics (after World War 2 and the Cold War), the political system of modern societies not only absorbed into itself all fragments of formal power immanent to social relationships and thus cemented itself as the definitive monopole of power means within society; it led society to a constantly increasing mobilisation and capitalisation of power in contexts of international competition between nationally unified modern polities.

Beyond this first phase, modern power began a process of self-emptying which ran parallel to the process that we termed as the de-polemisation or depoliticisation of politics. This means that the history of modern power shows a clear discontinuity in its evolution, which has no parallel in other social subsystems. To describe this process, the distinction democracy/non-democracy is of little use. It is in fact questionable whether we can use such a distinction to draw the line between modernising—in the sense of functionally differentiating—societies and non-modernising ones. During the first stage of the unfolding of modern power we see democratic as well as non-democratic differentiation, self-intensification and self-substitutiveness of power. While the first stage could appear as arming and the second as disarming power as the medium of politics, the disarmament of power is not characteristic of (all) democratic polities. There is also a set of democratic polities in which we can observe either a continuation of polemic politics or a re-politicisation of politics correlating with a re-empowerment of power. It is, however, notable that a de-politicisation of politics and an un-powering of power can only concretise in mature forms of functionally polycontexturalised and heterarchised societies. These can only be ('advanced') democracies. The ultimate unfolding of modern power then takes place in already thoroughly democratised polities.

The new divide along which late-modern politics is transmuting itself involves something which is not usually identified as a mutational edge. A criterion for defining the new age of non-power or of the post-polemical age of politics is what I called de-politicisation. This process, as I understand it, is essentially determined by a *doxic* structure. Between the two stages of modern power we find what constitutes their profound dissimilarity and stark antithesis: namely a difference in doxic dispositions—that is, in dispositions, abilities, proclivities to believe. Belief, in this sense, should be understood as a capacity to be affected by emphasis and to adhere to strong convictions.

The enshrining of democracy in modern political discourse as the absolute, unquestionable, non relativisable (political) value reintroduces emphasis into a process of political late modernisation that steers itself towards a systematic erosion of any enchantment of the social. Such a re-emphasising creates a confusion, blurring the divide between the political and the post-political, post-polemical understanding of power.

Modern democracy originally embodies the intelligence of a posture that virtualises directness, massiveness, onticity and distributes conflict through all domains of social communication, and renounces all postulates of unanimity, harmony and non-conflictuality as necessary conditions for public peace. It embodies the higher intelligence of an order founded on fluency, constant uncertainty and write-off of values as well as of truths, convictions, ways of thinking and paradigms of belief.[18] Modern democracy of this type, however, came under attack by authoritarian regimes. In that peril it came to embody a form of collective life and a shape of humanity whose loss would yield the peoples living under its regime to barbarity—meaning the absolutely rejected form of collective life. As a result of this, democracy became a sort of substantial value, a positive model of political organisation, a beloved form of social existence which cannot under any circumstances be renounced.

The *hole*, the void, at the centre of democratic order is the crucible where inrushing, and, in indefinite respects, conflicting, world-observations are processed, and provide the elements to constitute the variety necessary for a social order to live at a very high level of contingency. This hole at the centre, however, is transformed into the engulfing *whole* of an affirmative, ontologically filled structure. From a fabric of polymerised conflict and sustained contingency, modern democracy metamophoses into a *patria* mobilising *amor* for its earthen body and *odium* for its counter-figure.

DEMOCRACY AFTER THE AGE OF STRUGGLE: BETWEEN DE-POLITICISATION AND RE-POLITICISATION

Late-modern democracies have existed under the ambiguous doxic regime of relentless and emphatic self-affirmation while inwardly developing a tremendously intense self-insecurisation; this has at times taken such extreme shape as the paradoxical inclusion of difference (minorities) and a systematic application of the democratic programme allowing hetero-preference to prevail over self-preference. Such an evolution represents an intrinsic crisis of democracy after the age of struggle. Democracy is perplexed by the paradoxes of a sort of impossible self-affirmation. It can be militant and self-affirmative only in contexts in which it faces an external opponent challenging the world order.

Including differences is no longer restricted to the easy task of giving rights to those minorities who have been excluded on terms which are directly contradictory to the democratic principles of equality and non-discrimination: these

[18] On the foundation on fluency, see N Luhmann, *Soziologische Aufklärung 1* (Opladen, Westdeutscher Verlag 1967) 190. On the current write-off of truths, values, . . ., see J Clam, *Trajectoires de l'immatériel: Contributions à une théorie de la valeur et de sa dématérialisation* (Paris, CNRS-Editions, 2004).

minorities might include colonial *victi* (Indians, Blacks, Hispanics, etc) or groups under-privileged by the historical course of cultural evolution in which democracy has evolved (children, women, categories of people of minor status or reduced *manus* like the domesticity of the early liberal age).[19] It must also extend to fields of massive paradox. An example of this might be the inclusion of—so to speak—'intrinsic' others; ie people to whom we cannot give political satisfaction just by be-righting them,[20]—by giving them the (equal) rights which were unjustly withheld because they were not recognised as legitimate aspirants to them. Democracy has to provide such people with titles of tolerance and permit practices, ways of living, and convictions that conflict with the shape of public and private order that seems to flow from democratic spirit and design (deviant sexual practices, unfamiliar religious beliefs, peculiar customs and rituals . . .).This labour of democratic polities in the late stage of the un-folding of modern power has sharpened the sense of social contingency and it has deepened the doxic perplexity, which has come to be recognised as a major factor in the promoting and sustaining of innovation through adequate complexity: that is through the intelligence of fluent orders and the capacity to dispense with unity, identity, groundedness in stable foundations.

These are the criteria for the unfolding of de-politicisation as I understand it. Many advanced democracies did not provide it. The beginnings of the V Republic in France (De Gaulle's France) and Kennedy's presidency in the US stood under a doxic regime which was unable to give way to a de-politicised style of political communication. Charisma at the top, emphasis of political discourse, readiness for thymic resonance at the basis: these are the components of a political power which adheres to the idea of the Body of Many and of their unity in history. In a configuration of this kind, power and politics are embodied in the form of an accord and assent between top and base. This is not the monopoly of authoritarian regimes, nor is it a pertinent indication for a 'regressive' tendency hollowing the work of functional differentiation. Democratic consensuses can be maintained by such assents to the production and the use of power by a (highly personal) political leadership, which is able to nourish and profit from the emphatic momentum of its politics. The emphatic character of a political regime of this type stands here for the irreducible, non-elucidable character of the power-mediated decisions that the political summit makes in all situations where it senses provocation. The justness of the decision is entrusted to the political summit and expected from it. The unison of leadership and followers, of top and basis, is the image of the adhesion of both, of the seeing head and the trusting body, to the historical essence of the polity and the necessities of the hour.

[19] The legal theory of that age reflected (with Kant and Hegel) upon the reduced status of those categories and justified it by arguments based on the assumed (limited) capability of those categories to make a true and ordering use of reason. To access the status of a plain citizen one has to be able to act on principle, that means to base the conduct of ones own life on (universalisable) maxims of practical rationality.

[20] Like be-cloud, be-devil, be-dew . . .

It is quite manifest that the present international situation has some similarities with both these examples of the production and use of political power within the context of an advanced democracy. We might think here of George W Bush's America as a democratic polity undergoing a process of re-politicisation, with its characteristic elements of charisma, emphasis, the arcane privileging of power, the cementing of the non-elucidable decision and will as the sources of political action at the top, and the presence of strong emphatic beliefs in the non-centre, which lead the action at the top and provide for its affirmation at the base. Such politics always brings power back in and this has estranging effects on other polities anchored in the doxic structure of perplexity characteristic of the non-beliefs of the centre. Today, this contrast seems to be at the root of so much mutual incomprehension between the two sides of the Atlantic—the two sides of the post-war major alliance: beliefs of the non-centre, non-beliefs of the centre. The conditions of our late modernity put a sharp paradox at the centre of the self-understanding of our societies: they postulate the prevailing of heteropreference upon autopreference and enshrine such a postulate into their own self-definition and at the foundation of their legitimacy—thus restoring a possibility for their own autopreference. This figure explains why groups and intellectuals who have their standing in such a context cannot have simply beliefs, but only non-beliefs—that means floating views which can only crystallise into convictions when they are challenged in their own complex legitimacy. On the other side, a self-situation outside of this 'centre' make for a restored adhesion to simple beliefs and to drastic possibilities of action. This position is not embarrassed by paradoxical roundabouts and can steer into direct confrontation with those who challenge its declared autopreference.

Democratic polities of the developed world did not emerge from the—albeit very long—shadow of the polemical age until recently. As a matter of fact, both the persistence of polemical politics and the process of de-politicisation overlapped throughout the post-war period. By the end of the twentieth century however de-politicisation had reached a decisive stage. Against its background, politicisation appeared as a form of residual non-disenchantment (*Nicht Entzauberung*) of the social world. Social enchantedness has a definitively straggling or antiquated character.

Post-polemical politics is averse to emotion and emphasis. In the contexts and contests of late-modern politics, the emphatic discourse of traditional politics appears as a remnant whose artificiality is evident—and sometimes embarrassing—for any of its audiences (even at party conventions only a minority 'buys' the earnestness and vehemence of exaggerated speeches). It is however expected and tolerated, as are the passionate tonality of pleas for defence and the spiritual fervour of Sunday sermons.

Politics loses contact with the ground on which emphatic articulation of demands and exhortation to action occur when the stakes of political conflicts lose their hardness and when axial scarcities of goods, rights and opportunities are not contested. Late-modern society produces, on an ongoing basis, profusions of goods, rights and opportunities. It thus brings forth, as a matter of fact, the problem of how social products might be justly shared. At the same time, it inculcates into its members and groups the intelligence of contingency, the enhancement of which is the condition of such a profusiveness of production. Socially just distribution and redistribution is understood by all concerned as a technically demanding process of intelligent, and ultimately consensual, division of relative and changing preferences—and not of absolute values given in inelastic quantities.[21] No participant in such negotiations would earnestly seek to press the other side so much as to induce a blatantly unbalanced or unjust partition of goods. Nobody would indulge in the illusion that he or she could, for any length of time, take advantage of such an asymmetrical division of economic products. Long-term imbalances in this division would clearly have negative, disadvantaging effects for everybody. There is undoubtedly a sort of widespread common sense in the tendency of the 'system' towards a dogmatic and humanitarian idealisation of negotiation, equity, participation, consensus, mutual advantage, and the social responsibility of resource-holders.

The central stakes of national politics in the advanced democracies and welfare states of today are those of the redistributive division of monetary products of economic activity and of the access to socialised utilities. The emphatic style of the political contests over these is a traditional and genre-adequate façade behind which considerations of objectivity, legality and consistency have the greatest importance. There is no room for an emphasis which would suggest that the present moment could inaugurate a decisive transformation of the system itself. There is no room for a re-enchantment of the stakes themselves, since nobody can make out of calculatory reasonings with their robustly consensual structure a factor of radical change, opening a new promise of history.

In such contexts, however, there always remains a nostalgia for politics and political decisions which would be able to re-endow social communication with strong meaning; such a nostalgia flows in different directions depending on the national tradition in which it grows. In France, for instance, there is always a nostalgia for a '*grand dessein*' ('grand design' would be a pretty exact translation) which would awaken all the vital forces or the '*forces vives*' of the Nation and put them at work to build a voluntaristic future in which the community could believe. In today's Germany, the constitutional patriotism (*Verfassungspatriotismus*) in its Habermasian conception as the province of citizens' initiatives longs to restore agents to their status as authors of civic action, and enliven citizens with the consciousness of a true and full exercise of their rights. In the US, finally, such a nostalgia has little place to be expressed. In effect, US politics is intrinsically messianic. The Nation is a community led by

[21] About these processes of distribution of social products and the problematic of right and violence they imply, see N Luhmann, *Die Rückgabe des zwölften Kamels: Niklas Luhmann in der Diskussion über Gerechtigkeit*, above n 2 and J Clam *Trajectoires de l'immatériel: Contributions à une théorie de la valeur et de sa dématérialisation*, above n 18, 141–166.

God, living up to the epic of a *Landnahme* (land-settlement) and entrusted with the mission of upholding right and destroying evil.

Constant nostalgia for a salutary politics of radical change and establishment of a new (just and better) order does not lead, cannot lead and is not meant to lead to revolutionary dynamics. In our post-polemical democracies, such nostalgia plays a role in the legitimation of politics—political programmes, leaders, doctrinal *aggiornamentos*. It cannot be translated into drastic action. It remains a will for peaceful mobilisation of potentialities or a mobilisation of the possible in peace-time. It is a reaction against the anaesthetisation of politics in and through peace, against peacefulness, against the abatement of polemy and strife as the connatural elements of politics. Our societies are sewn with consistencies and continuities which are too strong to allow such revitalisations of their politics. They lack, most of all, the doxic constitution, complexion, for that. Not only are their social products always too scarce after redistribution to leave any real margins for politicising renovation. Dreams of re-authentificating the political are also, in fact, compensations for the impossibility of regaining an overall meaning for social existence—a meaning politics could pretend to provide only as long as the hierarchical order of society continued to shape mental life.

RE-POLITICISATION AND THE TOPOLOGY OF WORLD SOCIETY

The chance for a re-politicisation of communication is, one might think, most likely to arise from a specific situation. In urgent or perilous situations the primacy of action has binding effects on will and belief. Such a sense of emergency seems to have returned to international politics: offensive terrorism, and the war on it, renew situations of shock and polemic mobilisation. A reading of 9/11 as a *cataclysma* making it necessary to restore politics to its earnestness, emphatic character, wilfulness and enigmatic nature is strongly plausible. However, we should not forget that this is a political reading of the situation and not a reflective (theorising) reading of this reading itself. The 'situation' as the main factor in the revival of a doxic structure incompatible with what I described as the constitution of de-politicised politics in today's societies in the West does not explain everything. It is not the situation that is revitalising power-based politics, but the fact that the situation has enabled Western minorities (or American scarce majorities) to come to power who enhance its reading as a 'state of exception' (*Ausnahmezustand*). Reading the situation as a 'state of exception' deepens and restores divisions in the world that are not given anymore. It restores a world-image in the simple topology of the plane, with extensive parts, one outside the other (*partes extra partes*), lying side by side, with borders that could be shut or walls that could be built where those borders have to be shut hermetically. The world is not an extensive magnitude anymore, but an intensive, paradoxically involuted one in which the inside and the outside flow into each other. Their continuing separation is difficult to maintain.

The topology of world society is still unclear, or in the labour of birth. However, this topology is borne by every human mind, even the simplest and doxically staunchest. It is even borne by the intelligent weapons that try to prevent its emergence. It is borne by the intelligence of our differentiated social structures and by the democratisation of our polities. It is borne above all by the lack of alternative—the structural alternativelessness itself—of those structures.

The topology of world society is the topology of paradoxical surfaces, of surfaces which re-enter themselves and make it impossible to distinguish the inside from the outside, the engulfing from the engulfed, the penetrating from the penetrated. This topology is the re-entry of the world into itself: the world as an extensive, sequential space for a non-entangling deployment of self and other re-enters itself as an all-present, non sequential, paradoxical space of a constantly accomplished entanglement of a self and other. This is the description of a decline of alterity as an impossibility of a self-definition that does not re-import the defining difference into itself as a very relative one open to assimilation by the other or to change and disintegration by oneself.

De-politicised politics reflects the impossibility of affirming the self as extraneous to non-self, the impossibility of affirming self-preference as something which absolutely, radically invalidates heteropreference, and the impossibility of affirming self-certainty because of the irreducible uncertainties of self-choice. Self, in such a situation, is neither present nor given. It is a choice which is made with no premises—self-choice is always premise-less choice. There no grounds on which one could choose self. The pre-givenness of self reduces the scope of choices made, or ventured by self. A self which has to choose primarily what it wants to be, which self it should be, stands before an infinite, indeterminable, undecidable choice of a paradoxical identity.[22]

Western identity is paradoxical: it is not substantial, but composed of holes, places, functions, relationships of places and functions. Most profoundly, it is composed of this indeterminacy of identity itself, as a relationship of openness to what might temporarily fill the open space and suspend indeterminacy for a while. It is this opening for a steadily and irresistibly growing future and for its contingency, fluency, etc that constitutes the hollow identity of a self, which is nothing other than its self-emptying and self-indetermination as an openness and receptivity for determinations of identity. Western identity is the non-identity of being open to changing identitary determinations whose range is only limited by the constraint upon such determinations not to debar or exclude the initial openness to indeterminacy by re-substantialising moments of

[22] A Giddens, *Modernity and Self-Identity: Self and Society in the Late Modern Age* (Stanford, Stanford University Press, 1991) underlines, with a large section of present day sociology, the dis-embeddedness of self as the necessity for self to choose for itself every determination it would like to assume. However, he is not aware of the paradoxical structural of such choices, but only of their uneasiness and their liabilities for the individual.

essential identity. It is, in short, an identity 'without qualities' (*ohne Eigenschaften*).[23]

Such a paradoxic structure is felt most dramatically, in our own historical era, when Western polities enter a confrontation with historical-substantial identities with a strong affirmation of the self's absolute rights. Islam comes to the fore of international politics with the trappings of such fundamentalist self-absolutisation. The reaction to such a challenge has, in part, been a re-substantialisation of Western identity itself, although not quite identical with what I previously described as an emphaticisation of democracy in its struggle with fascism. The ambiguity of the present situation is that the confrontation does not bring into opposition distinct parties which represent branches of evolution of the same cultural and historical substrate. Defending the order of liberty today against Islamic fundamentalism cannot be restricted to the resolute affirmation of an order of disorder (ie democracy) in front of revitalisations of an order of mythic, historic and substantial order (fascism). Heavy, excessive re-politicisation of democracy—as in the US today—is mobilising, randomly and arbitrarily, an order of order against another order of order which is perceived to be of minor value and strength. The doxic structure which underscores and supports such a re-politicisation is rooted in the rootedness of politics in epics, culture and religion.

The struggle of the free world against Nazism and imperial dominationism took place on an apocalyptic scale. In such a struggle there was no alternative between destruction or rebirth, and the world was forced to choose between two absolutely exclusive orders. The measure of power mobilisation in that struggle was such that it conjured up the threat that the world would be annihilated by fire (*ekpurosis*) if that struggle were allowed to continue. The re-politicisation of democracy and the re-empowering of power in the West today lead to the construction of an image of an enemy (a *Feindbild*), which parallels the last gigantomachia of our civilisation. The construction of this image threatens to promote the advent of the reality which it conjures. Such re-politicisaiton is thus a re-substantialisation of politics and a re-vitalisation of an (undercomplex) order of order impeding the intelligence of the order of disorder to deploy its virtualities. It especially impedes a thorough vision of the modernising potentialities of the order of order with which it is clashing and with which it brings all the Western world into conflict. It is this misrecognition of the potentialities of Islam to promote in itself the energies of intelligent disorder that nourishes and is nourished by this re-politicisation.

Confrontation with a religious and social order which is perceived as radically anti-liberal, fanatical and intrinsically inclined to violence seems, under

[23] R Brague, *Europe, la voie romaine* (Paris, Criterion, 1992) pointed out the structural 'secundarity' of Christian / European culture. See my interpretation of his approach in terms of 'identity without qualities', J Clam, '*Une culture sans qualités: Autour d'Europe, la voie romaine*' (de R Brague) *Annales de Philosophie de l'Université Saint Joseph* (Beirut, 1998) 107–120.

these conditions, to be ineluctable. However, such a perception does not realise that its site of observation has shifted away from adequacy to the figure of world sociality which is our reality today, and which is characterised by the entanglement of self and other and the impossibility of self-preference (as the impossibility of a position of outward alterity in general); that it has shifted toward a regressive position where post-polemical non-identities are re-substantialised and traditional identities are prevented, owing to this re-substantialisation, from reflecting in themselves the loss of alterity as the loss of the sense that where alterity declines identity cannot be sustained as self-constituting. It is the loss for post-polemical identities of the horizon in which they could apprehend themselves as non-identities or self-differences.

The topology of world society is thus the structural background against which the problematics of international confrontation and civilisational conflict have to be situated. The topological description is quite difficult to perform: it makes strong demands on mental capacities for counter-intuitive thinking. It is a crucial and decisive undertaking, which is still in its first stages. Our ability to think of ourselves in adequacy to the post-historic and post-polemic posture which is ours today depends on this undertaking.

III.

Critical Responses

8

Some Observations on Social Anthropology and Niklas Luhmann's Concept of Society

ANNE FRIEDERIKE MÜLLER

INTRODUCTION

THIS ESSAY SETS out to accomplish two tasks. It looks firstly at Luhmann's concept of society, as it has emerged in his writings, and particularly in the monumental *Die Gesellschaft der Gesellschaft* (1997), from the point of view of social anthropology. Secondly, it examines certain received wisdoms in social anthropology from the perspective of Luhmann's theory.

Anthropology—literally the study of mankind—is a notion with a notoriously great number of meanings. For the purposes of this essay, it denotes the British and US-American university discipline of social (or cultural) anthropology, German *Ethnologie, Völkerkunde* or *Empirische Kulturwissenschaft*, and French *ethnologie* or *anthropologie*. Thus, 'anthropology' refers here to the corpus of theory and empirical research (ethnography) that constitutes the trading stock of these research orientations. This kind of anthropology has been felicitously defined as 'the comparative study of common sense'.[1] Why should it prove interesting to examine Luhmann's work from this angle? There are several reasons for this. Being traditionally grounded in participant observation and other fieldwork practices, anthropology is highly empirical and highly theoretical at the same time. As far as theory is concerned, anthropology and Luhmann's thought have a large number of references in common, including the work of classical sociological theorists such as Durkheim and Weber, but also more recent developments, such as Parsonian systems theory. Anthropologists have tested evolutionism, functionalism and structuralism on the ground (and more or less refuted or at least amended each of these theoretical orientations).

[1] M Herzfeld, *Anthropology: Theoretical Practice in Culture and Society* (London, Blackwell, 2001) *x*.

Anthropology deals with the micro- and the macro-level of social research and thought. It has traditionally been open to theories which situate themselves at such an abstract level as Luhmann's, while drawing its data from empirical engagement with social realities all over the world.

While Luhmann himself did quote anthropological work, mainly dating from the 1970s or 1980s, from time to time (Marshall Sahlins, Jack Goody, Louis Dumont, Pierre Bourdieu), there has been less theoretical transfer in the other direction. One aim of this chapter is to trace convergences between Luhmann's concept of society and recent developments in anthropological research and thought, as well as to examine in what ways Luhmann's approach might 'irritate' anthropology.

The other main aim of this essay is to attempt a critique of some aspects of Luhmann's work from the point of view of anthropology. This seems logical as many anthropologists conceive their task as that of critique of 'Western' sociological reason, and as many a 'Western' commonplace on the alleged workings or essence of society has been dismantled by means of intercultural comparison.

In Luhmann's terms, this social anthropological appreciation of aspects of his systems theory could be characterised as a third-order observation.[2] Luhmann could be described (and described himself) as a resolutely anti-anthropological thinker. In his introduction to *Die Gesellschaft der Gesellschaft*, Luhmann listed four tremendous obstacles to sociological knowledge with which his own theory purports to do away. At least two of these faulty premisses seem to be mainstays of anthropological thinking: the assumption that society is composed of human beings and their relations among each other; and the idea that societies exist in the plural, 'cross-cultural comparison' being the backbone of social anthropology.[3]

This chapter contrasts Luhmann's approach to the study of society to that of anthropology in a number of different ways. In the first section, it explores the limits of society as Luhmann conceived of it. The second section deals with the relation between society and the individual. The next two sections investigate the temporal dimension of society, that is social change, and functional differentiation as an evolutionary characteristic of modern society. The fifth section examines the issue of social integration and cohesion. This part of the essay goes on to look at how Luhmann's approach to the study of law compares with anthropological perspectives. Drawing the various strands of the argument together, the concluding section explores a possible convergence between Luhmann's thought and social anthropology, while pointing out the remaining differences.

[2] Ie The observation of an observation of an observation. Luhmann defines social theory as a second-order observation, ie an observation of social systems observing themselves and their environment, which can see the blind spots of that first-order observation, but not its own (G Kneer and A Nassehi, *Niklas Luhmanns Theorie sozialer Systeme: Eine Einführung*, 3rd edn (Munich, Wilhelm Fink Verlag, 1997) 100–11; N Luhmann, *Die Gesellschaft der Gesellschaft* (Frankfurt am Main, Suhrkamp, 1997) 115–28).

[3] *Ibid*, 24–5.

THE LIMITS OF SOCIETY

Luhmann conceived of society as the overarching social system that includes all other social systems. Society has no essence; its unity lies in the difference from what is outside itself. Being all-inclusive as far as social communication is concerned, society cannot be observed from the outside.[4] Despite recent, allegedly innovatory claims to 'postnational sociology' (cf. for example, various publications by Ulrich Beck and Jürgen Habermas from the 1990s), Luhmann was one of the first twentieth-century sociologists decidedly to overcome the national paradigm. In his 1971 paper on 'world-society', he stated that world-wide interaction had become a real possibility: an Argentinean may marry an Abyssinian, a Russian may use Japanese technology, a Berliner may tan in the Bahamas and so on.[5] By the 1970s, the economy, information, and the public sphere had reached an international dimension.

Obviously, some analyses to this effect had been proposed before (eg McLuhan about the 'electric age' ushering in the 'global village'[6] or Wallerstein's investigation taking the 'modern world-system' instead of the sovereign state or the national society as unit of analysis).[7] However, Luhmann was probably the first sociologist to apply this insight consistently in a great number of publications over more than two decades without relapsing into a 'national' framework. This achievement provides some common ground with recent developments in social anthropology.

Since the 1980s, anthropologists have insisted increasingly on the interdependence of 'social systems' or 'cultures'. Admittedly, introductory textbooks would state as late as 1985 that 'societies' in the plural were the basic units for anthropological research: 'We study *peoples* rather than *people*. Our primary units of reference are "societies", that is distinct and relatively autonomous communities whose members' mutual social relations are embedded in, and expressed through, the medium of a common culture'.[8]

However, at the same time, the idea that humanity as a whole has been parcelled up into a multitude of discrete cultural capsules was already coming under attack. This type of criticism of the concept of 'society' has been levelled vociferously by (mainly US-American) cultural anthropology and cultural studies. Marcus, Fischer, and Clifford have pointed at the interconnections between what were often portrayed as self-contained cultures or societies. They

[4] *Ibid*, 87–90.

[5] N Luhmann, 'Die Weltgesellschaft' (1971) in N Luhmann, *Soziologische Aufklärung*, vol 2 (Opladen, Westdeutscher Verlag, 1975) 51–71; 53.

[6] M McLuhan, *Understanding Media: The Extensions of Man* (Cambridge Mass, MIT Press, 1994).

[7] I Wallerstein, *The Modern World-System: Capitalist Agriculture and the Origins of the European World-Economy in the Sixteenth Century* (New York, Academic Press, 1974) 7.

[8] IM Lewis, *Social Anthropology in Perspective: The Relevance of Social Anthropology* (Cambridge, Cambridge University Press, 1985) 16.

have called for a 'multi-locale' ethnography with a focus on historical contacts, intercultural entanglements, and travellers' 'routes'.[9] Cosmopolitanism and creolisation in the 'global ecumene' provide new fields of research.[10] The isolated culture or society was revealed as a figment of the Western anthropological imagination. A recent compilation of anthropological research concludes that it 'might be more realistic, then, to say that people *live culturally* rather than that they *live in cultures*.'[11]

Moreover, it is possible to point out another convergence between social anthropological research and Luhmann's thought on the limits of society. Recent anthropological theory has placed great emphasis on the idea that the concept (or self-description) of society as an empirically delimited object derives from the ideology of the nation-state.

Obviously, it would be wrong to imagine that, in a world-historical perspective, all human beings used to think of themselves as constituting an open-ended social network, stretching as far as their geographical knowledge reached, until 'Western' explorers and colonialists imposed their own model of 'society' upon the rest of mankind, cutting the great unbounded nexus into arbitrary pieces. Intercultural contact, or (unsuccessful) 'communication', has always made people aware of their specificity: a language that is not shared by everybody else, a legal system that only applies to themselves, or a cultural practice that does not make sense to other people. The idea of 'society', in the sense of a group of rather similar and interdependent human beings as opposed to somehow different human beings, can hardly be seen as a specifically 'Western' concept. It is true, however, that the idea of 'societies' and 'cultures' underwent an important theoretical elaboration in eighteenth- and nineteenth-century Europe, and, more importantly still, that it achieved *political* significance on an unprecedented scale at this point of historical conjuncture. As a matter of fact, 'society' and 'culture' understood in a political sense, ie '*nation*', became the paramount political principle in nineteenth-century Europe, and spread rapidly over the rest of the world in the twentieth century.

'Society', 'culture', and 'nation' became objects of European and American philosophical and political thought at the end of the early modern period, and increasingly so through the nineteenth century, because they corresponded to more and more visible and politically effective realities. A series of intertwined political, socio-economical, demographic, technological, and cultural trans-

[9] J Clifford, *Routes: Travels and Translation in the Twentieth Century* (Cambridge Mass, Harvard University Press, 1997); GE Marcus and MJ Fischer, *Anthropology as Cultural Critique: An Experimental Moment in the Human Sciences* (Chicago, The University of Chicago Press, 1986).

[10] Cf U Hannerz, 'The Global Ecumene as a Network of Networks' in A Kuper (ed), *Conceptualizing Society*, (London, Routledge, 1992) 34–56. This self-proclaimed 'new paradigm' is, obviously, less radical than it may seem even in the field of anthropology; famously, Edmund Leach studied interactions between communities in Highland Burma as early as in 1954.

[11] Cf. T Ingold, 'Introduction to Culture' in T Ingold (ed), *Companion Encyclopedia of Anthropology*, (London, Routledge, 1994) 329–49. Similarly, the terms 'social life' and 'sociality' tend to replace 'society' in recent anthropological writing.

formations, which occurred at different times in the Euro-American part of the world from the eighteenth century onwards, produced societies and nations as political actors. With hindsight, one can establish the emergence of a historically different kind of 'societies' and 'nations' (ie of numerically grown, economically interrelated, and culturally relatively unified aggregates of people as opposed to the traditional ruling classes and as opposed to neighbouring, comparable aggregates) in eighteenth- and nineteenth-century Europe and America. The people who underwent the transformations described above resorted to the terminology of 'society', 'culture' (*Volk*), and 'nation' so as to make sense of their changed circumstances.

Luhmann sketched the emergence of this self-description of regional, politically and legally integrated social systems in a couple of pages of *Die Gesellschaft der Gesellschaft*.[12] According to him, the 'nation' is part of the galaxy of Old European thought, an epistemological hindrance to sociological insights.

From the point of view of anthropology, one crucial problem remains. If a 'world-society' is already in place, how do we account for cultural differences? Why does communication flow more easily between people speaking the same language and sharing similar cultural references, or 'expectations'? Why is the *Anschlußfähigkeit* empirically higher, the problem of double contingency less acute within a 'society' or 'culture' than between 'societies'/'cultures'? Luhmann seems to dismiss the evidence for varying probabilities that utterances (*Mitteilungen*) are understood. In his 1971 paper, he contended rather nonchalantly that, in world-society, one never enters into strange, completely unintelligible situations in which it becomes impossible to guess what others expect. Certainly, one has to learn something new in each country; for example, in Spain, train tickets have to be validated before starting the journey, while in Britain, some railway carriage doors have to be opened from the outside; but these difficulties are easily surmountable.[13] This treatment of the problem seems a bit too simple. It is certainly not a coincidence that Luhmann chose examples from nearby European countries and from the domain of transport and travel. Taking part, say, in a family celebration in Sri Lanka or a religious ritual in Polynesia would certainly be a different matter altogether.[14]

One keeps wondering if, all undeniable interconnections to the contrary, 'nations' and 'societies' in the Old European sense are not only self-descriptions, but (obviously leaky) frames for communication. Luhmann only hinted at an answer. Nations might be seen as remnants of segmentary differentiation.[15]

[12] N Luhmann, *Die Gesellschaft der Gesellschaft*, above n 2, 1045–55.

[13] N Luhmann, 'Die Weltgesellschaft', above n 5, 54.

[14] In a short paragraph in *Die Gesellschaft der Gesellschaft*, Luhmann tries, again rather unconvincingly, to do away with the problem of cultural differences: today, all cultures are known, and strangers are not blamed for problems of communication any more (*Die Gesellschaft der Gesellschaft*, above n 2, 170).

[15] N Luhmann, 'Die Weltgesellschaft', above n 5, 60; N Luhmann, *Die Gesellschaft der Gesellschaft*, above n 2, 1045.

However, segmentation, the most primitive form of social differentiation, is only discussed in association with traditional non-literate societies such as South African bushmen (*!Kung*) or Australian aboriginal tribes.[16] Luhmann has a clearly evolutionary view on this matter; segments are obsolete and doomed to disappear in the future. With the demise of the Soviet Union, the last (futile) attempt to build a relatively autonomous empire within world-society has failed.[17] Even if one wants to subscribe to the value judgement[18] that the remaining segmentary differentiations within the global systems of the economy, the law and so on will soon be a matter of the past, one cannot be satisfied with Luhmann's superficial treatment of this part of today's social reality. One problem lies in the fact that Luhmann dealt with language, the medium which enables the structural coupling between consciousness and the social system (ie social communications), only in the singular (for example in a long passage in *Die Gesellschaft der Gesellschaft*).[19] The fact that there are several hundred languages and several hundred sets of 'schemata' (the other medium which consciousness and social communication have in common)[20] in world-society is not sufficiently taken into account.

As often, criticism that might be levelled against Luhmann's thought concerns the degree of emphasis that he places on different elements of his theory. In descriptions and explanations of modern world-society, both transnational interconnections and national or cultural boundedness need to be taken into account. It was Luhmann's merit to call attention to the 'old-European' character of sociological thought and research within a national framework; this critique anticipates anthropological denouncement of ethnocentric 'Western' social thought imposing its categories on other parts of the world. However, this radical dismissing of national categories causes considerable problems for the investigation of 'social facts', 'phenomena' or instances of 'communication'. Luhmann's all-inclusive notion of society without social limits has not convinced some otherwise favourable commentators of his work.[21] Luhmann developed the concept of world-society because he was not satisfied with the kind of frontiers that sociologists assumed to exist between societies;[22] however, his reaction is not completely satisfying either. If anything, this impasse indicates a shortcoming of, and thence a desideratum for social theory.

[16] N Luhmann, 'Die Weltgesellschaft', above n 5, 60; N Luhmann, *Die Gesellschaft der Gesellschaft*, above n 2, 634–62.

[17] *Ibid*, 809–10.

[18] N Luhmann opined that national segmentations were harmful in today's society (*Ibid*, 1055)—surely a value judgement if ever there was one.

[19] *Ibid*, 205–29.

[20] *Ibid*, 110–1.

[21] Cf for instance R Greshoff, 'Kommunikation als subjekthaftes Handlungsgeschehen—behindern "traditionelle" Konzepte eine "genaue begriffliche Bestimmung des Gegenstandes Gesellschaft"?' in H-J Giegel and U Schimank (eds), *Beobachter der Moderne: Beiträge zu Niklas Luhmanns 'Die Gesellschaft der Gesellschaft'* (Frankfurt am Main, Suhrkamp, 2003), 71–113; 98–110.

[22] N Luhmann, 'Die Weltgesellschaft', above n 5, 53.

SOCIETY AND THE INDIVIDUAL

Society, according to Luhmann, includes all social systems, all social communications; however, it excludes an element that most previous social theory believed to be an essential constituent of society: the individual.

Luhmann himself analysed how the difference between state and society was replaced by the difference between state and the individual at the end of the nineteenth century.[23]

As a matter of fact, social theory has had to grapple with the problem of the relationship between 'individual' or 'subject' and 'society' from its (institutionalised) beginnings. The Brazilian anthropologist Eduardo Viveiros de Castro lists three theoretical orientations that have influenced social thought until today. Herbert Spencer saw society as a supra-individual (an organic whole that amounts to more than the sum of its parts) but natural phenomenon. Emile Durkheim also conceived of society as supra-individual ('collective representations', 'collective consciousness'), but thought that society distinguished humans from animals. Franz Boas defined culture as an extra-somatic and ideational reality, but not as one that makes up a distinct ontological realm. According to him, culture/society was individual (existing in human minds) and supra-biological.[24] Luhmann's redefinition of society as the sum of communications, and of individual consciousness or organic systems being part of society's environment rather than of society itself, could be considered as a radical break from concepts of society that retain an avowed or hidden transcendental element,[25] such as Spencerian or Durkheimian notions.

Are there any possible points of convergence with social anthropological research? Recently, the concept of 'society' has been unravelled by some anthropologists from a similar angle. Anthropologists working in Melanesia have pointed out that, from an emic point of view, the notion of 'society' does not make sense to at least some of the people among whom they studied. In the Papua New Guinean village of Hagen, Marilyn Strathern encountered neither ideas on 'individuals' nor on 'society'; rather, people thought and talked about interpersonal relations and potentialities for such relations. In Hagen, persons embody their relationships with others and are the outcome of acts of others.[26]

[23] N Luhmann, 'Tautologie und Paradoxie in den Selbstbeschreibungen der modernen Gesellschaft' (1987) in K-U Hellmann (ed), *Niklas Luhmann, Protest: Systemtheorie und soziale Bewegungen* (Frankfurt am Main, Suhrkamp, 1996) 79–106; 86–9; N Luhmann, *Die Gesellschaft der Gesellschaft*, above n 2, 1024–27.

[24] E Viveiros de Castro, 'Society', PE Britto (trans), in A Barnard and J Spencer (eds), *Encyclopedia of Social and Cultural Anthropology* (London, Routledge, 1996) 514–22.

[25] D Horster, *Niklas Luhmann* (München, CH Beck Verlag, 1997) 97.

[26] M Strathern, *The Gender of the Gift: Problems with Women and Problems with Society in Melanesia* (Berkeley, University of California Press, 1988); M Strathern, 'Parts and Wholes: Refiguring Relationships in a Post-plural World' in A Kuper (ed), *Conceptualizing Society* (London, Routledge, 1992) 75–104.

Similarly, Roy Wagner identified a Melanesian 'form of thought' which enables people to dispense with the dichotomy between individual and society. The Usen Barok in Central New Ireland, as well as some other Melanesian groups, conceptualise social and cultural phenomena like a 'holography', ie a form that is reproduced through all changes of scale, so that the smallest part always contains the whole. Thus, each phenomenon, including the 'person' and the 'aggregate', is fractal,[27] ie neither singular nor plural.[28]

This emphasis on exchange as the main constituent of society, and the concomitant relativisation of the individual or person, is intriguingly similar to Luhmann's view that society consists of communications, not of individuals. Like these (also supposedly post-modern)[29] anthropologists, Luhmann wondered if human beings can really be regarded as the agents and co-ordinators of societal development. Of course, Luhmann would never have denied that 'psychic systems' are involved in communication[30] and affected by it, but he would have attributed them very limited control over it.[31] This could be regarded as a devaluation of the individual, but also as a considerable liberation of the self.[32]

After a long period of rather rigid opposition between 'society' and 'community', *societas* and *universitas*, individualism and holism, a consensus has been reached in social anthropological thought that there are different kinds and degrees of cultural emphasis on individuality. Such variation exists both within and between societies and cultures. North Atlantic societies tend to place value

[27] Strictly speaking, 'holography' means the technique of producing holograms, ie images which appear three-dimensional when seen under a particularly source of light. It would be more consistent to always use the term 'fractal' to designate a self-similar object which remains invariant under changes of scale and whose component parts resemble the whole.

[28] Cf R Wagner, 'The fractal person' in M Godelier and M Strathern (eds), *Big Men and Great Men: Personifications of Power in Melanesia* (Cambridge, Cambridge University Press, 1991) 159–73. That Melanesian 'societies' consisted of fluid structures without boundaries had already been suggested by Peter Lawrence in the 1950s, to the dismay of his anthropological peers. Only relatively recently, the 'dissolution' of the 'dividual' and 'society' has become the dominant paradigm of Melanesian anthropology (M Strathern, 'Parts and Wholes' above n 26). Cf, also A Gell, 'Strathernograms' in E Hirsch (ed), *The Art of Anthropology: Essays and Diagrams* (London, The Athlone Press, 1999) 29–75 for more examples of fractal visions of societies and persons.

[29] On the erroneous classification of Luhmann with post-modernism see for instance J Soentgen 'Der Bau: Betrachtungen zu einer Metapher der Luhmannschen Systemtheorie' (1992) 21 *Zeitschrift für Soziologie*, 456.

[30] N Luhmann, *Die Gesellschaft der Gesellschaft*, above n 2, 103; G Kneer, *Rationalisierung, Disziplinierung und Differenzierung: Zum Zusammenhang von Sozialtheorie und Zeitdiagnose bei Jürgen Habermas, Michel Foucault und Niklas Luhmann* (Opladen, Westdeutscher Verlag, 1996) 360.

[31] N Luhmann was highly sceptical about the possibility of 'social engineering' or other aspects of human planning, which can never predict in what ways society will develop in the future (N Luhmann, *Die Gesellschaft der Gesellschaft*, above n 2, 430). Functionally differentiated society is so complex that the totality of the interdependencies between its subsystems is not transparent for any observer. Future developments are virtually impossible to calculate and foresee (*Ibid*, 763). If human organisms and psychic systems influence evolution in any way, this can only happen by coincidence ('Zufall'). A valid explanation for social change can only be found in the social system itself (*Ibid*, 457–8).

[32] I Blühdorn, 'An Offer One Might Prefer to Refuse: The Systems Theoretical Legacy of Niklas Luhmann' (2000) 51 *European Journal of Social Theory*, 339; 341.

upon each unique individual, while there are other societies which, as a matter of law and public ideology, place emphasis on the value of social relations.[33] Luhmann's reflections can be read as an indication for the perhaps surprising fact that Western social systems can produce self-descriptions in non-individualistic terms, while the friction caused by this approach shows that this view remains unusual and marginal. Interestingly, Luhmann discusses the genealogy of the terms '*universitas*' and '*societas*' himself: viewing society as a whole made out of parts, or of many parts assembling into a whole (which amounts to a slight shift in emphasis), belongs to the semantics of *Alteuropa*.[34] His own theory is intended to supersede such traditional self-descriptions of society.

If Western sociologists have criticised Luhmann for casting the model of a society without humans and without agency,[35] his concept appears less unrealistic from the point of view of social groups (and their anthropologists) that identify the social with exchange (without lapsing into interactionism, which takes individuals as its point of departure).[36] Despite all similarities, however, there would be disagreement on the concept of individual consciousness. Luhmann described consciousness as opaque. Psychic systems have their own operations which are distinct from communication in social systems. This is a theoretical choice that appears highly individualistic: each psychic system is completely isolated from the other.[37] Was Luhmann therefore an individualist *and* a curious sort of holist at the same time? The fact that his theory can be attacked from both sides, from a *societas* as well as from a *universitas* point of view, rather indicates that Luhmann transcends these dichotomies.

SOCIAL CHANGE

Having explored the limits of society and its relationship to the individual, it is necessary to approach Luhmann's concept of society from another angle: its temporal dimension.

According to Peter Burke, there are presently two main models of social change: a conflict one that understands social change as the result of

[33] M Carrithers, 'Person' in A Barnard and J Spencer (eds), *Encyclopedia of Social and Cultural Anthropology* (London, Routledge, 1996) 419–23.

[34] N Luhmann, *Die Gesellschaft der Gesellschaft*, above n 2, 912–21.

[35] For instance, J Habermas, *Der philosophische Diskurs der Moderne: Zwölf Vorlesungen* (Frankfurt am Main, Suhrkamp, 1985) 436; J-M Vincent, 'La société de Niklas Luhmann' (1999) 107 *Cahiers Internationaux de Sociologie*, 355.

[36] Cf also N Luhmann, *Social Systems*, J Bednarz, Jr with D Baecker (trans), (Stanford, Stanford University Press, 1995) 405.

[37] Very intriguingly, Luhmann suggested in response to his critics that his theoretical exclusion of human beings (psychic and organic systems) from the realm of society was a pre-condition for conceptualising the equality of all individuals and their equal human rights. If human beings were included in society, they would have to be included as belonging to different social classes, different nations, ethnicities and so on, ie not as equals: N Luhmann, *Die Gesellschaft der Gesellschaft*, above n 2, 30. In this passage, Luhmann seems to embrace the main tenets of individualism: the uniqueness and equal value of human beings.

confrontation between thesis and antithesis, and a consensual model that attributes change above all to internal factors and explains social change as growth, evolution or decay.[38] Once again, Luhmann's concept of social change confounds this dichotomy. His view of evolution, which has remained constant over the years,[39] incorporates elements of both models. The impulse to change is given by the complexity differential (*Komplexitätsgefälle*) between a system and its environment. Irritated by its environment, a system increases its own complexity in order to reduce the complexity of its environment. To take a historical example that Luhmann used, nomadic people domesticating horses, and thus attaining an increased mobility and military superiority, may force other people to build fortifications and adopt a more complex political organisation.[40]

If this approach follows the model of thesis and antithesis, Luhmann insisted nonetheless on the fact that the environment has no immediate contact with the system; it does not change anything in the system. Rather, 'all structural change is self-change'.[41] Social, ie structural change, falls into three main types: adaptation to the environment, as when a family reacts to its members growing older; self-adaptation, when a system eliminates internal difficulties that result from imbalances in how elements of the system relate to each other; and morphogenesis, when the system or parts of it are re-activated, dis-inhibited, or re-inhibited.[42]

Evolution follows a neo-Darwinian model: a number of variations are produced, a certain variation may be selected and then stabilised.[43] There are no obligatory phases through which an evolving social system has to pass. Evolution is hardly ever influenced by intentional processes—Luhmann accepts that there are attempts at social planning, but until recently, teleologically conceived sequences (goal-orientation) of structural change have been rare, he contends. On the whole structural changes are either *ad hoc* adaptations or morphogenetically uncontrolled.[44] Social evolution does not equate with 'progress' in any way; on the contrary, catastrophic developments are possible (see Luhmann's reflections on the deterioration of the natural environment discussed in the following section).

A few other approaches to historical change come somewhat close to this model. For instance, the art historian Gombrich contended that artists represent the world according to acquired schemata; they correct these schemata when they become aware of discrepancies between the model and reality.[45]

[38] P Burke, *History and Social Theory* (Cambridge, Polity Press, 1992).

[39] M Schmid, 'Evolution: Bemerkungen zu einer Theorie von Niklas Luhmann' in H-J Giegel and U Schimank (eds), *Beobachter der Moderne*, above n 21, 117–53; 117.

[40] N Luhmann, *A Sociological Theory of Law*, E King and M Albrow (trans), (London, Routledge, Kegan & Paul, 1985).

[41] N Luhmann, *Social Systems*, above n 36, 350.

[42] *Ibid*, 349–52.

[43] N Luhmann, *Die Gesellschaft der Gesellschaft*, above n 2, 454.

[44] N Luhmann, *Social Systems*, above n 36, 356.

[45] EH Gombrich, *Art and Illusion: A Study in the Psychology of Pictorial Representation* (London, Phaidon, 1977).

Comparably, Thomas Kuhn postulated that awareness of an anomaly usually precedes a paradigm shift in science.[46]

Marshall Sahlins is the social anthropologist who has probably reflected most on social change. According to Sahlins, people usually reproduce structures by acting according to their ingrained presuppositions. But sometimes, they stumble upon unusual occurrences. When they still apply their same old schemata to this new situation, the schemata (structures) are changed slightly. Surreptitiously, Sahlins introduces a distinction between *unique* events and *usual* events. Usual events reproduce structure, unique events (such as, to take Sahlins's famous example, the arrival of Captain Cook in Hawaii) transform structure.[47] However, compared to these models, Luhmann has suggested a more complete and sophisticated schema,[48] which historical social sciences would do well to engage with in depth.

Burke's two models correspond roughly to the two traditional views of society mentioned above. *Societas*, society seen as the sum of or a contract between individuals, is likely to develop conflictually, whereas *universitas*, society as a whole (metaphorically, as an organism), has rather been seen as evolving consensually. Given what we saw in the previous section, it seems logical that Luhmann's theory contrives to transcend this dichotomy. Change comes about in a constant interplay between irritation and communication reacting to this stimulus, and yet individuals, even collectively, are not agents of this change.

FUNCTIONAL DIFFERENTIATION

Although he cited and interpreted an impressive number of historical examples, Luhmann wanted to observe *modern society* above all else. Modern society, according to Luhmann, is characterised by functional differentiation. Functional differentiation constitutes a special case of the general principle of social evolution.

Social differentiation is a concept that dates back at least to the late eighteenth century. Famously, Adam Smith observed that the division of labour increased productivity. On the level of society as a whole, Spencer assumed that like any organism, society evolved from the simple to the complex. Inspired by German *Naturphilosophie* and Romanticism, he contended that the '[a]dvance from the

[46] T Kuhn, *The Essential Tension* (Chicago, The University of Chicago Press, 1997) *xvii*.

[47] M Sahlins, *Islands of History* (Chicago, The University of Chicago Press, 1985).

[48] The time dimension in Luhmann's work is of an importance that social theory has not even begun to grasp (see C Seyfarth, 'Die Gesellschaft als Gesellschaft in die Gesellschaft bringen: Annäherungen an ein Theorieprojekt' (1998) 21 *Soziologische Revue: Besprechungen neuer Literatur*, 153; for an invalid criticism of Luhmann's notion of time cf. S Brandt 'Systemzeit und Zeit sozialer Systeme: Zeitverständnis des Common sense als evidenzsichernde Größe?' in W Krawietz and M Welker (eds), *Kritik der Theorie sozialer Systeme: Auseinandersetzungen mit Luhmanns Hauptwerk* (Frankfurt am Main, Suhrkamp, 1992) 162–77). This issue deserves a more detailed treatment than is possible within the limits of this chapter.

homogeneous to the heterogeneous'[49] was a general principle. Durkheim was the first social thinker to characterise the difference between traditional and modern society in terms of differentiation theory; archaic societies were differentiated along segmentary lines (in families, clans, tribes), while modern society is differentiated functionally (into a political, an economic, a religious sector and so on). Weber conceived of different *Wertsphären*, each with its *Eigengesetzlichkeit*. In the process of the disenchantment of the world (increasing rationalisation) and under particular social circumstances, these spheres first disaggregated from religion and then came to differentiate themselves from each other. The sphere of politics is governed by the struggle for power, the sphere of economics by the struggle for profit, science by the struggle for truth and so on. The tension between these value spheres increases constantly.

Talcott Parsons, who had studied in Heidelberg five years after Weber's death, when the latter's influence was still considerable, developed another, less flexible model of functionally differentiated society. According to Parsons, every system has to fulfil four functions in order to persist: adaptation, goal-attainment, integration, and latent pattern-maintenance (AGIL). As far as the social system is concerned, these functions are performed by the economy (A), the polity (G), the social stratification system (I) and education/religion (L). Through 'double interchanges', these subsystems depend on each other. If Parsons has an explanation for the historical emergence of functional differentiation at all, it is teleological and circular: a functionally differentiated society simply works better than a non-differentiated one.[50]

Luhmann drew on these different strands of differentiation theory, but proposed an original model. He started out with a Durkheimian two-phase model of social differentiation (segmentary—functional). Subsequently, he introduced the concepts of stratificatory and centre-periphery differentiation.[51] Functional differentiation began in Europe in the late Middle Ages, but is difficult to date precisely.[52] There are about eleven subsystems (Schimank lists the economy, politics, the legal system, the military, science, art, mass communications, education, health, sports, the family, and intimacy).[53] Unlike Parsons, Luhmann would not pretend that the number and types of specialisation of subsystems are predictable; one can only determine empirically and retrospectively that a

[49] H Spencer, *First Principles*, 6th edition (London, Williams & Norgate, 1900) 312.

[50] On the history of differentiation theory cf. U Schimank, *Theorien gesellschaftlicher Differenzierung* (Opladen, Leske & Budrich, 1996); U Schimank and U Volkmann, *Gesellschaftliche Differenzierung* (Bielefeld, Transcript Verlag, 1999); G Kneer and G Nollmann, 'Funktional differenzierte Gesellschaft' in G Kneer, A Nassehi and M Schroer (eds), *Soziologische Gesellschaftsbegriffe: Konzepte moderner Zeitdiagnosen* (München, Wilhelm Fink Verlag, 1997) 76–100; H Tyrell 'Zur Diversität der Differenzierungstheorie: Soziologiehistorische Anmerkungen', (1998) 4 *Soziale Systeme*, 119.

[51] N Luhmann, *Die Gesellschaft der Gesellschaft*, above n 2, 613.

[52] *Ibid*, 707. N Luhmann, *Gesellschaftsstruktur und Semantik: Studien zur Wissenssoziologie der modernen Gesellschaft*, in 4 vols (Frankfurt am Main: Suhrkamp, 1995) *IV*: at 67 mentions the 16th and 17th centuries as the initial period of functional differentiation in Europe.

[53] U Schimank, *Theorien gesellschaftlicher Differenzierung*, above n 50, 154.

certain subsystem has emerged (such as sports in the late nineteenth century). For Luhmann, contrary to Parsons, subsystems are not primarily characterised, or differentiated, by their functions, but by their binary codes. Some 'islands' may resist functional differentiation, such as the religious system. Segmentary, stratificatory and centre-periphery differentiation may persist simultaneously with functional differentiation.

The subsystems are autonomous as they constantly produce their own elements (autopoeisis), but they are also linked to each other through 'structural coupling'. The relative autonomy of subsystems is responsible for some potentially catastrophic developments of modern society.[54] One such problem that Luhmann discussed at particular length is the impending environmental catastrophe (a theme close to the heart of German public opinion in the 1980s and 1990s). The natural environment may be spoilt by the economic subsystem, but the latter is unable to take this into account as it communicates exclusively with the code of having and not-having.[55]

Luhmann has been criticised intensively by his peers for downplaying the importance of interconnectedness and co-ordination between the subsystems (for instance by Richard Münch and Fritz Scharpf).[56] From Luhmann's point of view, this criticism is based on a distortion of his theory; it is precisely on account of their high functional specialisation that subsystems have to rely on each other.[57]

A criticism that could be levelled against Luhmann's model of functional differentiation from the viewpoint of social anthropology seems to be similar at first sight, but touches something closer to the core of Luhmann's unquestioned philosophical premisses. Anthropologists have spent a good deal of their energy demonstrating the actual embeddedness of 'subsystems'. Cultural domains such as kinship and social class, or gender and religion, are shown to be permeable and mutually structuring. 'Reading across domains [. . .] has been a standard analytic strategy of cultural anthropologists'.[58] The 'deconstruction of categories of thought, action and understanding has been a social anthropological skill and practice for many years'.[59] Seen from social anthropology, the splitting up

[54] N Luhmann, *Law as a Social System*, KA Ziegert trans (Oxford, Oxford University Press, 2004 [1993]) 466.

[55] See K-U Hellmann, 'Einleitung: Der Universalitätsanspruch der Systemtheorie' in K-U Hellmann (ed), *Niklas Luhmann, Protest*, above n 23, 7–45; 23.

[56] Cf also J Berger, 'Neuerliche Anfragen an die Theorie der funktionalen Differenzierung' in HJ Giegel and U Schimank (eds), *Beobachter der Moderne*, above n 21, 207–30; 224.

[57] N Luhmann was never short of illustrations for this phenomenon; cf, his account of the legal and political preconditions for the economic introductions of nuclear power stations; also a rather systematic series of examples in N Luhmann, *Die Gesellschaft der Gesellschaft*, above n 2, 781–7.

[58] S Yanagisako and C Delaney, 'Naturalizing Power' in S Yanagisako and C Delaney (eds), *Naturalizing Power: Essays in Feminist Cultural Analysis* (New York, London, Routledge, 1995) 1–22; 13.

[59] E Tonkin, M McDonald and M Chapman, 'Introduction' in E Tonkin, M McDonald and M Chapman (eds), *History and Ethnicity* (London, Routledge, 1989) 1–21; 5.

of modern society in relatively autonomous subsystems would be an (admittedly powerful) self-description of society.

Again, we are dealing here with a controversy that arises from a difference in emphasis that is placed on either of the two ends of a continuum. As we have seen before, Luhmann had come under attack for stressing too much the interconnectedness of—in his terms—the national segments of the economic and legal system, for example; in this case, the criticism arises from his placing emphasis on the autonomy of social subsystems. Obviously, Luhmann allows for structural coupling between subsystems; however, other (perhaps deeper) connections between subsystems may be thinkable. The sociologists mentioned above would hint at voluntary planning and organisation by human agents; many anthropologists would look elsewhere. Various anthropological research on socialisation, learning and cognition suggests that through engagement with their natural and social environment, human beings form—often unreflected, embodied—schemata or dispositions that they apply to different domains of their experience.[60] In this sense, the unity of the subject (or of the conglomerate of a psychic and an organic system) warrants a certain unity between domains that are allegedly separate and autonomous. Thus, Luhmann's black box approach to human consciousness not only prevents him from accepting a thorough account of the impact of cultural differences, but also leads him to underestimate structural similarities between social domains or subsystems.[61]

SOCIAL INTEGRATION

As Tyrell remarks, in most differentiation theory, at least from Spencer to Parsons, the reverse side of differentiation is integration.[62] How is social order possible? Or, to rephrase the question, concerning modern, functionally differentiated society: why is it that the different subsystems have not completely drifted away from, or entered into an inexorable conflict with one another? Luhmann raises the question himself in Die *Gesellschaft der Gesellschaft* when he mentions the problems widely known to result from social differentiation.[63] Again, a brief historical (necessarily incomplete) overview of how social theorists

[60] For example, N Quinn and C Strauss, *A Cognitive Theory of Cultural Meaning* (Cambridge, Cambridge University Press, 1997); P Bourdieu, *The Logic of Practice*, R Nice (trans), (Cambridge, Polity Press, 1990).

[61] Luhmann allowed for structural coupling between psychic and social systems through language and cognitive schemata (N Luhmann, *Die Gesellschaft der Gesellschaft*, above n 2, 110). Tellingly, his treatment of the latter ones is extremely short. Concerning embodied dispositions, cf, also R Dziewas, 'Der Mensch—ein Konglomerat autopoietischer Systeme?' in W Krawietz and M Welker (eds), *Kritik der Theorie sozialer Systeme*, above n 48, 113–32 about the problematic assumption of separated organic and psychic systems.

[62] H Tyrell, 'Emile Durkheim—Das Dilemma der organischen Solidarität' in N Luhmann (ed), *Soziale Differenzierung: Zur Geschichte einer Idee* (Opladen, Westdeutscher Verlag, 1985) 181–250; 181.

[63] N Luhmann, *Die Gesellschaft der Gesellschaft*, above n 2, 801.

have answered this question may help to situate Luhmann's solution to the problem. Durkheim assumed that members of modern society were bound together by 'organic solidarity'. The social division of labour caused interdependencies which made social cohesion necessary. However, it could also produce 'anomie' as a pathological misdevelopment.[64] Weber, who had a less harmonious view of modern society, thought that the legal state and bureaucracy tied the different social spheres together. Parsons was convinced that modern society was integrated by a common normative system, by shared symbols and values.[65]

This last opinion is a view that Luhmann rejected most decidedly.[66] According to Luhmann, society has neither a top nor a centre, it is polycentric or a-centric ('*ohne Spitze und ohne Zentrum*'[67]). The subsystems communicate in a multiplicity of codes, none of which speaks for society as a whole. Why is there no integration through common values? As opposed to Habermas, Luhmann did not think that social consensus was possible.[68] As for moral values, Luhmann made the lucid analysis that they claim universal relevance, but that hardly ever an agreement can be reached on them. Moral communication is articulated around the binary code of 'good' and 'bad', or 'esteem' and 'disesteem' (ie the attitudes adopted towards persons whose actions are seen to be either good or bad).[69] 'Good' and 'evil' are principally void of content, the relevant programmes are diverse and fluid as a consequence. Everybody can choose the programme that favours their own interests and opinions, while despising those who do not adhere to the same programme (and therefore, seemingly, not to the same code, which is an illusion). That is why moral communication is highly 'polemogeneous'.[70] Morality is dangerous in that it is likely to cause conflicts. In a counter-factual reflection, Luhmann contended that the social subsystems would collapse if they were integrated by moral values; their codes need to be amoral. For instance, the political system uses the code of government/opposition. If the government were to be declared to be 'good' and the opposition 'bad', democracy would perish. That is why, from a systems theory point of view, it

[64] E Durkheim, *De la division du travail social* (Paris, Félix Alcan, 1893) 118–41, 395–418.

[65] On slight changes in and a generally democratic orientation of Parsons's concept of normative integration cf, U Gerhardt 'Normative Integration moderner Gesellschaften als Problem der soziologischen Theorie Talcott Parsons', (1998) 4 *Soziale Systeme*, 281.

[66] N Luhmann, 'Die Weltgesellschaft', above n 5, 13.

[67] N Luhmann, *Die Gesellschaft der Gesellschaft*, above n 2, 803.

[68] J Clam, *Droit et société chez Niklas Luhmann: La contingence des normes* (Paris, Presses Universitaires de France, 1997) 98–100; D Horster, 'Gesellschaftsanalyse oder Gesellschaftsveränderung? Die Habermas-Luhmann-Kontroverse' in *Die Neue Gesellschaft/ Frankfurter Hefte*, May 1999, 432; 435.

[69] N Luhmann, *Paradigm Lost: Über die ethische Reflexion der Moral: Rede von Niklas Luhmann anläßlich der Verleihung des Hegel-Preises 1989* (Frankfurt am Main, Suhrkamp, 1989) 18.

[70] N Luhmann, *Paradigm Lost*, above n 69, 27; N Luhmann, 'The Sociology of the Morals and Ethics' (1996) 11 *International Sociology*, 27; 34; N Luhmann, *Die Gesellschaft der Gesellschaft*, above n 2, 404.

seems inordinate and superfluous that politicians judge each other in moral terms, at least in their speech acts and mass media communications.[71]

Semantically, Luhmann stipulated, 'value' is a term that spread from the economy to other spheres.[72] If values create conflict rather than cohesion, could it be useful to look at the economic sphere for a solution to the puzzle of social integration? Luhmann has been criticised for undervaluing the all-pervasive importance of the economic in modern society.[73] Schimank suggests that we could reformulate systems theory in a way that would explain the preponderance of the economic system by its fragility.[74] Luhmann himself intimated that the most fragile subsystem would probably dominate the others, and conceded that it was more likely that the economic and the legal system would have such a dominant position than science or religion, for example.[75]

Going further in his criticism than Schimank, Vincent questions the validity of the concept of autopoiesis and calls for an analysis of economic heteropoiesis, satellisation or contamination of other subsystems. This could be linked to Viskovatoff's criticism of Maturana's and Varela's, and consequently, of Luhmann's, misconception of the archetype of systems, the human cell: viruses can take over a cell's mechanisms for protein synthesis, substituting their own genetic instructions for those of the cell. The cell thus takes up information from the outside without any modification (the viral DNA) and lets it enter into its own internal operations.[76] Could economic considerations be seen as a virus that changes the programmes of other subsystems?

This reminds one of a sociological/anthropological description that resembles Luhmann's to some extent, but pays greater attention to the role of the economy in modern society (not only in its terminology as alleged by Kieserling).[77] Pierre Bourdieu's theory of self-referential and principally autonomous social fields which are increasingly concerned by economic heteronomisation could be a useful inspiration for a re-formulation of Luhmann's systems theory.[78] Luhmann seemed to admit that the economy is preponderant in modern society to some extent: three out of the six examples of structural coupling between subsystems which he gave in *Die Gesellschaft der Gesellschaft*

[71] N Luhmann, *Paradigm Lost*, 24, 40. *Die Gesellschaft der Gesellschaft* deals with values as (highly deficient) success media for the first time (P Beyer, 'Niklas Luhmann: Die Gesellschaft der Gesellschaft (review)' (2000) 51 *European Journal of Social Theory*, 369; 371; U Schimank, 'Einleitung' in H-J Giegel and U Schimank (eds), *Beobachter der Moderne*, above n 21, 7–18; 12).

[72] N Luhmann, 'Tautologie und Paradoxie in den Selbstbeschreibungen der modernen Gesellschaft' in *Niklas Luhmann, Protest*, above n 23, 79–106; 94–5; N Luhmann, *Die Gesellschaft der Gesellschaft*, above n 2, 340.

[73] For example, by Vincent, 'La société de Niklas Luhmann', above n 35.

[74] U Schimank, 'In Luhmanns Gesellschaft' (1998) 50 *Kölner Zeitschrift für Soziologie und Sozialpsychologie* 176; 178.

[75] N Luhmann, *Die Gesellschaft der Gesellschaft*, above n 2, 769.

[76] A Viskovatoff, 'Foundations of Niklas Luhmann's Theory of Social Systems' (1999) 29 *Philosophy of the Social Sciences*, 481; 490.

[77] A Kieserling, 'Zwischen Wirtschaft und Kultur: Zum siebzigsten Geburtstag von Pierre Bourdieu' (2000) 6 *Soziale Systeme*, 369.

[78] Cf. also U Schimank and U Volkmann, *Gesellschaftliche Differenzierung*, above n 50, 23–30.

concern the economic system,[79] and money, the medium of the economic system, is described as almost an archetype of media in general with its high flexibility and rapid turnover-rate. Money is a form of '*Weltkonstruktion*', a construction embracing the entire world.[80] However, Luhmann's main interest was focused on the autopoeisis and differentiation of subsystems, and even if he was prepared to concede that one of them dominated others, he would not have gone as far as to consider the possibility of heteropoeisis.

Of course, Luhmann spent much more time and effort discussing the legal than the economic system. To some extent, he seems to argue that positive law (and the inclusion of the entire population in the legal sphere) renders a better co-ordination between social subsystems possible. Functional differentiation was accompanied by the positivisation of law.[81] Modern, positive law is built on its difference from moral values; the code just/unjust of natural law is replaced by lawful/unlawful as code.[82] Conflicts emerging from other subsystems can be resolved more effectively (even if some conflicts only arise *because of* the availability of certain legal programmes).

Concerning social integration, Luhmann would mainly state in very general terms that all functional systems are linked to each other and are held in society through structural coupling: '*Faktisch sind alle Funktionssysteme durch strukturelle Kopplungen miteinander verbunden und in der Gesellschaft gehalten*'[83] (Luhmann admits that some couplings are more significant than others, and only discusses a few examples, such as the coupling between the political and the economic system). If we look for a more substantial answer, we learn that values are a particularly unlikely candidate as a factor for social cohesion. The economy may be a subsystem that has precedence over others, rendering possible a certain degree of coherence across society, but also causing considerable *Folgeprobleme* which are sometimes denounced by social protest movements. In a Weberian vein, should we assume that the legal system has a determining influence on the integration of functionally differentiated society?

Luhmann alluded to this possibility. He wanted to eschew the debate about a potential integrative social function of law.[84] However, law, according to Luhmann, has only one function: to stabilise normative expectations. This makes it possible to confront a principally unknown future, and above all to live in a complex society where trust cannot be secured effectively by any other means.[85]

[79] N Luhmann, *Die Gesellschaft der Gesellschaft*, above n 2, 781–8.

[80] *Ibid*, 349–51.

[81] N Luhmann, *A Sociological Theory of Law*, above n 40; N Luhmann, *Ausdifferenzierung des Rechts: Beiträge zur Rechtssoziologie und Rechtstheorie* (Frankfurt am Main, Suhrkamp, 1981) 129–30.

[82] Cf, N Luhmann 'La troisième question—de l'usage creative des paradoxes dans le droit et dans l'histoire du droit' (1993) 24 *Recherches sociologiques* 25; 36. Appearances to the contrary, fundamental rights are not values because values do not obey this new code (N Luhmann, *Grundrechte als Institution: Ein Beitrag zur politischen Soziologie* (Berlin, Duncker & Humblot, 1986) 213–215).

[83] N Luhmann, *Die Gesellschaft der Gesellschaft*, above n 2, 779.

[84] N Luhmann, *Law as a Social System*, above n 54, 143.

[85] *Ibid*, 146–8.

Luhmann chose to employ an organicist metaphor. According to him, law functions like an immune system. By providing counter-factual norms for society, it avoids the need to rely upon experience. In this way it deals with the extant 'pathologies' of society and prevents future 'infections', that is, it develops new programmes if necessary.[86]

Other subsystems can have stabilising effects as well. Operations of payment are used to exclude risks, for example.[87] The political system has the function of issuing collectively binding decisions. Luhmann went as far as to observe a certain 'functional synthesis' of law and politics,[88] but he would insist on the strict separation or differentiation of the two subsystems using different codes and programmes in modern society. On this point, many legal anthropologists would beg to disagree with Luhmann's analysis. The detection of the effects of power within the legal sphere is precisely one main objective of legal anthropological research. Even if law may sometimes protect the poor against the rich and the powerless against the powerful, as Luhmann argued,[89] legal resources are often used to achieve political ends, and, self-descriptions to the contrary, law is not always politically neutral.[90] Luhmann discusses the constitutional order as a structural coupling between law and politics, but assumes that the political sphere can only exert limited control over the sphere of law. Legal anthropologists emphasise the heteropoeisis of the legal sphere, even in complex society. Those working in the paradigm of 'legal pluralism' would even deny that there has to be only one single uniform legal system operating in a given social context.[91] However, concerns have been voiced about how to reasonably delineate the object of anthropological study when all instances of ordering, rule-making, and conflict-solving are understood as pertaining to the domain of 'law'. Rather than focussing on the presence of the binary code 'lawful/unlawful', which different (sub)subsystems may ascribe to themselves, it seems useful to concentrate on the central role of the state in law making and law enforcement so as to draw a boundary, while remaining attentive to recent transformations of the state in global contexts.[92]

[86] N Luhmann, *Law as a Social System*, above n 54, 171–2.

[87] *Ibid*, 154–5.

[88] *Ibid*, 165.

[89] *Ibid*, 163.

[90] Cf, for example J Starr and J F Collier, 'Introduction: Dialogues in Legal Anthropology' in J Starr and J F Collier (eds), *History and Power in the Study of Law: New Directions in Legal Anthropology* (Ithaca, Cornell University Press, 1998) 1–28.

[91] Cf, for example, P Sack and J Aleck 'Introduction' in P Sack and J Aleck (ed), *Law and Anthropology* (Aldershot, Dartmouth Publishing, 1992), *xiii–xxxi*. Legal pluralism could be described as a multiplicity of programmes working with the same code within one single legal system [I am indebted to Michael King for this observation]. The (hierarchical) co-existence of eternal/divine law, natural law and positive law in post-mediaeval Europe (N Luhmann, *Law as a Social System*, above n 54, 195) could be an example of such a phenomenon.

[92] S Falk Moore, 'Certainties Undone: Fifty Turbulent Years of Legal Anthropology, 1949–1999' (2001) 7, *The Journal of the Royal Anthropological Institute* 95; 107; and S Roberts, 'Law and Dispute Processes' in T Ingold (ed), *Companion Encyclopedia of Anthropology* (London, Routledge, 1994) 962–82; 979, referring to Gunther Teubner.

To some extent, Luhmann shared the same concerns as social anthropologists investigating the workings of law. Luhmann criticised the sociology of law for distinguishing between law and society. The very title of '*Das Recht der Gesellschaft*' (translated as 'Law as a Social System') was intended to stress the point that law operates within, not outside society. Many anthropologists would disagree about the actual degree of operational closure of the legal system, as outlined above, but they would obviously subscribe to Luhmann's view on its cognitive openness.[93] On the whole, however, it has to be stated that legal anthropologists pursue different research interests from Luhmann. Many of the former employ themselves in denouncing the persisting (operational) social 'embeddedness' of law even in differentiated, complex societies. Luhmann's questioning as to how the existence of law is at all possible in society[94] is closer to the concerns of the early, evolutionary anthropology of law (Maine, Morgan) than to recent research.

CONCLUSION

Luhmann's theory is much less incompatible with recent social anthropological research than one would assume at first sight. His reflections on the role of time in society and on social evolution are of great interest for social science and cultural history, which are still stuck in the sterile opposition of structure and agency for an explanation of social change.

Moreover, Luhmann's writings on world-society can constitute an interesting theoretical framework for those who study social phenomena across territorial frontiers. Luhmann made a convincing case for the fact that function systems do not stop at national borders. However, accounting for remaining differences between regional segments of the social system virtually only in terms of 'inclusion' and 'exclusion' is hardly satisfactory for the anthropologist. Anthropological fieldwork on the ground paints a picture of social life in the contemporary world which is, arguably, much richer than a passing reference to Brazilian slums and the assumption that most of the rest of world society functions in exactly the same way, or at least is going to do so in the near future.

Grand theories, like Luhmann's, tend to bring forth simplifying and unifying rules. There are, however, seeds in Luhmann's thought that could be brought to fruition in a more anthropological reformulation of his work. Luhmann was very dismissive of the term 'culture'. The fact that there are many (often differing) attempts to define this word[95] was recognised by anthropologists themselves as early as in 1952, when a study listed and analysed 164 definitions of the concept.[96] If a similar study were carried out for the term 'society', it

93 N Luhmann, *Law as a Social System*, above n 54, 90.

94 *Ibid*, 73.

95 N Luhmann, *Die Gesellschaft der Gesellschaft*, above n 2, 881.

96 AL Kroeber and C Kluckhohn, *Culture: A Critical Review of Concepts and Definitions* (Cambridge Mass, The Peabody Museum of American Archaeology and Ethnology, 1952).

would probably be found that this word is just as ill-defined in social studies as the term 'culture' has proven to be. However, Luhmann would not have regarded this as a sufficient reason to discard the concept altogether. Disagreement about an exact definition will most probably persist as long as people research and write about sociocultural topics, and it is not within the scope of this essay to resolve this problem. However, one would like to point out an intriguing parallel between what most anthropologists designate as 'culture' and two concepts which Luhmann used: 'semantics' and 'social memory'. According to Luhmann, meaning ('*Sinn*') is 'stored' in language and objects.[97] Social memory preserves possible meanings which are not presently actualised. Thus, its function is to maintain latent patterns (the 'L', which 'culture', religion and education carried out in the scheme devised by Parsons).[98] 'Culture' is a term invented in the second half of the eighteenth century in order to refer to this memory function of social communication.[99] The stock of possible themes and forms makes up the 'semantics' of society. Luhmann discussed the semantics of Old Europe at length.[100] If Old Europe had or still has a semantics of its own, logically, other parts of the world must have different semantics. Luhmann never talked about these other semantics, but his terminology implies their existence. A Luhmannian theory dealing with languages and semantics in the plural would make sense to most anthropologists.

In particular, Luhmann operated an intriguing deconstruction of Old European ideas of society and the individual. Conceiving of society as constituted of communications or relations between persons and institutions would meet with the approval of anthropologists working in Melanesia and some other parts of the world. However, the emphasis on the opaqueness of human consciousness for any observer, on the separation of the psychic system and the organic system, and their distinctiveness from the 'person' (ie the human being included in some sort of social communication) would not be accepted by anthropologists working in the 'embodiment' paradigm. Even those open to systems theory *à la* Maturana and Varela in general, such as Christina Toren, would refute Luhmann's application of it to anything else but the human being seen in its entirety.[101] Anthropologists working with the concept of 'embodiment' seek to overcome the (Old European!) duality between mind and body, which Luhmann's theory seems to reinforce. The perceptual experience of the individual, its 'embodied mind',[102] and its 'being-in-the-world' are taken as a

[97] N Luhmann, *Die Gesellschaft der Gesellschaft*, above n 2, 47–8.

[98] *Ibid*, 587.

[99] *Ibid*, 587; cf, also N Luhmann, *Gesellschaftsstruktur und Semantik IV*, above n 52, 31–54.

[100] N Luhmann, *Die Gesellschaft der Gesellschaft*, above n 2, 893–957.

[101] C Toren, 'Anthropology as the Whole Science of What It Is to Be Human' in RG Fox and BJ King (eds), *Anthropology beyond Culture* (Oxford, New York, Berg, 2002) 105–24; 123, n 3.

[102] C Toren, 'Comparison and ontogeny' in A Gingrich and RG Fox (eds), *Anthropology, by Comparison* (London, Routledge, 2002) 187–203; 192.

point of departure for this research informed by phenomenology.[103] The equally influential anthropological research inspired by Bourdieu's concepts of 'practice' and 'habitus' attempts to elucidate socially inculcated, rather unconscious mental and bodily dispositions, ie 'semantics' stored in the body and the consciousness, so to speak. The emphasis is decidedly on the connections between mind, body, and society.

To observe in Luhmann's sense means to draw a distinction between two terms of which only one is seen. Many critics who have accused Luhmann of placing exaggerated emphasis on the autonomy of social or consciousness systems have not paid sufficient attention to his distinction between *Autonomie* and *Autarkie* and his elaborations on interpenetration/structural coupling. The crucial question would be whether the concept of structural coupling is sufficient to describe the close interdependence between mind, body, and society highlighted by the majority of anthropologists sympathetic to the embodiment and/or practice paradigms.

[103] Cf, TJ Csordas, 'The Body's Career in Anthropology' in HL Moore (ed), *Anthropological Theory Today* (Cambridge, Polity Press, 1999) 172–205, for an introductory overview.

9

The Theoretical Context and Foundations of Luhmann's Legal and Political Sociology

BERND R HORNUNG

THE LEGAL AND political sociology to be discussed in the present volume covers two themes with which Niklas Luhmann was particularly concerned, but which are fully integrated into his broader theory of society and social systems. His legal sociology and his political sociology are two particular applications of his general theory of society ('*Theorie der Gesellschaft*'); this theory, however, is applied to virtually all subsystems of society, such as medicine, aesthetics, education, economy, religion, which are usually the topics of specialised sociologies. This means that his legal sociology and his political sociology can only be understood in the framework of his more general theories about social systems, autopoietic systems, society, and its functional differentiation. Therefore, the present contribution will both outline this general context and explain a series of theoretical concepts used by Luhmann in his legal and political sociology as well as in his treatment of the other functional subsystems of society. The intention of this text is not just to provide a kind of glossary for a better understanding of the contributions in this volume, but a coherent, and at some points critical, view of Luhmann's generic approach to social systems and the application of his theoretical concepts.

LUHMANN

Niklas Luhmann (1927–1998) is certainly one of the most important contemporary sociologists, and he has left us a huge number of published works.[1] His

[1] Important books, on which the present paper is also largely based, are: N Luhmann, *Soziologische Aufklärung*, in 6 vols (Opladen, Westdeutscher Verlag, 1974, 1975, 1981, 1987, 1993, 1995); N Luhmann, *Soziale Systeme. Grundriß einer allgemeinen Theorie* (Frankfurt/Main, Suhrkamp Verlag, 1987), which appeared in English as *Social Systems*, John Bednarz, Jr with Dirk Baecker (trans), Foreword by EM Knodt, (Stanford, Stanford University Press, 1995); N Luhmann, *Zweckbegriff und Systemrationalität. Über die Funktion von Zwecken in sozialen Systemen* (Frankfurt/Main, Suhrkamp Verlag, 1973); N Luhmann, *Ökologische Kommunikation. Kann die*

book, *Social Systems*, which appeared in 1984 and was translated into English in 1995 is among the most important. The fact that this book became available in English relatively quickly may well have been one reason why many authors outside Germany focus largely on the autopoietic theory of social systems which he develops in that work. Another reason may have been that *Social Systems* is indeed written as a kind of synthesis, summary, and systematic presentation of an important part of Luhmann's work. This means that it makes access to his theories relatively easy.

Before we outline the key concepts of Luhmann's theories, it is appropriate to explain why his 'theories'—in the plural—seem to be so impenetrable and why his analyses of specific systems, such as legal and political sociology, seem to be so inaccessible. Both points are closely related. In my view they are also closely related to Luhmann's style of working.

Luhmann's theories are difficult, first of all, because of the sheer quantity of his writings. Second, there is the problem of *his language*, which, even in German is not easy to understand. It seems that he demonstrates with his own writing a basic principle he used to profess: 'Only complexity can reduce complexity' or only a complex language can describe complex phenomena, for example, social systems. Moreover, and this seems related to his professional background as a lawyer and administrator, his language is not as precise and unequivocal as he himself claims. It is not like the language of mathematics which, beyond any doubt, is also highly complex. A key element in achieving precision in complexity, as in mathematics (to which Luhmann was never favourable), is the use of precise and explicit definitions. Although definitions can be found in Luhmann's writings, even in abundance, these are rather entire concepts and not concise definitions in the usual scientific and mathematical sense. Thus one might say, *Luhmann's definitions* or concepts do not seem to be precise, unequivocal, or, most especially, stable. That is to say, they seem to be formulated for the moment and the present context, already changing a few pages later. He seems to argue in the manner of a lawyer referring to case law, whereby each new case changes the law, and where it is necessary to know the history of cases and juridical decisions, not just the codified law.

This problem becomes even more serious, when we consider that much of Luhmann's work was *written in articles*, not books. In many cases his books were put together only later or by combining a series of articles. The consequence is that each article covers only a small area and a particular problem. It presupposes, of course, that the readers know what Luhmann had said previously and what the theoretical preconditions of each particular issue are.

moderne Gesellschaft sich auf ökologische Gefährdungen einstellen ? (Opladen, Wiesbaden, Westdeutscher Verlag, 1988); N Luhmann, *Rechtssoziologie*, 2 vols (Reinbek, Rowohlt Verlag, 1972); N Luhmann, *Das Recht der Gesellschaft* (Frankfurt/Main, Suhrkamp Verlag, 1995), which appeared in English under the title *Law As a Social System*, K Ziegert (trans) (Oxford, Oxford University Press, 2004); very useful for the beginner and specialist alike is C Baraldi, G Corsi and E Esposito, *GLU. Glossar zu Niklas Luhmanns Theorie sozialer Systeme* (Frankfurt/Main, Suhrkamp Verlag, 1998).

Naturally, all of that cannot be repeated in the article itself, but it becomes evident in the numerous footnotes and references, of which Luhmann was very fond. Again, this seems to illustrate the holistic principle that you cannot understand one item of Luhmann's theories, a single article, his legal sociology or his political sociology, without knowing all his previous works and his general theories. This, however, is once more rendered even more complex, as Luhmann was not and did not intend to be a 'systematic' sociologist aiming at designing one coherent and consistent building of thought. *Luhmann's work is science in progress*. In consequence, legal sociology and political sociology are both topics that run through from his early writings, still inspired by Parsons, to his late works on autopoietic systems.

His two volumes on the sociology of law were published as early as May 1972, while his major book on *Law as a Social System* (originally: *Das Recht der Gesellschaft*) only came out in 1993. Similarly, an early volume on the political system, the first edition of which came out in 1971,[2] contains a collection of papers published individually between 1964 and 1971.[3] Luhmann's late works on political sociology are documented in a volume edited by André Kieserling, which was only published after his death.[4] Early texts on legal sociology and political sociology are furthermore published in the first volumes of the series on 'Sociological Enlightenment', volume 1 (1st edition 1970) and volume 3 (1st edition 1981).[5]

In later articles and works Luhmann tends to develop his ideas further, introducing new complexities, always looking at new and different cases and examples. Luhmann discards few of his old ideas;[6] instead, he either tends to see them in a new light, or, alternatively, he simply does not come back to them again. Therefore, one cannot really say that Luhmann developed 'a' theory. Rather, his writings document the constant development of his theoretical thinking while passing from one functional subsystem to the next. He never provides a picture of the full theory which he might have had in mind when writing a particular piece. For this reason, his theory is not systematic in a theoretical sense, although he hardly left out any aspect of society worth consideration as the

[2] N Luhmann, *Politische Planung. Aufsätze zur Soziologie von Politik und Verwaltung* (Frankfurt/Main, Suhrkamp Verlag, 1971).

[3] Two of these (both first published as individual papers in 1969) are of particular interest in the present context, one on complexity and democracy: N Luhmann 'Komplexität und Demokratie', in N Luhmann, *Politische Planung* (Opladen, Westdeutscher Verlag, 1975, 1971) 35–45; the other one on the function of jurisdiction in the political system: see N Luhmann, 'Funktionen der Rechtsprechung im politischen System', in Luhmann, *Politische Planung*, 46–52.

[4] N Luhmann, *Die Politik der Gesellschaft*, edited by A Kieserling (Frankfurt/Main, Suhrkamp Verlag, 2000).

[5] N Luhmann, 'Soziologie des politischen Systems', in N Luhmann, *Soziologische Aufklärung*, vol 1 (Opladen, Westdeutscher Verlag, 1974) 154–177; N Luhmann, 'Positives Recht und Ideologie', in N Luhmann, *Soziologische Aufklärung*, vol 1, 178–203; N Luhmann 'Der politische Code "Konservativ" und "progressiv" in systemtheoretischer Sicht', in N Luhmann, *Soziologische Aufklärung*, vol 3 (Opladen, Westdeutscher Verlag, 1974), 267–286; N Luhmann, 'Theoretische Orientierung der Politik', in N Luhmann, *Soziologische Aufklärung*, vol 3, 287–292.

[6] This is also confirmed by Kieserling in his editorial note about Luhmann's posthumously published works: N Luhmann, *Die Politik der Gesellschaft*, above n 4, 435.

object of a 'special' sociology, such as, for instance, the sociology of law and the sociology of the political system.

FOUR THEMES AND PHASES OF THEORY BUILDING

Although we said earlier that *Social Systems* is a major summary, it represents only one of four themes and three main phases which can be distinguished in Luhmann's works. Luhmann initially studied law and worked in the legal profession, spending many of his private hours studying philosophy, in particular Husserl, before going to the US where he studied sociology with Talcott Parsons.[7] Consequently his first phase of scientific work after returning to Germany was strongly influenced by functionalism, although Luhmann extricated himself from Parsons's intellectual influence very soon, developing his own ideas about functionalism. This led to a second phase in which he concentrated on another theme, complexity. At this stage, he developed the concepts of complexity and reduction of complexity into a magic formula, even a world-formula, or, as less charitable commentators might say, an empty formula.[8] Then came the 'autopoietic turn', when Luhmann adopted and again, as with Parsons's theory, immediately 'Luhmannified' autopoietic theory. Autopoietic theory had originally been developed by Maturana and Varela, two Chilean biologists and physiologists, as a theory of life for living systems.[9] It is this third phase which is basically documented in a condensed form in *Social Systems*. With his new focus on autopoiesis and communication, another issue became very prominent, which, however, had been there already for quite a while. This is what we might see as a fourth big theme of Luhmann's theorising—semantics.

Although for purposes of presentation we have divided Luhmann's scientific legacy into four themes and three phases, the phases are by no means clear cut. They are rather determined by emphases of focus and by the predominance of certain themes and issues, which can also be found in much earlier or much later writings. Moreover, as he developed his ideas in articles, talks, and conferences rather than in monographs, it should not be surprising that we find a variety of topics in parallel. Writings about legal and political sociology can be found, with more or less prominence, in all phases. Chapters on law, politics, and the state are also to be found in his volumes on 'Societal Structure and Semantics'.[10]

7 BR Hornung, 'In Memoriam: Niklas Luhmann (1927–1998)', in (1999) 78–79 *ISA Bulletin, International Sociological Association* 24.

8 Cf, E Topitsch, 'Sprachlogische Probleme der sozialwissenschaftlichen Theoriebildung', in E Topitsch, *Logik der Sozialwissenschaften* (Köln, Berlin, Kiepenheuer & Witsch, 1972) 17–36.

9 HR Maturana and FJ Varela, *Autopoiesis and Cognition. The Realisation of the Living* (Dordrecht NL; Boston USA, D Reidel Publishing Company, 1980); HR Maturana and FJ Varela, *Der Baum der Erkenntnis; Die biologischen Wurzeln menschlichen Erkennens* (München, Goldmann Verlag, 1987).

10 N Luhmann, *Gesellschaftsstruktur und Semantik: Studien zur Wissenssoziologie der Modernen Gesellschaft*, in 4 vols. (Frankfurt/Main, Suhrkamp Verlag, vol 1 1998/1st edn 1980, vol 2 1993/1st edn 1981, vol 3 1998/1st edn 1989, vol 4 1999/1st edn 1995).

Functionalism

In this first phase of his work, Luhmann wrote a number of books, including his two volumes on the sociology of law. Luhmann's mentor, Parsons, was certainly functionalist, but not all functionalism is necessarily Parsonian functionalism.[11] Luhmann recognised that the basic principles of functional analysis are indispensable for an adequate sociological theory,[12] yet he was also aware that Parsons's structural-functionalism had its drawbacks and that something else was needed in order to advance and elaborate upon a sociological theory which also includes, albeit at a less abstract level, theories about the legal system and the political system.

Hence he made a first strategic shift, albeit one which is generally not well recognised in the secondary literature. He switched from structural-functionalist theory to functional-structuralist theory.[13] Apparently only playing with words, this turn permitted him to break away from the conservatism inherent in much of Parsons's theory. If structural-functionalist theory means that structures exist, such as society, which require certain functions in order to be maintained, this results in either structure-maintenance or structural breakdown, depending on whether the functions are or are not adequately fulfilled. Such a theory does not provide for structural change and adaptation, and does not enable us to envisage structural alternatives. This is the conservatism for which Parsons is often reproached. Responding critically to this, Luhmann's functional-structuralist switch means that if a function needs to be fulfilled, there have to be structures (and processes) to do this. Consequently, to maintain a function structures can and often even have to be modified, adapted, or completely replaced. This means that we must also recognise the existence of structural dynamics, adaptation, development and, one of Luhmann's key concepts, the functional equivalence of different kinds of structures. From this point of view the function of law is to reduce complexity and to arrive at (juridical) decisions that stabilise counter-factual expectations,[14] ie

[11] N Luhmann, 'Soziologie als Theorie sozialer Systeme', in N Luhmann, *Soziologische Aufklärung*, vol 1, above n 1, 113–136; 116. For a detailed discussion of functionalism and the theories of Parsons, see: KD Bailey, *Sociology and the New Systems Theory: Toward a Theoretical Synthesis* (Albany NY, State University of New York Press, 1994) in particular, 73–80, 176, 201–202, 219–220.

[12] The indispensability of functional analysis for social and sociological theory is also asserted, for instance, by M Thompson, R Ellis and A Wildavsky, *Cultural Theory* (Boulder Co, San Francisco/Oxford, Westview Press, 1990).

[13] N Luhmann, 'Soziologie als Theorie sozialer Systeme', above n 11, 113–114.

[14] A function is an aspect under which mechanisms of a system or also of entire (sub-)systems can be compared to each other; in problem-functionalism (see below) this aspect is a solution to a reference problem. In *Law as a Social System* (above n 1, 167ff), Luhmann distinguishes between the specific 'function' a subsystem, eg the legal system, has with regard to society and the functions such a subsystem has, eg, for other subsystems. This latter kind of functions Luhmann designates as 'services' (*Leistungen*). However, one might as well designate them as 'secondary functions' or something similar, as this distinction seems to depend mainly on the system and research reference and does not indicate a difference in quality but in priority.

norms.[15] This can be accomplished by means of quite different but functionally equivalent structures, for example, codified law on the one hand and case law on the other, or also by religious law, etc.

Functional-structuralism was extended to become problem-functionalism, although this was never really systematically elaborated by Luhmann himself.[16] In this concept, Luhmann added the idea of a 'reference problem'—another one of his key concepts—to his functional-structural theory. The category of 'reference problem', or sometimes 'reference system', provides, according to Luhmann, orientation to functions—that is, it provides a clear point of reference or criterion under which different structures or mechanisms can be compared whether they are functionally equivalent or not under this particular aspect. This is a *sine qua non* of Luhmann's functionalist analysis because the use of the reference problem allows him to avoid a central critique of earlier functionalism. The fact that early functionalism did not see this is the reason why these versions of functionalism see almost everything as either functional or dysfunctional. As Luhmann never tires of insisting, it is only by stating a clear reference problem that criteria for 'functionality' can be given. The 'reference problem', however, does not have any normative implication in Luhmann's writings. He explicitly rejects normative statements in theory.

Luhmann's problem-functionalist analysis of modern society and its functional differentiation, of which the legal system and the political system are two prominent examples, leads inevitably to the issue of complexity.

Complexity

Looking for a most general and most abstract reference problem—which for Parsons was the maintenance of social structure—Luhmann discovered complexity.[17] Complexity, as a reference problem, is indeed highly abstract and highly general, in particular in Luhmann's theory of social complexity which is the over-arching theoretical framework for his specific analyses of how particular functional subsystems reduce complexity. As a reference problem at the level of social systems in general, it is abstractly intangible to the extent that it risks

[15] See N Luhmann, *Law as a Social System*, above n 1, esp. 142–147, for the function of law; for the concept of norms see 60; justice is strictly speaking not a *function* of the legal system, although some formulations, eg on 393, seem to say so. However, Luhmann clearly considers justice, as a systems concept (see especially 60), as something which is very closely related to the function proper of the legal system. Justice is the 'formula of contingency' (*Kontingenzformel*) of the legal system and as such occupying a very central place (218).

[16] At least not to this author's knowledge. For a further development of problem-functionalism towards applications cf. BR Hornung and FT Adilova, 'Conceptual Modelling for Technology Assessment of IT Systems: Smart Cards, and Health Information Systems', (1997) 26 *Kybernetes* 787.

[17] N Luhmann, 'Komplexität', in N Luhmann, *Soziologische Aufklärung*, vol 2, above n 1, 204–220, see 205 for the analysis of complexity as the ultimate reference problem of society, cf, also 210ff.

turning out to be an 'empty formula', that is, a blanket concept covering everything and, therefore, incapable of explaining anything. Whatever exists consists of structures or processes, or a combination thereof, and is one instance selected from a range of possibilities.[18] As such it is contingent, that is, it could be different and is already a reduction of complexity. In the same way any observation, any cognition, any meaning, and any model—in the widest sense—is a selection and consequently already a reduction of complexity. The legal system, of course, reduces complexity, the political system reduces complexity, but so do all the other functional subsystems that Luhmann identifies (see Table 1 below). The particular way in which each one of these functional subsystems does so is quite specific to that system. Luhmann's basic idea was that the world is complex, ie it contains a multitude of components and relations, to the extent that it cannot be understood (ie given meaning), described or handled anymore. Otherwise it would be only complicated, not complex. There is only one way to deal with complexity, namely to reduce it, that is to manage it, or give it meaning. Reduction of complexity is necessary both for the individual to act and get along in the world and for other kinds of systems to exist and survive. It is a key theorem of Luhmann that the reduction of (environmental) complexity is only possible if the system builds up its own internal system complexity. Only system complexity can reduce environmental complexity.[19] Only the build-up of (internal) complexity permits the reduction of (environmental) complexity. This evidently sets into motion a cycle of circular causality in the course of which more and more complexity is built up on all sides, ie it leads to a development towards constantly increasing complexity.

Complexity has been recognised as a serious problem in contemporary society for a long time. Luhmann sets out a number of fascinating studies on how different mechanisms, e.g. the legal system, reduce complexity. The problem, however, has already been mentioned: 'Reduction of complexity' seems to be too general and too abstract to provide reliable, operational, and non-arbitrary criteria to determine appropriate functions, dysfunctions, etc. After all, it can be said that everything is complex, and after all, nearly everything can be said to reduce complexity in some way. We are thus confronted once again with the problem of early functionalism because complexity does not turn out to be a reference problem which can really provide guidance at more concrete, more empirical levels.

[18] N Luhmann, *Social Systems*, above n 1, for theory as a reduction of complexity; 25 for selection as a reduction of complexity; 60 for information as reduction of complexity; N Luhmann, 'Komplexität', above n 17 206 for structure as selectivity and reduction of complexity.

[19] N Luhmann, *Social Systems*, above n 1, 26f—only complexity can reduce complexity, also N Luhmann, 'Komplexität', above n 17, 211—only system complexity can reduce environmental complexity; N Luhmann, 'Soziologie des politischen Systems,' above n 5, 160–161; N Luhmann, 'Soziologie als Theorie sozialer Systeme,' above n 11, 116–117; in a certain way reduction of complexity is also a condition for the build-up of (internal) complexity as selections have to be made which provide a basis and starting point for building up, for example, complex structures which depend on these particular selections, see N Luhmann, *Law as a Social System*, above n 1, 219ff.

I would suggest that one reason why the theory of autopoiesis was so suitable to Luhmann was perhaps that it promised to provide a more tangible, yet still highly abstract, reference problem. Autopoiesis is a quite different phenomenon in this respect. Although it is also a highly abstract theoretical concept, the conditions under which autopoiesis continues can be clearly specified as can the cases where autopoiesis has ceased or did not exist from the very beginning. Luhmann emphatically insists on this characteristic of the all-or-nothingness of autopoiesis. All of this does not mean, however, that the issue of complexity disappeared from Luhmann's later writings.

Autopoiesis and Selectivity

As mentioned earlier, the concept of autopoiesis was originally coined and developed by Maturana and Varela in a biological context to describe living systems. For these authors, if society is a living system, it is a system composed of individuals, ie biological organisms that make up society. Autopoiesis is defined by Maturana and Varela as a particular kind of 'organisation' of a system. It is distinct from the system's 'structure' and can be maintained by different, or, in Luhmann's terms, 'functionally equivalent', structures. Hence the 'organisation' of an autopoietic system is not simply the particular pattern of its structural components. It is rather what in functionalist theory we might call the functional organisation of a system, ie the set of its functionalities and of their interdependencies.

The particular characteristics of an autopoietic system are:

a) that this functional organisation is circular and closed in such a way that the components of which the system consists reproduce, in their operation, the same components and thus the system itself. As long as this circular process goes on, autopoiesis continues and life goes on. This circular operation is the phenomenon to which 'operational closure' refers.
b) that autopoietic systems are, according to Maturana and Varela, energetically open (biological systems obviously have a metabolism) but that they are informationally closed. Luhmann, after generalising autopoietic theory, speaks of operational closure and openness in other respects. This means that for each system or type of system it is necessary to specify the kind of operations which are closed as well as the aspects in that the system or type of system is open.

Nonetheless, some kind of 'communication' is possible by what is called 'structural coupling'. To what extent this view of informational closure can be accepted depends to a very large degree on the concept of information being used. Most authors, including Luhmann,[20] refer to Shannon's concept of

[20] N Luhmann, *Social Systems*, above n 1, 529; CE Shannon and W Weaver, *The Mathematical Theory of Communication* (Urbana, Ill, University of Illinois Press, 1964).

information. This was developed by Shannon for a quite different purpose, namely as a technical theory of communication,[21] and is rather problematic if it is used for other purposes. Luhmann abstracts from (physical) action as a component of social life and restricts the social to 'communication'. Consequently, he analyses social systems as pure communication systems, even abstracting from the communicators, who, according to Luhmann, are psychological or 'psychic' systems. Psychological systems exist, however, outside the social systems—which exist purely as their environment. Hence, in the logic of autopoiesis, psychological systems do not communicate with social systems. There is only 'structural coupling' or 'interpenetration'. The latter is another concept borrowed originally from Parsons.

On the basis of Shannon's concept of information and his own view of social systems as communication systems, Luhmann sets out to identify and analyse different social subsystems in accordance with his logic of autopoiesis. He describes the political system, the economic system, the legal system and other systems, as informationally closed systems of communications. In this he focuses on the communications themselves while abstracting from the communicators. All of this is situated in the theoretical context of the functional differentiation of modern societies. Functional differentiation is indispensable for building up and reducing complexity and it makes modern societies highly complex and interdependent. Most sociologists would say, in spite of the autopoietic theorem of informational closure, that functional differentiation requires a high level of information flows and information exchange in order to ensure a certain level of coordination. According to autopoietic theory, however, there is no information flow, eg between politics, law, and economy—only structural coupling.

Following the logic of informational and operational closure of societal subsystems, Luhmann develops theories about the specific 'media of communication', that each functional subsystem possesses . These media are bound up, in each instance, with different 'codes'. According to Luhmann these are binary codes which follow the model *yes/no* or *exists/does not exist*. They are not the elaborate codes of information technology, like eg ASCII or EBCDIC. The latter, although being binary at the electronic and basic logical level (consisting of bits = binary digits), enable the building of complex texts, images, movies, and even music on computers. Luhmann's theoretical framework becomes complete and consistent once he links all of this to his concepts of different kinds of 'programmes', which serve to steer and guide social life. The concept of 'programmes' provides an over-arching context to the micro-operations of a social system which follow a code step by step. It permits the linking of these

[21] For a more extensive discussion see BR Hornung, 'Structural Coupling and Concepts of Data and Information Exchange. Integrating Luhmann into Information Science' (2001) 2 *Journal of Sociocybernetics* <http://www.unizar.es/sociocybernetics> last accessed 4 Sept 2005; MS Blois, *Information and Medicine: The Nature of Medical Descriptions* (Berkeley, University of California Press, 1984).

micro-operations to meso- or macro-properties of social systems and their operations. Although all types of social systems share the same properties of social systems in general, the different kinds of specific social systems, also of functional subsystems, are characterised, according to Luhmann, by the predominance of different types of programmes that permit these systems to fulfil their specific reference functions. Luhmann distinguishes in particular between conditional programmes, typical of the legal system, and goal-oriented programmes (*Zweckprogramme*), that prevail in the political system. The notion of programmes dates back to his functionalist phase. Nonetheless, considering his 'empirical' analyses and examples of analysing different areas of social life in this way, it becomes evident that the original concept of 'one functional subsystem, one medium, one code' cannot be maintained.[22] This is demonstrated in Table 1 below, showing codes, media, and functional subsystems as they exist in Luhmann's writings. It could, however, be argued that different areas of social life are simply not equally suitable to be described in this way.

In a certain sense autopoiesis can be seen as a logical outcome of the complexification of other system concepts. The most basic one, circular causality, is simply a causal chain closed back to itself. At a higher level, however, more complex feedback mechanisms steer and control loops, and they thus imply some kind of information processing, which, at the very least, consists of a comparison between a target state and a real state—a comparison that guides feed-back or feed-forward. A further step, particularly developed in the works of Heinz von Foerster,[23] is self-organisation. Self-organisation is not simply feedback, but also the build up of new structures and new systems by feedback processes. A self-organising system is not yet autopoietic; it lives, as it organises itself, but it does not (necessarily) reproduce itself. Self-reproductive systems are at a last level of complexification, found in autopoietic systems, which are self-reproducing systems.

Luhmann speaks about self-reference rather than self-organisation, as he is concerned not with material, physical or biological systems, but with communication systems. In his discussion of communication, media, and codes, based on whatever concept of information, the issue of organising communications (or information and knowledge) becomes prominent, and the concepts of 'meaning' and 'semantics' become central. This opens the door to the fourth big theme in Luhmann's works.

[22] For example, N Luhmann, *Law as a Social System*, above n 1, 100–101. Here Luhmann states that the operational closure of a system requires the use of one single binary code.

[23] For example, H von Foerster and B Poerksen, *Understanding Systems: Conversations on Epistemology and Ethics* (New York, Boston, Dordrecht, London, Moscow, Heidelberg, Kluwer Academic Publishers / Plenum Publishers / Carl-Auer-Systeme Verlag, 2002); H von Foerster, *Sicht und Einsicht. Versuche zu einer operativen Erkenntnistheorie* (Heidelberg, Carl-Auer-Systeme Verlag, 1999).

Semantics

Luhmann also turns his attention towards the sociology of knowledge, or towards what in other theoretical approaches, for instance in those of Leslie White or Claude Levi Strauss, is called culture, the knowledge base of social systems and societies, or knowledge management. Sequences of communications are not arbitrary. They follow a certain logic, certain paths that connect some concepts to each other and not—or not directly—to others. Meaning, so to speak, is the horizontal network of concepts along which communications can move, for instance inside the autopoietic legal or political system, or across the different subsystems by means of their structural coupling. Consequently for Luhmann 'society' is 'all that is communicably reachable' (across networks of meanings). That is why for Luhmann there can be only one society nowadays, which is 'world society'. Everything (within the world) is communicably reachable. The 'world', for Luhmann, is not a system as it does not have a boundary. It has no boundary, because it is impossible to go beyond it, to go on the other side. If a communication were to go 'outside' it, it would make whatever is there communicably reachable—hence, that part would also be inside.

Complementary to the horizontal concept of meaning as a network is the concept of semantics. In certain ways, semantics can be understood as the content of the concepts that constitute the nodes of the network of meaning.[24] As such, it is a content which, so to speak, connects and anchors language, knowledge, and the network of meaning in the world they describe and to which the concepts refer. Luhmann, however, does not necessarily use 'semantics' in its ordinary meaning, referring to the content of a concept, and perhaps to its definition and context. Luhmann uses the word in this sense, but frequently he goes beyond this, and he refers instead to an entire style of thinking and arguing, or to an 'everyday theory' of a particular social group or a historical epoch. This is the case, for example, when he speaks about the 'semantics of romantic love' or the 'semantics of the subject'. Semantics in this wider meaning does not concern a single concept, but rather a whole lifestyle or cognitive style constructed around a concept like 'romantic love' or 'subject'.

As a result of this shift towards semantics, meaning, knowledge, or, as others would say, towards the cognitive and informational domain which can be interpreted as culture, it was only to be expected that Luhmann would use the concept of self-reference rather than that of self-organisation. Self-reference is a term that carries fewer connotations regarding matter/energy than self-organisation. The latter, in the context of thermodynamics, evolution, physics, and biology, is heavily loaded with implications of this type. Moreover, self-reference is more associated with the problems of hermeneutics, like the hermeneutic circle and the more general problem of understanding (etics/emics,

[24] See N Luhmann, *Law as a Social System*, above n 1, 143f. The original German word for meaning, '*Sinn*', has both connotations: That of a definition or contents of a word/concept (semantics) and that of references into a network of concepts (meaning in its relational sense).

inside/outside), which bring the supposedly ultra modern and nearly esoteric autopoietic theory into a much older context of occidental philosophy.[25] In a certain way, therefore, Luhmann's long march through sociology and social systems, which set out from Husserl's phenomenology and passed through Talcott Parsons's rigid functionalism, onward to the world formula of complexity and to theories of life and social life, ultimately points back (self-referentially?) to the issues of culture and philosophy.

After this outline of Luhmann's science in progress, the evolution of his works and theories in four themes and three phases, in all of which legal and political sociology are present, a more systematic attempt will be made to reconstruct the core of his theoretical approach from a number of key concepts. In this, we have to bear in mind what has been described so far. The concepts on which the following attempt is based are derived from different themes and phases of Luhmann's thinking, and they do not really constitute a finished, completed, systematic, authoritative theoretical construct: They do not form 'Luhmann's sociological system', as the old philosophers would have said. Luhmann was not and did not claim to be an axiomatic, mathematically oriented systems thinker.

KEY CONCEPTS IN LUHMANN'S THEORY

Luhmann was always a systems theorist, so an attempt at a systematic explanation of his work should begin with the concept of the system.

System and System Boundary

A *system*, according to Luhmann, is characterised above all by the fact that it has and maintains a *boundary*. All other characteristics of systems are merely secondary. This means that issues which are not legal matters are outside the legal system, issues that are not political remain outside the political system. For instance, the legal system maintains its boundary not by deciding whether a political decision was good or bad but by dealing solely with the legal question whether a political decision was legal or illegal, ie whether it was in accordance with or contravention of the law.

Environment and World

The existence of a boundary means the existence of an *environment* for a system. In the environment there can be other systems, but not everything in the envir-

[25] Cf, BR Hornung and R Hornung, 'Implications of Autopoiesis and Cognitive Mapping for a Methodology of Comparative Cross-cultural Research: Unity of Science and the Etics-Emics Controversy' in F Geyer and J Van der Zouwen (eds), *Sociocybernetics: Complexity, Autopoiesis, and Observation of Social Systems* (Westport Conn., Greenwood, 2000) 173–189.

onment is necessarily a system. The *reference system* and its environment together constitute the *world*, or in different terms, the observer and whatever the observer observes constitute the world. After all, the observer is always in the world. The world is not a system itself, because the world includes everything and therefore it has no outside, and thus no boundary.[26] A boundary is something which delimits one thing from another or, in cognitive terms, it is a distinction. Because in this sense there are always two sides to a boundary, the world has no boundary. The legal system, for example, sees the political system (which in Luhmann's terms is a system), as part of its environment. But the environment of the legal system includes much more than just the political system.

Reference Problems

If a scientist or somebody else deals with a system in order to resolve a theoretical or a practical issue, this system is called the *reference system*. According to Luhmann we cannot talk meaningfully about systems unless we reveal which system we are talking about,[27] that is, unless we give a reference. Indicating the reference system makes clear what is the environment, what are subsystems, etc. Similarly, if we talk about *functions* we need to indicate and make explicit our *reference problem* (or research interest) and the resulting *reference function*. Only in that case we can meaningfully state what is functional, dysfunctional, *functionally equivalent*, etc. If the legal system is our reference system the political system is part of the environment. If, however, the political system is our reference system, then the legal system is part of the environment.

When analysing functional subsystems, the reference system for Luhmann is society. The legal and the political functional subsystem of society, for example, should be viewed in light of the reference problems that they resolve for society. One such reference problem, to be resolved by the legal system, is to communicate expectations (over time) and enable them to be accepted throughout society.[28] As a result, the reference function of the legal system is defined by Luhmann as the systemic stabilisation of normative behavioural expectations, that is behavioural expectations not based on experience.[29] Another reference problem at the level of society is to make and implement collectively binding decisions.[30] Hence, the reference function of the political subsystem is to provide sufficient capacities of power to enable the implementation of collectively binding decision-making.[31]

[26] N Luhmann, 'Soziologie als Theorie sozialer Systeme', above n 11, 114–115; N Luhmann, *Soziologische Aufklärung*, vol 5, above n 1, 7.

[27] N Luhmann, 'Soziale Aufklärung', in N Luhmann, *Soziologische Aufklärung*, vol 1, above n 1, 66–91; 72; N Luhmann, *Social Systems*, above n 1, 136, 177.

[28] N Luhmann, *Law as a Social System*, above n 1, 143.

[29] *Ibid*, 467, also 142ff.

[30] N Luhmann, *Die Politik der Gesellschaft*, above n 4, 87.

[31] *Ibid*, 84–87, cf, 190, see also nn 15 and 16.

Build-up and Reduction of Complexity

For a system, the environment, and, above all, the world (which consists of other systems and other things), is complex. To be able to handle this *complexity* and to manage its effects, a system has to reduce the environmental complexity. A *reduction of external complexity* can, however, only be accomplished through *building up internal complexity*. This is provoked by the irritations coming from the environment and this in turn increases the complexity of the world. For example, a build-up of greater complexity in the reference system in order to reduce environmental complexity makes it necessary for other systems in the environment to do the same thing, and for the same reason. Reduction of complexity is a central reference problem for any system in a complex world. In order to deal with the increasing complexity of its environment, the legal system, for example, is required to develop more and more laws covering more and more areas of society in ever increasing detail. Thus the complexity of legal regulations becomes a problem in itself.

Communication

Social systems are defined by Luhmann, at least after his turn towards autopoiesis, as *communication systems*, abstracted from any material substrate of physical action or interaction. As autopoietic systems they constitute themselves by their very operations which are communications. Most sociologists would probably agree that in social life there is no physical action which does not incorporate at least indirect or long-term communicational/informational aspects. Most, however, would also argue that communication and information exchange are not possible without a material substrate. Even the Internet, for example, is made of wires and electromagnetic waves. Luhmann, however, restricts his concept of what a social system is to pure communication (without denying the existence of a material substrate). For Luhmann communication is an over-arching category closely linked to the concept of autopoiesis of social systems. Communication systems consequently have boundaries, and their first reference problem is the reduction of complexity. What Luhmann calls *interaction systems* are merely particular kinds of communication system, and they are characterised by the presence of the participants. Luhmann distinguishes *machines* (or one might call them technical systems),[32] *organisms*, that is, biological systems, *psychological systems*, and *social* systems, all of which he classifies as distinct types of systems. He then differentiates between social systems by distinguishing between *interaction systems*, *organisations*, and *societies*. On the whole, taking into account that he constantly seeks ever higher abstraction and ever higher complexity, especially in the composition of his own

[32] N Luhmann, *Social Systems*, above n 1, 16.

sociological theory, this is a very sparse *typology of systems*, even if he at times adds cells, brains, and organisms to this list in the category of living (biological) systems. According to this typology, functional subsystems such as the legal and the political subsystem have to be conceived as social systems. In addition to functional subsystems, Luhmann distinguishes the three types of social systems mentioned already—societies, interaction systems and organisations. This is shown in one of the few diagrams that can be found in Luhmann's works.[33]

Functional Differentiation

To reduce complexity, systems and in particular social systems use *functional differentiation*. Functional differentiation creates particular, specialised secondary reference problems for the particular *functional subsystems* or *function systems*. Complexity is reduced, as each functional subsystem has to deal only with one part of the total complexity. The political system has to deal with decision-making and power management, the legal system with legal issues, and the economic system with providing and distributing resources.

Symbolically Generalised Media and Codes

Functional differentiation leads to the formation of functional subsystems, such as, for instance, the legal system and the political system. These functional subsystems are delimited by boundaries, and each of them tends to its own business and treats all other subsystems as environment. To do this, subsystems develop particular mechanisms for coordinating their own internal lives. Originally, in Parsons's theory, these were the symbolically '*generalised media of exchange*', of which money in the economic system is an example: Money, for Parsons, combined the material aspect, of exchange of goods, values or tokens, with the informational, or, in Luhmann's terms, the communicational aspect of co-ordinating by providing networks of information. Media relate meaning to things and depend in their operation on normatively stabilised expectations, including expectations of expectations. In the economy, then, scarcity and abundance are communicated through such networks by means of prices. Luhmann abstracts from the material aspect and considers media strictly as media of communication. A medium in this sense is just a bearer of communications. It is necessary to send communications by means of a *medium* and to express them in (or impress them onto) a medium, using some kind of code. According to Luhmann, *binary codes* are used, and these are also specific to each

[33] N Luhmann, 'Sociologie als Thearie soziater Systeme' in N Luhmann (ed) *Sociologische Aufklärung*, 4th edn (Oplachen, Westdenuscher Verlag, 1974) 113–136, see pp 114–115; N Luhmann *Sociologische Aufklärung 5. Konstrucktiristische Perspektiven* (Opladen, Westdeutscher Verlag, 1993), 1, p 7 (Introduction).

medium. Communication takes place according to a code within the respective subsystem by means of the respective medium. The way in which the codes operate (or are operated) depends on the different kinds of *programmes* used by the respective subsystem, for instance conditional programmes or goal-oriented, purposeful programmes. With regard to the political system Luhmann also talks about the opposition government/opposition as a code, and in a text published as early as 1974 he discusses the opposition conservative/progressive as a code.[34] The latter example, however, might be considered as an early trial rather than a definitive formulation.

The relation between codes, media and functions is set out in the table below.

Table 1: Luhmann's Media, Codes, and Functional Social Systems[35]

CODE	MEDIUM	FUNCT/SYSTEM
Payment/Non-payment	Property/Money	Economy
Power/No-power	Power	Political System
Government/Opposition	Power	Political System
Legal/Illegal	Law	Legal System
True/Not true	Truth	Science
Beautiful/Ugly or Fitting/Non-fitting	Art	Art System
Love/No love	Love	Family *
Pass/Fail	Selection of Students**	Education
	Concept of Child***	
Values	Values	
Respect/Disrespect		Morals
Good/Bad		Morals
Good/Evil		Morals
Observable/Not observable		Religion
Immanence/Transcendence		Religion
Health/Disease		Medical System
Ascription/Non-ascription		
Risk/Danger		
Risk/Safety		
Pleasant/Unpleasant		

* Multiple codes.
** Not really a medium, but a functional equivalent for a medium.
*** A kind of supplementary construction, as there is no real medium.

[34] N Luhmann, 'Der politische Code, "Konservativ" und "progressiv" in "systemtheoreitischer" Sicht', above n 5 267–286.

[35] This table is largely based on C Baraldi, G Corsi and E Esposito, *GLU*, above n 1, 190, 193; and G Kneer and A Nassehi, *Niklas Luhmanns Theorie sozialer Systeme: Eine Einführung*, third edn (München, Wilhelm Fink Verlag, 1997) 170ff. For analysis of political codes, see also N Luhmann, *Law as a Social System*, above n 1, 378. The legal code, in German 'Recht/Unrecht', 60, 436; the legal code '*Recht/Unrecht*' and the two political codes '*machtüberlegen/machtunterlegen*' and '*Regierung/Opposition*' are mentioned also in N Luhmann, *Die Politik der Gesellschaft*, above n 4, 99.

Autopoiesis

Autopoiesis can be considered the most complex case of *circular causality*, in which causal chains are not simply folded back onto themselves, but constitute in a complex array of different *feedback loops* a closed system with a kind of *self-organisation*, that not only organises but reproduces the very components of which it itself consists. Essential for this reproduction or auto-(re-) construction are not the concrete parts, structures (and processes), but their (functional) organisation and coherence. This means that, just as in Luhmann's original switch to functional-structural theory, autopoietic theory professes that *functional organisation* remains stable, although the structures maintaining such functional organisation may change. This means that it is possible for different, yet functionally equivalent, structures to maintain the same functional organisation that permits operations to go on, ie to maintain autopoiesis. A business company, for example, can use a strict line structure to operate or it can use a team oriented structure. In both cases it will be able to operate, but the secondary consequences will, of course, be different, as the former implies a top down chain of command and communication, while the latter implies decentralised decision making and communication.

Of great importance for autopoiesis is *closure*. In its autopoietic operation the system is closed—in other aspects, however, it is open and highly interdependent with other systems.[36] Building once more on Maturana and Varela, Luhmann considers autopoietic systems to be informationally or operationally closed but energetically and in other aspects open. This means that Luhmann accepts that systems can have a metabolism and that the laws of physics, in particular the second law of thermodynamics concerning entropy and negentropy, are valid. All of this, however, is not of central interest to Luhmann as he deals with social systems which he conceives as communication systems. These he considers communicationally closed to correspond with Maturana and Varela's informational closure.[37] In this sense both the legal system and the political

[36] N Luhmann, *Soziologische Aufklärung*, vol. 5, above n 1, 11—self-referential functional subsystems have to be conceived as operationally closed but in other aspects highly interdependent.

[37] For example, in N Luhmann, *Law as a Social System*, above n 1, 112, Luhmann explains that on the one hand there is no such thing as information transfer but that the system itself produces information. On the other hand, it does so by 'reference to differences in the environment'. This is impossible unless the system 'knows' somehow about those differences that are properties of the environment, ie outside the system. A 'difference', if perceived, is a 'distinction', and both a difference and a distinction are at a basic level binary, ie yes/no, green/red, or formulated more abstractly: A binary digit which is the essence of contemporary information theory and informatics. At 80, Luhmann states that communication contains information as a component, at 315 information is defined as 'surprise value' which corresponds to the information concept of Shannon and Weaver and which indeed, by definition, cannot be an 'input' or 'output' of a system. However, it clearly does depend on the input and output of signals. See also the formulations at 353f regarding loss of information (caused by an ill-functioning transmission system) and the claim that: 'Everything that cannot be brought under the controlling scheme legal/illegal does not belong to the legal system but its . . . environment' (94).

system are closed systems, and each one processes its own affairs by means of its own medium and using its own code. The political system operates, ie communicates, by means of power using the code power/non-power, and the legal system communicates by means of law as a medium using the code of legal/illegal. Whatever is not a matter of power in one case and not a question of legal/illegal in the other cannot be processed by the respective functional subsystem and is not part of the political or legal system. In order to render an economic issue, such as a payment, processable in politics or law, it is necessary first to translate or transform it into a question of power in one case and a question of legality in the other. According to autopoietic theory, a transformation of this kind is effected by the mechanism of structural coupling between the functional subsystems involved.

Structural Coupling and Interpenetration

In spite of the constant assertion that there is no information exchange between two autopoietic systems, for example between the political and the legal system, there is a phenomenon known as *structural coupling*, which makes cooperation and co-evolution possible between systems, thus permitting the system to construct its own internal information and to make sense of what is going on. Although there is no 'information flowing from one system to the other', in a certain way this nevertheless makes possible some kind of communication.[38] Both systems can construct their own respective information on their own respective terms and due to this both can coordinate and operate effectively together. The latter, as will be argued below, is the constructivist criterion of truth. The concept of structural coupling, developed already by Maturana and Varela, refers to the fact that a system always exists in an environment and is in principle always threatened by events in the environment. These events, as they are perceived by the system, are called *irritations* (or *perturbations*).[39] The system reacts to these by means of internal events. If two systems, seen from outside by an observer, are in a relationship of mutual irritation over a longer period of time, *co-evolution* comes into existence. This means, regularities in the patterns of irritations appear and each system begins internally to adapt to the irritations it perceives. In this way a kind of communication becomes possible, analogous to when two humans, who do not understand each other's language, start to act, to interact, to develop regular patterns of interaction—even of linguistic interaction, albeit at a rudimentary level. This is, in fact, the process through which linguists can learn hitherto unknown native languages.[40] Instances of structural coupling are

[38] For more detail, see: BR Hornung, Structural Coupling and Concepts of Data and Information Exchange, above n 21.

[39] Other terms used besides 'irritations' are 'perturbations', 'disturbances', 'noise', but also 'resonance', 'impulse', and Leibniz's 'pre-stabilised harmony' pertain to this context.

[40] See TN Headland, KL Pike and M Harris (eds), *Emics and Etics: The Insider/Outsider Debate* (London, Newbury Park, New Delhi, Sage Publications, 1990).

the influence of legal regulations, for example a constitution, on politics, or the effects of political decision-making in legislation on the legal system. Autopoietic theory nonetheless insists that in structural coupling there is no information exchange, just irritations or perturbations.

Information and meaning are, according to autopoietic theory, only constructed or reconstructed internally—within the system.

A particular kind of structural coupling is *interpenetration*, a concept also derived originally from Parsons. In my view, this is another rather unclear concept. It designates a kind of symbiosis between two systems. The concept of symbiosis implies that the systems concerned cannot live without each other. In contrast to interpenetration, the concepts of symbiosis and especially parasitism (which is a one-sided symbiosis) imply some kind of input-output relation between the systems concerned. Interpenetration, however, deals with closed systems which are connected exclusively by mutual 'irritations'; that is to say that they provide for each other a mutually indispensable environment, yet without input-output relations and without information exchange. This is because they are autopoietic social systems, which Luhmann construes as pure communication systems.

The two examples of interpenetration which are most commonly mentioned, including by Luhmann himself, are those between psychological systems and social systems and between the brain and the psychological system (or between the brain and the mind, as it is usually described). A particular feature of these two examples is that one case refers to an interface between thinking (psychological, symbolic, inside) and the brain (biological, material, outside), and the other one to an interface between thinking and social communication. In both cases the interaction between the two kinds of system does not occur by means of a well-defined interface, but, one might suggest, by a parallelism. In both examples the brain/mind or matter/information hiatus seems to be somehow involved. The terminology of interpenetration might simply hide the fundamental problem involved in this latter issue, which is as yet scientifically unresolved, in spite of all neurophysiological brain research.[41]

Semantics

Semantics, as the term is employed by Luhmann, refers to the concepts used in a society, and to their *meanings* and contents. It is not simply language, but those concepts and parts of social knowledge which are generalised from the

[41] See also RM Bilder and FF Lefever (eds), *Neuroscience of the Mind on the Centennial of Freud's Project for a Scientific Psychology* (New York, The New York Academy of Sciences, 1998); AR Damasio, *Descartes' Irrtum: Fühlen, Denken und das menschliche Gehirn* (München, DTV, 2000); H Atmanspacher and GJ Dalenoort (eds), *Inside Versus Outside: Endo- and Exo-Concepts of Observation and Knowledge in Physics, Philosophy and Cognitive Science* (Berlin, Heidelberg, New York, Tokyo, Springer-Verlag, 1994).

particular and used to guide communication and social processes. It is the cultural stock of concepts, perspectives, ways of seeing and perceiving, which include what other authors sometimes call 'ideology' or 'world-view' ('*Weltanschauung*'). It is also, moreover, the stock of socially available topics for communication, which are themselves generalised and typified from particular, concrete communications. As a premise for communication, semantics provides *selectivity*: It means that certain topics will be more likely than others to occur in a communication, or that one way of continuing the communication will be more likely than others. Semantics is not directly related to *social structure* or (social) reality. Indeed, it even may lose its contact with them. In this case, however, its function of orienting communication will no longer be successful. Luhmann is extremely interested in the relationship between social evolution and the evolution of semantics. He tries to analyse the indirect and intricate relationships between changes in semantics and social change. In this sense, the semantics of the 'subject' and the changes it undergoes in the course of history are essential for the evolution both of the legal system and the political system, for instance in the change from natural law to positive law or in the development of concepts of individual human rights.[42]

Contingency and Double Contingency

The importance of the role of semantics in reducing complexity by providing selectivity becomes evident if we look at what happens in social interaction. Social action, understood as communication by Luhmann, is always selected out of a larger range of possible actions in a situation. Already in a dyadic interaction system, in which only *ego* and *alter* are involved, the behavioural dispositions of *ego*, in terms of social norms and role structures for example, are complex. Hence social action and communication as a selection out of this complexity is highly contingent: It could always be completely different. This means that such action and communication is also (im-)probable, as the possibility of selection always involves probabilities.

The *contingency* and *improbability* of *ego*'s social action multiply when we consider the fact that the same condition exists in *alter*, and that *ego*, as an observer of *alter*, takes into account the contingency of *alter* including the expectations of *alter*. Thus double contingency in social systems implies expectations of expectations. Mathematically two (im-)probabilities do not add up, but are in a multiplicative relation. This contingency and improbability of *reciprocal behavioral expectations* and the actual behavior based on them can be increased once more by adding more levels of *reflexivity*. Under these conditions a social system is necessary in order to coordinate the highly contingent actions of *ego* and *alter* and to make otherwise highly improbable coordinated action

[42] See Gert Verschraegen's chapter in this book.

and communication more probable. According to Luhmann, this *double contingency* provides the condition for autopoiesis to emerge in social systems.

Constructivism and Observers

Luhmann's concern with observers and the double contingency resulting from *ego* and *alter* observing each other is rooted in philosophical constructivism. Yet he strongly emphasises the sociological level when he talks about autopoietic systems, or about what takes place when systems observe each other.[43]

Constructivism is a philosophical view which offers an epistemological alternative both to ontological realism and to idealism, which results in solipsism. While realism asserts that the world 'out there' is perceived by an observer (or subject) more or less the way it really is and that finding truth means finding an image of reality which corresponds more accurately to what is really out there, solipsism asserts that the world is a mere invention of the observer. This invention has no correspondence whatsoever outside it and no external criterion of truth. Constructivism rejects both the image and mapping approach of realism and the pure subjectivity of solipsism.

According to the constructivist view what an observer knows about the world is strictly the observer's own construction. The observer can never know what 'is really out there'. However, for constructivists there does exist a negative criterion of truth which indicates which constructions are *not* viable, to use an expression of Glasersfeld, or which are *not* working or useful for practical purposes. Thus, constructivism obtains a practical criterion of truth by means of a negative selection. This conception of constructivism resembles the concept of structural coupling, autopoietic closure, and the philosophical problems of understanding and hermeneutics.

As in many other cases in which Luhmann adopted theories or parts of theories from somebody else, also in the case of constructivism he set out to develop his own 'Luhmannified' version of constructivism. Like the philosophical constructivists, for example Glasersfeld, von Foerster or Wallner,[44]

[43] He explicitly deals with constructivism and its epistemological foundations in N Luhmann, *Erkenntnis als Konstruktion* (Wabern, Beuteli Verlag, 1996); N Luhmann, *Soziologische Aufklärung*, vol. 5, above n 1; see the introduction of this volume, in particular 9–11, and 'Das Erkenntnisprogramm des Konstruktivismus und die unbekannt bleibende Realität', in N Luhmann, *Soziologische Aufklärung*, vol 5, above n 1, 31–58.

[44] E von Glasersfeld, *Radikaler Konstruktivismus. Ideen, Ergebnisse, Probleme* (Frankfurt/Main, Suhrkamp Verlag, 1998) see in particular 200–205, 210; E von Glasersfeld, in SJ Schmidt (ed), *Der Diskurs des Radikalen Konstruktivismus* (Frankfurt/Main, Suhrkamp Verlag, 1996), 219–221, 404; H von Foerster, *Sicht und Einsicht: Versuche zu einer operativen Erkenntnistheorie*, above n 23; H von Foerster and B Poerksen, *Understanding Systems. Conversations on Epistemology and Ethics* above n 23; F Wallner, *Acht Vorlesungen über den Konstruktiven Realismus, Cognitive Science* vol 1, third edn (Wien, WUV—Universitätsverlag, 1990); B Poerksen, *The Certainty of Uncertainty. Dialogues Introducing Constructivism* (Exeter UK, Charlottesville, VA/Heidelberg, Imprint Academic/Carl-Auer-Systeme Verlag, 2004).

Luhmann considered the ontological world (not to be confounded with Luhmann's concept of 'world' as explained above) as real but in principle inaccessible. While constructivists usually consider practical success and usefulness of knowledge as a criterion for indirect access to the ontological reality, Luhmann saw some possibility of, also indirect, access through social systems, their self-reference and self-stabilisation. These differences are related to Luhmann's focus on communication and his neglect of (or disinterest in) the material substrate of communication systems, that is social systems. To discuss these differences in detail and to analyse to what extent Luhmann succeeded in developing a new and different kind of constructivism clearly goes beyond the scope of the present chapter.[45]

Paradoxes

A paradox appears, if the condition for the possibility of an operation is at the same time the condition for its impossibility. This means, that a paradox is not simply a logical contradiction, but rather a contradiction in a two-step process or operation, in which the assumption 'true' in the first step leads to a 'false' in the second step and a 'false' in the first step leads to a 'true' in the second.[46] A famous classical example is the liar's paradox in the version which is assumed to date back to Eubulides from Megara who said 'If a liar says that he lies, this means that he says both the truth and a lie, because if he says the truth he lies, and if he lies he does not lie but he says the truth'. Supposing (1) the sentence is true that he is a liar, the speaker would say the truth, thus (2) it would not be true that he is a liar. Supposing (1) the sentence is false, the speaker would indeed say a lie, thus (2) after all the sentence would be true, as the honest man would say a lie. Thinking through this kind of paradoxes leads to oscillations as the question is not decidable and one answer, 'true', leads to the other one, 'false' and back again in a circular fashion.

In this way each distinction is inherently paradoxical, as each side of a distinction necessarily refers to and implies the other side. This turns out to be a key phenomenon in Luhmann's theory of self-reference and autopoiesis with regard to the distinction between system and environment.[47] A self-referential system can establish and maintain its own identity only by distinguishing itself from the environment, an operation which, however, is possible only inside the system itself.[48] The same problem emerges in all functionally differentiated subsystems, as these are, according to Luhmann, self-referential or autopoietic systems. In the case of the legal system the specific paradox is that decisions have

[45] For example, N Luhmann, *Soziologische Aufklärung*, vol 5, above n 1, where Luhmann explains his position quite clearly in the introduction. See in particular, 9–11.

[46] N Luhmann, *Social Systems*, above n 1, 150.

[47] *Ibid*, 33, 411–12.

[48] *Ibid*, 363.

to be taken that are binding, although they cannot be binding.[49] There exist paradoxes not only with regard to self-description but also with regard to the specific binary codes used, as also a binary code applied to itself results in a paradox.[50] Therefore self-observation and reflexivity can never be complete, as, to be complete, they should also observe the very distinctions they apply to themselves. Attempting to do this, however, they inevitably run into paradoxes.

Paradoxes are a problem of the observer not a problem of operations, which can simply happen without (self-)observation.[51] At the level of observers, however, paradoxes lead to what Luhmann calls the 'blind spot' of the observer, that which the observer cannot observe unless he shifts his operation, thus creating a black spot in a different place. To deal with paradoxes and blind spots, systems need to develop strategies of deparadoxation which can take a number of different forms, eg asymmetrisation, unfolding, invisibilisation, civilisation or hierarchisation—which in itself leads to a paradox.[52]

Paradoxes and deparadoxation seem all-pervasive, as they are indeed, according to Luhmann, an essential property of self-reference and autopoiesis, but possibly also a much more fundamental phenomenon inherent in epistemological constructivism—which indeed has to be considered a self-referential and closed system without the possibility 'to look outside' and yet as constructing a reality precisely in order to cope effectively with that 'outside'.

CONCLUSION: DISCUSSION AND CRITIQUE OF LUHMANN'S THEORIES

In the previous paragraphs it was argued that Luhmann's theories are based on constructivism which consequently has to be accepted as a basic premise of his theory design. Therefore, one could describe his work as a post-ontological theory of society. In a similar way, autopoietic theory has to be accepted as a basic premise of the major part of Luhmann's works. A number of problems that show up when one analyses Luhmann's theories, and in particular when one tries to apply them, points back to these basic decisions and premises. Moreover, these basic decisions, in particular Luhmann's so-called autopoietic turn, make a partial or eclectic use of his theories extremely difficult. Such a use runs a high risk of applying mere jargon, not theory. As Paterson points out in his contribution to the present volume, one has to be convinced of autopoietic theory in the first place, otherwise Luhmann's analyses will not make sense.

While I am convinced of the constructivist point of departure and largely adopt autopoietic theory in its original formulation for living systems as presented by Maturana and Varela, I nevertheless question aspects of Luhmann's

[49] Luhman, *Law as a Social System*, above n 1, 282–84.
[50] *Ibid*, 459–462.
[51] *Ibid*, 182.
[52] *Ibid*, 64.

application of autopoietic theory to social systems and several of his other theory-technical decisions and concepts. Two issues arise in the original formulation of autopoietic theory. One is that the concept of structural coupling focuses on structure and tends to disregard process. This, however, might ultimately be a problem of terminology and a lack of clearly defined concepts rather than a problem of substance. However, Paterson's discussion of openness/closedness and of the problems of steering and control as related to autopoiesis and structural coupling (this volume) supports the impression that it is necessary to substantially modify our understanding of causality, as he suggests, and his discussion also calls into question other concepts that tend to lose their meanings. This issue is closely related to the discussion of Luhmann's kind of definitions at the beginning of this chapter and might turn out to be essential for the further development of the theory of autopoietic social systems. Just as essential is that the concept of information used both by Luhmann and by Maturana and Varela is based on the concept of information developed by Shannon and Weaver in the context of their theory of (technical) communication. Moreover, this concept has a number of well-known drawbacks. In the context of structural coupling it is used by Luhmann without adopting Shannon and Weaver's concept of signal transmission, which, in their theory, is essential for communication. Instead, this clearly defined concept is replaced by vague and general notions like disturbances, perturbations or irritations, with other terms used synonymously. The question then is, how it is possible to conceptualise theoretically what is going on between two systems that somehow react to each other. Structural coupling produces some kind of reaction due to something, and this something one might call irritation, reinforcement, or simply *xyz*. But why not call it information or, perhaps even better, signal? It is certainly possible to say things in different terminologies, but the terminology of 'irritations' etc opens a gap between autopoietic theory and the wide field of information science. This might not be necessary and it might be even counterproductive.

Other fundamental issues concern Luhmann's own strategic decisions for the design of his theories. One of these is the question whether autopoietic theory can indeed be applied to social systems. A second one, closely related to this, is the question of what social systems are. Luhmann opts for communications as the basic units or rather operations of social systems, not for actions and not for subjects or individuals which are usually considered as basic constituents of society. According to Luhmann a communication as a unit of analysis and operation is something three-dimensional which, in a certain way, incorporates the components of a communication *system,* as conceived by Shannon and Weaver, under a different perspective. According to Luhmann a communication is the synthesis of three aspects, namely of utterance (*Mitteilung*), information, and understanding. Such communications are the basic elements (*Letztelemente*) of social systems. Social systems operate by means of communications which result in communications which result in communications etc. In this way the communication units create and maintain the autopoiesis of social systems by reproducing themselves. Consequently, and in the strict sense of autopoiesis, social systems are systems *of* communications creating the very communications they are constituted of, and incorporating in the communication unit itself what Shannon and Weaver distinguish as different components of the *communication system*, namely sender, receiver, and the message consisting of signals coming across a channel. The channel itself has no correspondence in Luhmann's concept of the communication as a unit but is implied in the notion of social system as a relational concept. As psychic systems remain outside the social system, which operates autopoietically and self-referentially, and are seen by Luhmann as an environment connected to the social system only by means of structural coupling, one might question where in such a system the dynamics—the process of communicating, the movement, the operation—comes from. In many instances, Luhmann writes about systems that 'operate', 'do', 'react', 'select', etc, just like other authors write about individuals or subjects. But what does this mean in the case of a social system consisting of communications as defined above?

This might be considered an illegitimate question about causality in Luhmann's functionalist framework. But after all, functionalism implies causality, even if it is not of primary concern, and also, in an evolutionary framework for sociology, causality cannot be avoided altogether, even if the mechanism of evolution itself does not work with causality but with the production of variety, conditions for selectivity, and conditions for retaining and stabilising what is selected. These aspects, however, cannot be further developed here. Luhmann professes very clearly such an evolutionary view of (social) systems that also implies causality, and he presents a lot of historical material in support of his theoretical arguments. In a narrow sense, causality can be interpreted as an unequivocal clearly specifiable sequence of cause and effect. Luhmann, and others, are perfectly right, of course, in asserting that this kind of causality cannot be found in social systems and that it is not possible to 'determine' and control an (autopoietic) system from the outside in such a way. In a wider sense, however, causality also includes weaker forms of only probabilistic effects, even at the level of logics, where so-called fuzzy logics is widely accepted and applied. While causality in the narrow sense is often hard to apply to sociological phenomena, a probabilistic approach is quite common. This is also the direction indicated by the discussion of reflexive law between Luhmann, Teubner, and Paterson as outlined by Paterson (this volume).

I do not have the space here to discuss whether these fundamental issues are basic flaws that discredit the theories built upon them, or whether they are only weaknesses that need further elaboration. The problems I have raised with regard to structural coupling and causality are also relevant for the question of how the subsystems of society can be integrated to constitute society. After all, the subsystems are autopoietic themselves, that is, they are operationally closed, and they use their specific media and their specific codes. Luhmann clearly rules out value-integration, but co-evolution alone—based on structural coupling and mutual irritations—does not look like a very convincing alternative. In particular, because Luhmann is very clear about the autonomy functional differentiation provides on the one hand and the increased interdependencies and needs for coordination it requires on the other, especially as complexity increases. If not by co-evolution and structural coupling, can this be achieved by those aspects of systems under which they are not closed but about which Luhmann does not tell us very much?

The autopoietic closure of social systems depends on codes that operate as criteria and decision-making aspects, guiding the operations, ie the processes and decisions, in their respective subsystems. Talking about operations of a (sub)system, it is evident that by definition such operations cannot step outside the system, as Luhmann asserts. Although economic processes or business processes, for example, are strictly internal as processes, whatever they are processing is connected, at least in a non-Luhmannian view, somehow to the outside, that is usually to similar business processes in other organisations or to events in other functional subsystems which depend on resources. In other words, there is, as in biological living systems, some kind of metabolism. This is not inconsistent with autopoietic theory in general and Luhmann's views in particular.[53] Nonetheless, it raises the question whether Luhmann's abstraction from (or neglect of?) such a metabolism in favour of pure communication is justified and acceptable in sociology, or whether the principal interest of sociological analysis should not be devoted precisely to the connections *between* such processes and their intersections.[54] On the other hand, Luhmann also concedes that issues can be brought into or taken out of a functional subsystem like the legal system.[55]

The integration and closure of functional subsystems inevitably becomes an issue as soon as applied research is carried out within a framework of theory of society, as this implies a look beyond the boundaries of a particular functional subsystem. This refers us to the theoretical status of Luhmann's statements. Although they are not clearly and systematically distinguished by Luhmann himself, four different levels of statements can be found. There are three theoretical levels and one empirical level, whereby in Luhmann's case 'empirical' refers largely to second order analysis of empirical and historical literature, as explained in the beginning of this chapter:

[53] N Luhmann sometimes talks about the 'internal environment' of a system. This, however, refers to autonomous subsystems rather than something 'external' passing through the system, as in the case of a metabolism. In case of the organism and its digestive tract, eg, it would hardly make sense to consider this passage through the organism as part of the 'external' environment.

[54] See, for example, E Buchinger, 'Innovation Policy as a Governance Problem: Systemic and Cybernetic Principles', Paper presented at the 4th International Conference of Sociocybernetics (Corfu, Greece, June 30–July 5, 2003). In this study Luhmann's autopoietic theory is heuristically used to investigate the process of innovation. Heuristic use seems to be a common solution among those who try to apply Luhmann's theories in applied or empirical research.

[55] N Luhmann, *Law as a Social System*, above n 1, 102.

1) *Theory of social systems*, which includes statements like social systems being communication systems, being autopoietic systems, etc. Such statements should be valid for all social systems including society, organisations, and interaction systems.
2) *Theory of society*, to which belong statements like society existing only at the world level, including whatever is communicably reachable, etc. Such statements should be valid only for societies as a particular type of social system.
3) Theory of functionally differentiated society, which includes statements about the different types of functional subsystems, eg the legal system, the codes and media such specific subsystems are using, etc. As a theoretical model this should apply to the fully functionally differentiated contemporary or even future society, that is, a particular type of society only. This raises the question of historicity and of the relation of such a theory to the fourth, the empirical level.
4) *Empirical description and analysis of contemporary functionally differentiated society as a historical instance of a theoretical model.* This includes statements about which types of functional subsystems are already differentiated, what their historical evolution was, to what extent they are differentiated, what kinds of media and codes they use more or less successfully, etc.

Many of Luhmann's statements are indeed of the fourth, empirical, category, that is, a diagnosis of contemporary (historical) modern society. This is distinct from a theory of functionally differentiated society, that is, level 3. In Luhmann's writings, however, these two levels are usually not very clearly distinguished. To what extent Luhmann's theory of functional differentiation is indeed limited to society, or more precisely a particular historical or empirical type of it, and not applicable, for instance, to organisations, which according to Luhmann are one particular type of social system, and to what extent this is the case with his autopoietic approach, is by no means clear. This is particularly the case, as Luhmann on the one hand insists that society nowadays can only be world society, but on the other hand professes a theory of functional differentiation, which is most obviously inspired by (empirical) 'national societies'. Moreover, Luhmann's theory of functional differentiation fits best to such 'national' social units, whatever one might call them after all. At the global level even economy, the most advanced of the functional subsystems, is not (yet) fully differentiated and integrated as a coherent gobal economic system, not to mention at all the still very rudimentary global legal and political systems, etc. It might clarify the issue considerably, if the analysis in the dimension of social units were to be clearly distinguished from the analysis in the dimension of variables or functions cutting across the social units. This is what Bailey describes as 'Q-R analysis' of social systems.[56]

[56] KD Bailey, *Sociology and the New Systems Theory*, above n 11, 54–57, 60–62, 66–69, 223–227.

We might say that the concept of functional codes and media, and the view of different functional subsystems of society as autopoietic systems with their particular media and codes, is plausible up to a point. The concept of autopoietic closure, however, seems to be problematic, as is also suggested by Paterson (this volume)—at least as long as the dimensions in which social systems are open are not specified and explicitly dealt with. The idea of pure communication systems, without including communicators which, according to Luhmann, are connected to the communication systems only by structural coupling and irritations, is not necessarily convincing.

Conceiving the functional subsystems of society indeed as autopoietic subsystems of world society, which is according to Luhmann the only society that exists nowadays, requires answers to the questions of where and how these subsystems intersect, whether structural coupling and co-evolution are indeed appropriate concepts, and last not least, whether 'the communication', which according to Luhmann 'processes', 'does', 'selects', etc is indeed an appropriate basic unit for sociological analysis.[57] Society, as world society, is extremely impractical for most purposes of applied research and analysis. A finer granularity of analysis is usually needed. But also the question of information and irritation seems to be, after all, a matter of granularity and, of course, of the information concept used. If what gets across the boundaries of autopoietic systems by means of structural coupling are irritations that are highly specific and patterned, why not call them 'information' as Stonier suggests,[58] or at least stick to the clear theory and terminology of Shannon and Weaver, in the context of which it would be a matter of signals travelling along a channel which after all are or are not interpreted as information by the receiver. In autopoietic terms, signals could be re-interpreted as patterned disturbances used by the system to distil meaning and to build up (internal) information. Talking about 'information' instead of disturbances or signals would be appropriate, in particular, if the reference system is an organisation or an even larger social system and not the micro-level of the transfer of bits and bytes through computer networks or of the intricacies of human understanding and hermeneutics.[59] Nevertheless, there exist, meanwhile, attempts to measure (at those higher levels) information exchange and communication in terms of bits and bytes, eg by means of 'Transaction Byte Analysis' (TBA).[60]

[57] This has been strongly called into question, for example by J Klüver, 'Auf der Suche nach dem Kaninchen von Fibonacci oder: Wie geschlossen ist das Wissenschaftssystem?', in W Krohn and G Küppers (eds), *Selbstorganisation: Aspekte einer Wissenschaftlichen Revolution* (Braunschweig, Wiesbaden, Friedrich Vieweg Verlag, 1990), 201–229.

[58] T Stonier, *Information and the Internal Structure of the Universe: An Exploration into Information Physics* (Berlin, Heidelberg, New York, Tokyo, Springer-Verlag, 1990) *vs* the information theory in CE Shannon and W Weaver, *The Mathematical Theory of Communication*, above n 20.

[59] Cf, BR Hornung, Structural Coupling and Concepts of Data and Information Exchange, above n 21; BR Hornung and R Hornung, 'Implications of Autopoiesis and Cognitive Mapping for a Methodology of Comparative Cross-cultural Research', above n 25.

[60] S Turnbull, 'Grounding Sociology in Cybernetics', Paper presented at the *XV*th ISA World Congress of Sociology 2002, Research Committee 51 on Sociocybernetics (Brisbane, Australia,

The previous considerations indicate that some of the difficulties with Luhmann's autopoietic theory of social systems and its application to empirical cases might be reduced or even overcome if:

— the distinction between epistemology and sociology is taken seriously and if at both levels the implications and consequences of Luhmann's constructivism are clearly specified and taken into account,
— a clear distinction is made between micro-levels, at which structural coupling may be the correct model, and (emergent) meso- and macro-levels, at which the concepts of signal flow or information exchange are likely to be more appropriate,[61]
— the diffuse concept of 'irritations' etc is replaced either by Shannon's clear concept of 'signals' and signal transmission or by an entirely different information theoretical foundation, eg Stonier's 'information physics',[62] which avoids the drawbacks of the information theory of Shannon and Weaver,
— the dimension of functional analysis is clearly distinguished from the dimension of analysis of social structures and processes, ie the analysis of social systems as units, aggregates, and empirical phenomena,[63] taking into account Q-R analysis,
— Luhmann's analysis of autopoietic closure is more closely linked to other contexts. One such context is the original theory of Maturana and Varela, which is well aware that autopoietic closure and autopoietic organisation are but one aspect of living systems (although a central one), and that living systems include many more aspects without which the respective systems cannot be understood. Another context might be First Order Cybernetics, in the guise of Ashby's 'essential variables'.[64] A certain organisation of the essential variables, eg their autopoietic organisation, without any doubt, constitutes the core of a system. To understand only the core, however, is not enough. A third context is the theory of self-organisation, which can be conceived as a less rigid, less constrained, and more open theoretical framework than autopoietic theory, although being very close to the latter.

Nevertheless, Luhmann's great achievement lies in his attempt to develop an encompassing theory of society. This he considered possible only as a highly generalised and highly abstract theory. In achieving this, Luhmann spans the

July 7–13, 2002) <http://ssrn.com/abstract=321203> last accessed 04 Sept 05; S Turnbull, 'Governing the Management of Complexity', Paper presented at the 19th EGOS Colloquium (July 4, 2003) <http://ssrn.com/abstract=436380>, last accessed 04 Sept 05.

[61] See BR Hornung, Structural Coupling and Concepts of Data and Information Exchange, above n 21; BR Hornung, *Emergence. A Key Concept for Sociocybernetic Theory of Information Society*: Paper presented at the 15th World Congress of Sociology (Brisbane, July 8–13, 2002).

[62] CE Shannon and W Weaver, *The Mathematical Theory of Communication*, above n 20; T Stonier, *Information and the Internal Structure of the Universe*, above n 58.

[63] Cf. BR Hornung and FT Adilova, 'Conceptual Modelling for Technology Assessment of IT Systems. Smart Cards, and Health Information Systems', above n 16.

[64] WR Ashby, *Einführung in die Kybernetik* (Frankfurt/Main, Suhrkamp Verlag, 1974) 284–291.

full scope from the micro to the macro level, for example from the double contingency of the social relation between *ego* and *alter* to the world society and the world, and from theories about particular social phenomena, like the family, to his general theory of social systems and even beyond, for example with his further generalisation and abstraction of autopoietic theory. The latter is situated at the level of general system theory. This enormous theoretical apparatus Luhmann applies to practically all areas of social life, not just to the political system and the legal system. In this way, his works cover, indeed, the entire field of sociology.

10

Dealing (with) Paradoxes: On Law, Justice and Cheating

ANDREAS PHILIPPOPOULOS-MIHALOPOULOS

IN *EL ALEPH*, Borges mentions his short story *Los naipes del tahúr*, which, according to the author, has been short-listed for the Argentinian National Literature Prise but, quite unbelievably, got no votes whatsoever.[1] As far as we know, this story has never been written. It appears nowhere in Borges's collected works and no manuscript has ever been found. The only thing that exists of the story is its title, which can be translated as *The Cards of the Cheat*. One purrs in delight when thinking how Borges must have enjoyed identifying with the card cheat. By inventing a cheat about someone who cheats and referring to it in his own work, Borges dealt with a paradoxical self-reference (since the only place in which the story is to be found is its reference) by dealing the cards of a cheat to the unsuspected reader. Borges's hands remain free from sleight: it is the reader who deals with the paradox of a non-existent story as dealt to her by the author. Indeed, Borges passes the paradox onto his reader, offering only one clue: a deck of cards.

Dealing *with* the paradox is not the same as *dealing* the paradox. In fact, the two may well be mutually exclusive. But never too far from each other. A linguistic sleight, achieved by the parenthetical invisibilisation of a seemingly insignificant preposition, allows one almost to play with both sides of the paradox. 'Almost', since any decent card game is based on the premise that dealer and recipient see different sides of the card. Unless, of course, one is a cheat.

My purpose here is entirely dishonourable: I am going to cheat by looking at both sides of the cards. I will deal with the paradox by dealing it. This is not quite giving in to the paradox. It is rather an understanding that the paradox always returns. In this sense, this chapter is a performance: the text itself is a paradox, at the same time dealt to the reader, and dealt with by cheating. 'Cheating', for the purposes of the present analysis, entails simultaneously 'marking' or prioritising both system and environment. The system of interest here is law; its environment is the void of all things unutterable, including law's legitimacy and justice. The paradox links system and environment in a form

[1] JL Borges, *El Aleph* (Buenos Aires, Alianza, 1971).

that is inoperable, except perhaps through a skilful dealing! But before that, a discussion is reserved on why paradoxes—and cheating—are things one would not want to do without.

PARADOX

Etymologically, paradox is 'the other belief' (*para-doxa*). Paradox is the first and last instance of dialectics. It initiates the other speech, the other speaking, their expressing a belief contrary to the belief of their interlocutor. This contrary belief, however, is equally valid, with the result that the discussion returns to itself without ever concluding anywhere. The adverb must be taken literally: the discussion concludes neither anywhere outside the *doxa* and the *paradoxa* (say, a third *doxa*); nor anywhere within the initial dialectics. Instead, it carries on whirling between the two initial *doxae*, without ever reaching a conclusion . But this irritates a dialectics habitually guided by reason, and (paradoxically) begets a *necessity* of coming to a conclusion—a moral, phenomenological, logical, phenomenal, evolutionary, transcendental, operational, attributional, some sort of necessity anyway, which seems to be called upon by a whole constellation of known -logies to the effect that the discussion *carries on*.[2] And quite rightly so: paradoxes are frightful things, they bring boredom, obsession, counter-productive repetition, paralysis, inability to communicate, inability to distinguish, no sense, nonsense.[3] They are facile excuses and unlaborious shoulder shrugs, they obscure determination and encourage determinism, they force one to give up, to grin embarrassingly, to abandon battle, to take a nap under the trees. Paradoxes are too much hard work to be taken seriously and too easily unresolvable to be attempted.

Except for recently that is. Theory's turn to paradoxes is not surprising.[4] Paradoxes emerge as epiphenomena of a generalised lack of direction. World society is turning upon itself, systems bite their own operations, individuals

[2] One of the few times that to my knowledge Luhmann employs the concept of necessity is when referring to paradox as a 'transcendental necessity': *Die Religion der Gesellschaft* (Frankfurt, Suhrkamp, 2000), 132.

[3] See P Goodrich, 'Anti-Teubner: Autopoiesis, Paradox, and the Theory of Law', (1999) 13 *Social Epistemology*, 197 for a reference to Tacitus with regard to legal paradox; also G Teubner, 'The King's Many Bodies: The Self-Deconstruction of Law's Hierarchy' (1997) 31 *Law and Society Review* 763, and 'Economics of Gift-Positivity of Justice', (2001) 18 *Theory, Culture & Society* 29.

[4] Theory has always been preoccupied with paradoxes, but mostly about how to solve them. It is only lately that an embracing of the paradox has emerged. For a contextualised account see N Luhmann 'The Paradoxy of Observing', (1995) 31 *Cultural Critique* 37. For non-autopoietic theory, see eg, G Bateson, *Steps to an Ecology of Mind* (New York, Ballantine, 1972) on the immanence of totality; JF Lyotard and JL Thebaud, *Just Gaming*, W Godzich (trans), (Minneapolis University of Minnesota Press, 1985) on the linguistic impossibility of deriving the prescriptive from the descriptive in justice; E Levinas, *Otherwise than Being or Beyond Essence*, A Lingis (trans), (The Hague, Martinus Nijhoff, 1981) on the phenomenological self-interruption in the name of ethics; C Schmitt's 'love your enemy' and the subjection of rule to its exception: *The Concept of the Political*, G Schwab (trans), (New Brunswick Rudgers, 1976); etc.

throw away their psychoanalytical couch (with themselves on it), and the word 'paradox' finds its way into the world's worried whispering. *Aporias* and *epoche*, *together in difference* and *in-betweens*, *infinity*, *collective unconscious* and *unknown*, are adequately complex concepts that address the complex inadequacy of the world. Gaps everywhere render any conceptual bridging problematic: human rights theory and practice, chasms between north and south, terrorism, justification and guilt, technology and ecological catastrophe, sovereignty and naked bodies, system and subject. The world wakes up to her paradox and shuts her eyes before her reflection.

Paradoxes are painful. The impossibility of solution is embarrassing, suffocating, incarcerating. So one finds that one has to deal with it. Dealing *with* paradox can sometimes seem conveniently close to *dealing* the paradox, passing it on, pushing it into somewhere spacious, airy, breezy, full of cathedral light: where better than religion? Luhmann dreams of a moment of *au-delà* when he equates paradox with the transcendental subject: it is through paradox that knowledge is given in its absolute form, unconditionally and *a priori*.[5] A paradox pushed into the divine is luminous, blinding, invisible in its radiating visibility. But above all, it is dealt, it is passed on and allowed to be, since its impossibility is not our weakness. The collapse of the divine as an apothecary of our impossibility has not affected the dealings. *Loci* of transcendence have cropped up all around and inside the human that receive the paradox as gallantly as god. However, such dispersion has made the invisibility of paradox less visible. God's shadow was enough to cover it, but human shadows tend to fly erratically away,[6] and social systems cast no shadow over their environment. The paradox returns and its visibility becomes, once again, embarrassing. Theory can no longer ignore this, as it has done ever since enlightenment. One's gaze has progressively shifted from the lamp to the floor, and the battle of the shadows is well underway.

This does not mean that the fascination with paradoxes is merely the desire to be rid of them. Agreed, paradoxes are prone to de-paradoxification; but arguably because they expose themselves in all their fragile omnipotence:[7] they are omnipotent, of course, because there is no reference from which they draw their power except for themselves. But, while one's second reaction is to kick them, the first reaction is nearly always to admire them. Paradoxes are perfection. A paradox contains the world in one autonomous, autocephalous, autologous, *auto-générée/ générative* form.[8] *Paradox is autopoiesis*, in all its lithe

[5] N Luhmann, *Religion der Gesellschaft*, above n 2; see also N Luhmann, 'Notes on the Project "Poetry and Social Theory" ' (2001) 18 *Theory, Culture & Society* 15, on the transcendental.

[6] From *Peter Pan* to *Die Frau ohne Schatten*, shadows are obviously not to be trusted!

[7] On omnipotence and self-reference see P Suber, 'The Paradox of Self-Amendment in Constitutional Law' (1990) 7 *Stanford Literature Review* 53.

[8] '[S]elf-generating/generative', E Morin, *La Méthode: La Nature de la Nature* (Paris, Seuil, 1977) 258.

claustrophobia.[9] Paradoxes afford a glimpse of the impossible, the unity, the illusion of being together, the unstoppable becoming, the time before time when no apple had been bitten and no horizon was ever to limit infinity. Paradoxes are pre-edenic *forms* in that they include both marked and unmarked space in one inoperable unity—'inoperable' because the system cannot operate with unities: only by marking itself against the environment, or by marking the observed against the unobservable, can the system deal with unity. Unity expresses an omnipresent impossibility, both alluring and threatening in its inoperable perfection.

The fascination with the form in the sense of unity, impasse and impossibility, is a radical motivation behind theory's paradoxical engagement. And theory generates something out of this fascination: it obliges paradoxes with its attempts at deparadoxification.[10] Luhmann identifies the following modes of deparadoxification: 'unfolding, making invisible, civilizing, making asymmetrical.'[11] One could comment on all four of them and amuse oneself especially by questioning the ramifications of the third;[12] still, one has to *carry on*, only to discover that all four are emanations of one primordial operation: that of *distinction* (decision, asymmetrisation, marking, prioritisation).[13] The world was an unbearable (no one could possibly bear it, as much as no one was there to bear it) mêlée of divine-demonic, godly-human, light-darkness, this-and-that. And then came the operation of distinction, the wand that marked the marked from the unmarked, the this from the that, the side of the card where the queen rests from the other side where a *fleur-de-lis* averts and confounds nosy stares. This was the end of the paradox, once and for all: a paradox torn into two, a fitful interruption of the irritating perfection. But where did this operation come from? Who dealt it? Surely not god: too busy being marked this side of being marked. Then from distinction itself? Can distinction distinguish? And isn't this paradoxical? 'What about the paradoxicality inherent in the very act of

[9] This point goes somewhat further than J Clam's assertion that 'without paradox, there is no autopoiesis' ['The Specific Autopoiesis of Law' in J Pribáñ and D Nelken (eds), *Law's New Boundaries* (Aldershot Ashgate, 2001)] in the sense of the Derridean use of the cupola, resonant of 'deconstruction is justice' in J Derrida, 'Force of Law: The 'Mystical Foundation of Authority'', M Quaintance (trans), in D Cornell *et al.* (eds), *Deconstruction and the Possibility of Justice* (New York, Routledge, 1992), and the Levinas-inspired 'intentionality is hospitality' in J Derrida, *Adieu*, P Brault and M Naas (trans), (Stanford, Stanford University Press, 1999).

[10] There is nothing untoward about this: every man kills the thing he loves, etc. For an expansion on deparadoxification based on a confluence between Derrida and Luhmann, see my 'The Suspension of Suspension: Settling for the Improbable' (2004) 15 *Law and Literature* 345.

[11] N Luhmann, *Law as a Social System*, K Ziegert (trans), F Kastner, R Nobles, D Schiff and R Zieger (eds), (Oxford, Oxford University Press, 2004) 64. In the original, the phrase reads: '*Entfaltung, Invisibilisierung, Zivilisierung, Assymmetrisierung*', N Luhmann, *Das Recht der Gesellschaft* (Frankfurt am Main: Suhrkamp, 1993), 23. Also N Luhmann, *Ecological Communication*, J Bednarz, Jr (trans), (Cambridge, Polity Press, 1989), 144–145.

[12] Since, interestingly, 'the paradoxicalization of civilization has not led to the civilizing of paradoxicality.' N Luhmann, 'Sthenography' (1990) 7 *Stanford Literature Review* 133; 134.

[13] See eg N Luhmann, *Observations on Modernity*, W Whobney (trans), (Stanford California, Stanford University Press, 1998), 108*ff*.

distinguishing that makes its appearance, for instance when one thinks of the beginning or the end of the process of distinguishing.'[14] Paradox returns, and renders the process of deparadoxification a jolly pastime with temporally limited validity.

So what? Paradox, just as everything else, is temporally conditioned. Paradox, just as everything else, has to refrain itself from asking the foundational question: is paradox paradoxical? *Idem* for distinctions, systems, individuals: do I do what I do? Does the distinction distinguish, is law lawful, am I me: all frightfully relevant questions that the questioner can only answer by creating another distinction, taking distance and invisibilising the suspicion of the whole. One will rightfully wonder whether this is answering or simply postponing the answer. Regardless, I choose to postpone the answer here by saying that any answer to this is simply a postponement, not so much of giving the answer but *of asking the question.*[15] Dealing with paradox is a catenation of negative steps, backward steps forward as it were, which lead inexorably but non-causally away from the question and nowhere closer to the answer. But enough with all these self-confounding witticisms. Because a paradox does have its use: in all its irritability, through and because of it, a paradox demands structural reconsiderations, resemiologisations, shiftings, adjustments, self-searchings, comparisons, new positionings.[16] It is not through the *question* that a paradox does all that (anathema to the question which is to remain unuttered), but through the *fear* of the question. It is the desire to reveal it in its terror, and the subsequent fear of such magnificence, that the one who turns away from the paradox shifts uncomfortably and finds new ways of becoming. To find an answer is to find oneself, to emplace oneself in the world and expose oneself to the flow of communication/perception. To find the question is to suspect that there are other emplacements, all equally contingent, all equally markable. To find that one should never find the question is the sublime torment of becoming, the halo of knowledge around the abyss of ignorance, the only communication with the self—however negative, prohibiting or limiting. The impossibility of asking the question is what makes being avoid the question and revolve around a negative becoming. Avoidance is, just as everything else, temporally conditioned; so every time once, the avoidability of the question arises and keeps one becoming. Through their need to remain invisible, paradoxes are the *élan vital* of autopoiesis. They are the ones who wake us up by asking the facetious, all-too-avoidable question: 'Are you asleep?'

[14] N Luhmann, 'Sthenography', above n 12, 136.

[15] It is said that in her deathbed, Gertrude Stein asked her companion 'what is the answer?' And when she got no answer, she asked 'anyway, what is the question?'.

[16] '[The paradox] can be understood as an inducement, even a compulsion to solution. This means: as a challenge to reconstruction with the help of distinctions that enable stable identification.' N Luhmann, *Observations on Modernity*, above n 13, 112.

LAW AND PARADOX

What is the question that the law can never ask itself? Simply, whether law is lawful or unlawful.[17] The question immobilises the legal system and may even cause its eventual collapse. The question echoes the primordial never-to-be-uttered question: who dealt the first distinction? For law, this translates into the first moment of violence.[18] Law followed that moment by preceding it: the law justified one side of the violence, thereby marking itself this side of the law. The law legitimised itself by legitimising violence—or could it be that the law legitimised violence by self-legitimisation? In other words, which came first, law or violence? But this is perilously close to the unutterable first question. The law cannot deal with its own limitations, let alone with what lies beyond its limits (that there exists something beyond its limits would be a surprise for law).

So let me return to the law, to the security of ignorance as guaranteed by the system's boundaries. Law's paradoxes are always a fractal reiteration of the unutterable question. Nevertheless, they are asked. Not because they are less 'paradoxical', but because their 'unfolding' is always a step away from the unutterable; in other words, their distinction does not coincide with the unutterable or first distinction. These paradoxes –I will call them *utterable*[19]—can be dealt with from within the system, through its own operations and systemic observations.[20] Some of them are common amongst social systems. Some are peculiar to law. Most of them engage with themselves in the usual narcissistic disregard towards the world. All of them are dealt with through the usual mechanisms: distinction in the form of decision that enables unfolding, asymmetrisation, prioritisation, invisibilisation. None of them is solved forever: they are merely postponed.

A rudimentary Luhmannian list necessarily includes instances of self-reference, most of them founded on biological autopoiesis. Thus, an autopoietic system has been originally defined as a system that reproduces itself, all its

[17] N Luhmann, 'Law as a Social System', (1989) 83 *Northwestern University Law Review*, 136.

[18] See R Rogowski, 'The Paradox of Law and Violence: Modern and Postmodern Readings of Benjamin's "Critique of Violence"' (1994) 18, *New Comparison* 131; Luhmann has also discussed the connection between law and violence in *A Sociological Theory of Law*, E King and M Albrow (trans), (Boston, Routledge & Kegan Paul, 1985), as well as more recently in *Law as a Social System* above n 11, where he suggests the coding of the legal paradox as the difference between law and violence.

[19] This is reminiscent of J Clam's (see above n 9) distinction between pure and derivative paradox. If I read Clam correctly, the difficulty with the derivative (here, utterable) paradox is its correspondence with the represented real. In the distinction un/utterable, however, the correspondence is circular and confined in the binarism itself. The 'real' in all its theatricality only appears in the following section in this chapter.

[20] This does not imply that the unutterable paradox cannot be dealt with from within the system. Nor, however, that it can. To start with, the unutterable can only be dealt, not dealt with. But whatever the dealings, they are necessarily observed from within a system, even if no system has an adequate vocabulary for them. In other words, the system is the sole entity *(in)capable* of dealing the unutterable.

constituent elements, and even the processes of its reproduction.[21] The immediate systemic interpretation of such circularity is that a system recognises no *telos*. There is no inherent purpose in the system except for its own operations. An autopoietic system exists and the product of its existence is itself: in autopoiesis being is becoming,[22] whereby the tautology between the given of existence and the beyond of creation constitute the schizophrenia of the autopoietic paradox. The system's identity is defined in opposition to the system's environment ('I am what I am not'); the latter is supplemented by the tautological definition from within the system's boundaries ('I am what I am'). However, since the system has no access to its environment due to its normative closure,[23] the only identity description to which the system has access is self-description.[24] Systemic self-description introduces the unity of the system within the system. Self-description is the operationalised version of self-observation, namely the observation of the system by the system itself (on the level of second-order observation) in order for links and attributions to be established. This means that observations are observed ('We ourselves may be observing systems observing observing systems'),[25] in exactly the same way as levels of operations appear as emerging clusters of self-referentiality: thus, in the legal system, norms are created on how to create norms, and decisions are taken on decisions in a manner reminiscent of a DNA helix.[26] All this, of course, as long as it fits in with the ubiquitous systemic code (in law, the form lawful/unlawful) which can be imagined as a watchdog on the borders of the system, guaranteeing systemic closure while simultaneously (another paradox: open because closed) underscoring the system's cognitive openness and selectivity towards its environment.[27]

It is obvious from the above instances of paradoxical self-reference that tautology is not far from paradox. Tautologies are expressed predicatively (lawful *is* lawful), whereas paradoxes attributively (lawful *because* unlawful).[28] Their common point is a lack of any external reference.[29] Consequently, a paradox (or

[21] H Maturana and F Varela, *Autopoiesis and Cognition: the Realization of the Living* (Dordecht, Reidel, 1972).

[22] *Ibid*; see also A Schütz, 'The Twilight of Global Polis: On Losing Paradigms, Environing systems and Observing World Society' in G Teubner (ed) *Global Law without a State* (Aldershot, Ashgate, 1996).

[23] N Luhmann, 'The Unity of the Legal System' in G Teubner (ed), *Autopoietic Law: A New Approach to Law and Society* (Berlin, Walter de Gruyter, 1988), at 20.

[24] N Luhmann, 'Closure and Structural Coupling' (1992) 13 *Cardozo Law Review* 1419.

[25] *Ibid*, 1420.

[26] N Luhmann, *The Differentiation of Society*, S Holmes and C Larmore (trans). (NY, Columbia University Press, 1982) 100.

[27] Selectivity refers to the ability of a system to reduce the possibilities that originate in its environment (*Ibid*, 213).

[28] N Luhmann, 'Some Problems with Reflexive Law' in G Teubner and A Febbrajo (eds), *State, Law and Economy as Autopoietic Systems* (Milan, Guiffre, 1992) 395*ff*.

[29] 'Tautologies are distinctions that do not distinguish. They explicitly negate that what they distinguish really makes a difference.' N Luhmann, *Essays on Self-Reference* (New York, Columbia University Press, 1990) 136.

a tautology) cannot communicate anything with any certainty: 'a paradox exists when communication, as soon as it is embarked upon, generates the opposite of what it intends as communication.'[30] The opposite of communication can be either miscommunication or simply the break up of communication.[31] This is another way of conceptualising the systemic aversion to paradoxes: since all social systems operate with communications, and a paradox disrupts or interrupts communication, the system takes recourse to methods of invisibilisation of the paradox. Here, however, we are faced with an apparent conflict of paradoxes. Luhmann tells us that communication is also an autopoietic system in its own right: '[c]ommunication recursively recalls and anticipates further communications, and solely within the network of self-created communications can it produce communications as the operative elements of its own system.'[32] How is it then that the same thing that enables communication also interrupts communication?

The conflict is only impressionistic. All paradoxes are echoes of the unutterable question. Every utterable paradox contains a negative (prohibiting) reference to the unutterable, in the sense that every utterable is another step away from the unutterable. Every utterance of a paradox visibilises the invisibility of the unutterable paradox by maintaining its inoperability. Imagine every utterable as temporarily adequate (but only just) chunks of meat that keep the great beast calm. In every paradox, the unutterable is found *sous rature*, never to be found, in a *form* with the utterable, on a level at the same time simultaneous and nonsimultaneous to the utterable. 'Simultaneous' because it is constitutive of the form; 'nonsimultaneous' because it can never be evoked while the utterable is speaking. The gregarious, sociable, communicative utterable paradox is the only way in which the unutterable paradox can be kept at bay. Thus, every apparent conflict of paradoxes is resolved by recourse to the different levels of paradoxification, as a strategy of distanciation from the unutterable.

This is precisely the reason for which every system abounds in utterable paradoxes. Indeed, the law keeps itself busy and mostly safely away from the big 'existential' questions by dedicating itself to particular utterabilities. To carry on with the ones peculiar to law, the form of norm and its interpretation can be added to the list of paradoxical equilibria. The form can helpfully be put in the Luhmannian parlance of core and 'periphery'. Courts are to be found in the former, in contradistinction to other kinds of legal communication, such as the legislature, that correspond to the 'periphery' of the system.[33] As expected,

[30] N Luhmann, 'Notes on the Project "Poetry and Social Theory"' *Theory, Culture and Society* 22.

[31] Luhmann has referred to silence as the opposite of communication; see *ibid* and 'Speaking and Silence' (1994) 61 *New German Critique* 25.

[32] N Luhmann, *Art as A Social System*, E Knodt (trans), (Stanford California, Stanford University Press, 2000) 9.

[33] N Luhmann, *Law as a Social System*, above n 11. One can see that this is a turn from the usual continental centrality of the norm, to a more common law-friendly judicial centrality: compare with N Luhmann, *A Sociological Theory of Law*, E King and M Albrow (trans) (Boston, Routledge & Kegan Paul, 1985) where such division does not appear.

Luhmann was quick to dispel any impression of hierarchy between core and periphery, since hierarchy would be a misinterpretation of autopoietic circularity.[34] The courts are simply the elements of the legal system that deparadoxify law's utterable paradoxes, not least because their operation itself is based on a constant expectation of deparadoxification (that of the legal obligation to decide);[35] but also because courts are the guards of systemic memory, the facilitators of its evocation.[36] This means that the form norm/decision is deparadoxified through differentiated prioritisation between what can also be referred to as the internal and external sides of the form.

Indeed, courts link the internal with the external. This is better observed through the concept of *programme*: the courts are the main applicators of the computation between an *if* and a *then*, or else a fact (external) and a legal rule (internal).[37] The conditionality of the application (*if . . . then . . .*) is what a programme is. This conditionality renders the programme more flexible than the binary code lawful/unlawful and facilitates a more practice-informed application of the code. Needless to say, a programme is another method of deparadoxification. When a court employs a programme, it links the internal self-referentiality of the code with the avenue of external connection as provided by a programme.

The same internal/external differentiation can be witnessed in another Luhmannian binarism, that between *redundancy* and *variation*.[38] Variation is the systemic accommodation of surprise, whereas redundancy is akin to the memory of the system. While there is little doubt that the system accommodates surprises according to its memory, variation triggers not only evocation but also new combinations—in other words, intelligence. Redundancy, on the other hand, is the process of banalisation of external perturbations that takes place in strict accordance with the system's memory. The system is expected to balance both functions without compromising either its ability of cognitive openness to innovations, or its structural unity. In balancing, the system takes into consideration two kinds of consequences: the intrasystemic consequences which refer to future legal decisions, and the external consequences, or the effects a decision has on the legal environment.[39] It is not as if redundancy and variation have respectively internal and external consequences, or that the legal system can

[34] N Luhmann, *Law as a Social System*, above n 11, 277.

[35] *Ibid*, 292.

[36] In 'Boundaries of Exclusions Past: The Memory of Waste' in R Lippens (ed), *Imaginary Boundaries of Justice* (Oxford, Hart, 2004) I have argued on the mnemonic function of the courts in relation to differentiated levels of systemic forgetting.

[37] See N Luhmann, *Law as a Social System*, above n 11; also N Luhmann, *Ecological Communication*, J Bednarz, Jr (trans), (Cambridge, Polity Press, 1989) and N Luhmann, 'Law as a Social System' (1989) 83 *Northwestern University Law Review* 136; for a comprehensive explanation and application of the concept see M King, 'An Autopoietic Approach to "Parental Alienation Syndrome"' (2002) 13 *The Journal of Forensic Psychiatry* 609.

[38] N Luhmann, 'Legal Argumentation: An Analysis of its Form' I Fraser (trans), WT Murphy and G Teubner (eds), (1995) 58 *Modern Law Review* 285.

[39] *Ibid*, 294.

consciously select which mode of reaction it will employ. Rather, the connection is one of contingently balancing one binarism against and through the other without any prioritisation—otherwise known as a paradox.

The list of utterable paradoxes could carry on for a few more pages. But I fear that by indulging the system's fears, the text will melt away in some sort of polite description of noble badinage. The system's move away from the unutterable and into the semantic jungle of Luhmannian prestidigitations can be alluring but ultimately misleading. We are being presented with one side of the form, the side that shows the innocuous *fleur-de-lis*. But I said I want to cheat, and cheat I will: I am going to take a peak on 'the other side of the air: pure, boundless, no longer habitable.'[40] I want to turn to the echoing environment, where even the queen has abandoned her throne.

ENVIRONMENT

Some phrases mark their reader. The following phrase by Anton Schütz has marked this reader: 'The environment is too powerful but unable to choose at all. There is nobody in the environment.'[41] The combination of power and frailty, the echoing absence of a *pantokrator*, the never occupied throne: there is something that evokes a 'sense' of *justice* due, an urge to help, to sympathise with the clumsy giant who is '*too* powerful'—in a way, the *only one* who is powerful enough to hold the wand and deal the distinction, any distinction, with all the violence of the origin, and to 'call it the first distinction.'[42] So powerful that all the power that there is, is in her hands; *too* powerful to stop herself from collapsing under the inoperable burden of her own *gravitas*. Such images come to mind and make it gaze towards the unmarked environment.

Of course, the environment *per se* cannot be observed. The environment can never be 'marked' as a whole—only as an object of a distinction. Environment is simply what is not (the) system. Law's environment is everything to which the legal code does not apply. Agreed, the legal system is cognitively open, it accepts (albeit in a self-referential way) environmental perturbations, it evolves by taking into consideration its (self-) observations. It even engulfs its environment in the manner of *re-entry*, that is the inclusion in the system of the difference between system and environment.[43] But the system wields the wand. It is the grand subject *and* the grand object, the Cartesian marriage of a historically necessary distinction: the system observes, the system is observed. A 'flattened' society where hierarchy has been replaced by contingent and temporal

[40] Extract from 'An die Musik', RM Rilke, *Ahead of All Parting*, S Mitchell (trans and ed), (New York, Modern Library, 1995).

[41] A Schütz, 'Desiring Society: Autopoiesis beyond the Paradigm of Mastership' (1994) 5 *Law and Critique* 149; 161.

[42] G Spencer Brown, *Laws of Form* (New York, Dutton, 1979) 3.

[43] N Luhmann, 'Observing Re-entries' (1993) 16 *Graduate Faculty Philosophy Journal* 485.

prioritisation.[44] All there is, is (in) the system. Whatever remains, is (in) the environment—but there is *nothing* in the environment, except perhaps for the answer to the question.[45]

The unutterable raises its head the deeper one peers into the environment. Law's foundational paradox is whether law is lawful or unlawful. If law is lawful, all is well. But what if law is unlawful? Societally speaking, lawfulness is expected, whereas unlawfulness is expected to turn into lawfulness. Even so, who is to turn unlawful into lawful, if not law? But how can an unlawful law turn anything into lawful? Logical impossibilities are usually solved in a Gordian way: bring in the sword! Take a deep breath in and dismiss it as nonsense! Look the other way! Anything that will break the symmetry of the paradox would do—however, nothing of the above is of the system. They are all imported from a garrulous environment whose tirades are silence to the system. Any legitimacy of deparadoxification vanishes before the incommunicability between the system and the environment. Nothing can legitimise the systemic paradox, because the only communicable legitimation originates in and returns 'outside', to the external side of the form law/justice, to the façade *of* legitimacy as well as to legitimacy *as* façade.[46] As Pribáñ puts it, 'the social space of instability and constant confrontation is the space in which legitimation takes place . . . [N]oise is not only contingent, but also subversive.'[47] Since self-legitimation cannot be accepted as the answer, the question must never be asked. But the question *is* asked: maybe not in these terms, but the terms are shaken. In a society that questions its self-description and allows the suspicion of other descriptions to enter its night sweats, the question is repeatedly asked from numerous sides and in numerous ways.[48] It is no longer an issue of theoretical description, but of practical prescription. It is the gap between law as it describes itself, and law as it is being described. It is the gradual corrosion of law's self-description as the institutionaliser of normative expectations, and its embarrassment before an overabundance of cognitive expectations.[49] It is also

[44] W Rasch, *Niklas Luhmann's Modernity: The Paradoxes of Differentiation* (Stanford, Stanford University Press, 2000) 102.

[45] Nothing worthy of observation: conscious systems, the grand *manqué* of society, are not worthy of observation, since, as Luhmann rather inelegantly puts it 'there are too many of them' (!) in 'Deconstruction as Second-Order Observing' (1993) 24 *New Literary History* 763; 773.

[46] '[C]ommunicable' being the operative term that differentiates this thesis from Luhmann's *Legitimation durch Verfahren* (Darmstadt, Luchterhand, 1975); see also S Machura *The Individual in the Shadow of Powerful Institutions* in K Röhl and S Machura (eds), *Procedural Justice* (Aldershot, Ashgate, 1997).

[47] J Pribáñ, 'Legitimation between the Noise of Politics and the Order of Law' in J Pribáñ and D Nelken (eds), *Law's New Boundaries*, above n 9.

[48] See N Luhmann, 'Why Does Society Describe Itself as Postmodern' (1995) 30 *Cultural Critique* 180; also P Goodrich, 'Anti-Teubner: Autopoiesis, Paradox, and the Theory of Law' (1999) 13 *Social Epistemology* 197.

[49] Normative expectations rarely change: their normativity is expected to be able to stabilise expectations. Cognitive expectations, on the other hand, can change in the form of adaptation to disappointment. The legal system reduces complexity by fixing normative expectations that have the ability to maintain and perpetuate themselves (N Luhmann, 'Law as a Social System', above

the theory observing itself changing, softening, pluralising.[50] To put it in terms that the legal system could not understand (but everyone else would), it is a question of why law is not just.[51]

Luhmann puts it bluntly: 'The traditional question on the justice of law loses all practical meaning'[52]—it belongs to the *nothing* outside the system. The passage from natural to positive law unequivocally entailed the disruption of theoretical constructions of continuity between law and justice.[53] Their contribution to the understanding of the legal system is inadequate because they cannot account for the presence of, as well as need for, complexity. Instead, justice is to be seen as a *supra-programme* of the legal system, namely a criterion that applies to the code lawful/unlawful and determines its selection, leaving the gates open for a filtered complexity to be understood by the system. Justice 'guides' legal decisions from outside of the process, as 'a programme of (all) programmes on the level of the programmes of the system',[54] or as a *circular formula of contingency*.[55] However, the criteria for justice are to be found within law: '[s]ince only positive law is "valid", namely able to use the symbol of legal validity, one must not look for criteria outside ("*rechtsexternen*") but within law ("*rechtsinternen*").'[56] There are two things worth noting about these criteria: first, the legal system does not employ them in order to be just, but to be consistent: 'these criteria become relevant through the question as to how, in the face of the increasing complexity of law, it is possible to continue taking consistent decisions (that is, distinguishing between cases that are alike from ones that are not).'[57] Second, the criteria may well be inside the system, but justice itself as a value remains outside the legal system, in its environment, at a safe

n 11. The two categories of expectations, in direct analogy to a system's structural closure and cognitive openness, are combined by the system to achieve its evolution; see N Luhmann, *Law as a Social System*, 106–108. Thus, although the selection of whether a disappointment will be handled normatively or cognitively is made by the system, specifically for the legal system the processing of expectations entails institutionalisation, and this occurs predominantly through normative expectations. However, the production of cognitive expectations is on the rise: see *malgré soi* G Teubner (ed), *Global Law without a State* (Aldershot, Ashgate, 1996).

[50] N Luhmann himself, especially post-90s; G Teubner *in toto* as a valiant ambassador of autopoietic pluralism; K-H Ladeur, *The Theory of Autopoiesis as an Approach to a Better Understanding of Postmodern Law*, 99/3 EUI Working Paper (Florence, European University Institute, 1999).

[51] G Teubner in 'Alienating Justice: On the Surplus Value of the Twelfth Camel' in J Přibáň and D Nelken (eds), *Law's New Boundaries*, above n 9, looks at the gap between the legal and the external through what, reluctantly, he calls 'a chance for another re-entry' (at 35) or, following Luhmann, a partial self-transparence of the legal re-entry. The obvious connection with Derrida's position of justice is explored by P Fitzpatrick, 'Abiding the World' in J Přibáň and D Nelken (eds), *Law's New Boundaries*, above n 9.

[52] N Luhmann, *Law as a Social System*, above n 11, 212.

[53] *Ibid*, 212.

[54] *Ibid*, 213.

[55] This circular formula appears on the level of programmes. Circular formulae are self-referential modes of crossing the boundary between determinacy and indeterminacy; see N Luhmann, *Die Wissenschaft der Gesellschaft*, vol *II* (Frankfurt am Main, Suhrkamp, 1990) 879*ff*.

[56] *Ibid*, 225.

[57] *Ibid*, 225, footnote omitted.

distance from its code.[58] This can only mean that the legal system *may* be just. What is surprising about the last statement is that it is not surprising, even on a level of second-order observation where attributions in the sense of causalities and responsibilities are demanded.

Let me return to the environment, to the security of ignorance as guaranteed by the system's boundaries. For although the question remains unuttered in law's self-description, it is vociferously murmured everywhere else—but then again, nowhere else matters. Or maybe it does. Maybe law's propensity for paradoxes allows the paradox between legal self-description and societal expectations of continuity between law and justice to seep into the systemic operations and expose itself ready to be severed. Goodrich points to the environment of the law in the following: 'Law remains the site in which the social drama of affect is acted out in resilient theatrical forms. Ethic and antagonism, identity and alterity, are staged in the symbolic forum of law and that staging too deserves study.'[59] If, even at times of doubt and questioning, when the unutterable becomes threatening in view of the proliferation of legal representations from outside the legal system, justice (as the external side of legitimation) remains excommunicated in the legal environment, then it is questionable whether law can carry on ignoring the open-air theatre of its social enactment where arguably not so virile but definitely relevant satires are being performed. This is not merely an epistemological point: if on the level of theory, the theoretical self-reference of the law is being disputed in its role as a validation avenue, then the unutterable paradox stops being unutterable and the system is at risk. For there is indeed an operation of the legal system that the autopoietic self-description of the law does not seem to be taking into consideration: legal theory.[60] And while theory (in the form of self-observation) can make a positive change by engaging with the 'formulation and criticism of the cultural practice of law',[61] it can also embody a threat and put the system at risk from the inside by bringing the very foundational paradox to the fore.

DEALING

When a paradox is dealt, a paradox is passed on to 'a less sensitive spot'.[62] Luhmann has described this process a few times, with the usual end-receiver

[58] The terms 'just/unjust' are not to be found in the vocabulary of the legal system, for otherwise justice would have to be added as a third term to the existing code—N Luhmann, *Law as a Social System*, above n 11.

[59] P Goodrich, 'Anti-Teubner: Autopoiesis, Paradox, and the Theory of Law', above n 48; 212.

[60] '[T]he theory of autopoietic systems powerfully relativises the practical significance of legal dogmatics and even more so the practical significance of legal theory.' N Luhmann, 'Some Problems with Reflexive Law' in G Teubner and A Febbrajo (eds), *State, Law and Economy as Autopoietic Systems* (Milan, Guiffre, 1992) 409.

[61] P Goodrich, 'Anti-Teubner: Autopoiesis, Paradox, and the Theory of Law' above n 48, 212.

[62] N Luhmann, 'Sthenography', in *Stanford Literature Review*, above n 12, 135.

being politics.[63] When systems cannot deal with the question, they simply deal it to the most vocal system around. Politics seems to be the locus of legitimacy too,[64] arguably because it is easier for the political system to compromise the concept of truth and replace it with self-reference.[65] Truth is presumed to need a reference to an external world, whereas political self-reference combines the illusion of externality within its self-referential form. Politics flirts successfully with the internal/external side of legitimation—for what else is legitimation if not the communicative ability of a system to organise its operations in such a way that they appear required—arguably by encouraging individuals to be more liberal with their cognitive expectations. The somewhat inevitable price of this is a lowering of the system's credibility threshold that translates into apathy. But, while politics seems more resilient to such minimum legitimation, law does not allow this to enter its self-description for the reasons I gave in the previous section. So law has to deal by dealing with it through self-questioning; but it does not *seem* to deal very convincingly. Observing law dealing reveals a rupture between itself and justice, or else the internal and external side of legitimation. Even on the level of second-order observation, where attributions can be established between legal operations and considerations of justice, the rupture remains—or at least the link is shaken.

Second-order observation is Luhmann's preferred avenue of dealing with the paradox. For reasons that will become obvious below, second-order observation is also the gaming table for dealing the paradox. Second-order observation visibilises the paradox of distinction of first-order observation. Every observation is a distinction and every distinction divides the marked from the unmarked. The unmarked always includes the observer: 'one thing the observer must avoid is wanting to see himself and the world. He must be able to respect intransparency.'[66] The observer cannot see *the* unity—he can only see what remains after the unity has been severed. What he sees may well be *a* unity, but it will not include himself. He remains in a *blind spot*, namely the point of observation that enables observation to take place. The unity of the first order observation (the unity that includes the observer and the observed) can only be observed by means of a further distinction, that is, via a different observer, who will also, however, operate from his blind spot. First and second-order observation necessarily function together: 'observation is possible only in a recursive network of the observation of observations, not in the form of a singular spontaneous, "subjective" act.'[67]

[63] In *Ecological Communication* (see above n 11), risk is dealt by the legal system to politics; human rights and democracy are also passed onto politics; see, eg *Die Gesellschaft der Gesellschaft* (Frankfurt, Suhrkamp, 1998). See also my *Absent Environments: Theorising Environmental Law and the City* (London, UCL Press, 2006).

[64] J Pribáň, 'Legitimation between the Noise of Politics and the Order of Law' in J Pribáň and D Nelken (eds), *Law's New Boundaries*, above n 9.

[65] N Luhmann distinguishes between the two by prioritising the latter as the way to understand modernity in 'The Modernity of Science', in (1994) 61 *New German Critique* 9–24.

[66] N Luhmann, *Observations on Modernity*, above n 13, 111.

[67] *Ibid*, 111.

Dealing is like second-order observation: one is under the illusion of an overview of the game. But there is no *über*observer—'there is nobody in the environment.' There is always the other side of the card that even the one who deals cannot see. The blind spot of the second-order is as teasing as the hidden cards. But it is precisely this teasing, the intransparency that players have to respect, that enables the game to carry on. Dealing the paradox—just like dealing the cards- is an invitation to the other to have a look at your blind spot. In fact, the blind spot is the ground on which the invitation takes place—the blind spot *is* the invitation, has always been there, a protended appellation to the other, an awareness of the form invisibilised by its unutterabillity, in short: an inviting void in the shadow of the game where one can project dreams of unity. Luhmann does exactly that when saying 'this imaginary space replaces the classical a priori of transcendental philosophy.'[68] And somewhere else: 'the systemic keystone of epistemology—taking the place of its a priori foundation.'[69] And somewhere else: 'the blind spot is [the second-order observer's] a priori, *as it were*.'[70] The blind spot replacing the *a priori*, the origin, the foundational phrase, the first gesture, the paradox of unutterability; yes, but only '*as it were*'—not really. Not in reality, not even in the theory. The origin is replaced by its supplant, the necessity is covered up as non-necessity, as the opposite of desire, as Luhmann's yo-yo jolted to the time where no outside could ever be, and then quickly rolled back, to the safety of ignorance '*as it were*'. This is Luhmann's—and everyone's- desire both to break the rules *and* to carry on playing. The necessity invisibilises itself as the blind spot of playing: the necessity does not exist. Or better, it has always existed, in blinding unutterability.

Hence justice. In second-order observation, in the society of two, where necessity translates into its needlessness, and—to recall Levinas[71]—justice is society because forgiveness replaces the need for law, law is only introduced with the plurality of observers. The circuit of second-order observers, Luhmann's solution to paradoxical paralysis,[72] organises the invisibility of blind spots in a self-referring circuit of paradoxical postponement. But one cannot fail to see that, in so doing, a network of second-order observation enables the *form*: on the 'inside' of the form, there is law, prancing amongst the observers, a stabilising system of virile communications that manages to leave his unutterable paradox at home. And, on the 'outside' of the form, there is justice, nowhere to be seen, a blind spot of theatricality, a social stage of needless necessity, the home that always remains unoccupied, an unmarked environment, a throne saturated with a scent of absence. Law is marked, visible and

[68] N Luhmann, 'The Modernity of Science', above n 65, at 21.

[69] N Luhmann, 'The Cognitive Program of Constructivism' in W Krohn *et al* (ed), *Selforganization: Portrait of a Scientific Revolution* (Dordrecht, Kluwer, 1990) 75.

[70] N Luhmann, 'Speaking and Silence', above n 31 at 28, my emphasis.

[71] E Levinas, *Entre Nous*, M Smith and B Harshav (trans), (London, Athlone Press, 2000) 19*ff*.

[72] N Luhmann, 'Sthenography', above n 12, 133–137.

deparadoxicalised, but only *because* and *through* its unutterable form with justice which law so cleverly hides away.

The form remains inoperational. Distinction on behalf of the system will always orient itself away from its blind spot—not teleologically nor transcendentally, but operationally. The invitation and its complementary distanciation, is always 'open', always preceding observation, in another form where distinction presupposes paradoxicality.[73] The invitation leaves an echo in the system, a 'resonance',[74] which cannot be introduced properly in the legal operations: precisely because of this, the incomprehensibility of invitation (who invited you?) remains nagging and irritating. But you are here now, and I know this, not because I see you, but because I do not see you: because you blind me.[75] Theory, legitimacy, justice: all blindingly irritating, all bouncing back from the identity of difference between the system and its environment.

Cheating, therefore, for law is to be simultaneously with law and justice, to observe the plurality of observers observing each other, while solely concentrating on the blind spot of one's sole observer, to spread one leg on the system and the other on the environment. Cheating is nothing more than observing carefully. Of course, it always helps if the cheat is also the one who deals. Because dealing necessarily precedes playing, and it is only through dealing that one invites the other to one's blind spots—the game must begin, after all! All players sitting around each other, one observing the way others observe their cards, one putting together the observer and the blind spot in a façade of unity. Perhaps the only way to do something about that stuffy table is to cheat. Everyone can cheat—and difficulties help, irritate, make someone devise ways of coping with them; in short, difficulties (in the sense of ruptures, internal criticism, overabundance of cognitive expectations) enable the player to evolve cognitively.

Asking law to cheat is nothing more than asking law to observe carefully—observe what others do and learn from it. The legal system cannot observe what it cannot observe. It cannot observe its blind spot, nor can it observe its unity. However, it observes others observing, offering their blind spots, welcoming before even inviting. The legal system itself links blind spots with their observing systems, as well as exposing its own blind spot to the invitations of other systems. On top of this, the legal system observes itself observing, and describes itself accordingly. And while the unutterable paradox of law is never to be uttered within law, *this* can be uttered: that it is never to be uttered. And this indeed is uttered through law's utterabilities, for every utterable is a reiteration of the unutterability of the unutterable. Law will carry on dealing with the paradox by dealing it, but the act of dealing is the beginning of law's cheating.

[73] *Ibid*, 133–137.

[74] N Luhmann, *Ecological Communication*, above n 11.

[75] This is the gaze of God for Derrida, which remains invisible despite the fact that is directed to my face. See J Derrida, *The Gift of Death*, D Wills (trans), (Chicago, University of Chicago Press, 1996).

Theory is here to remind law of its blind spot, to echo the invitation and to help law cheat without exposing itself. By including in its self-description a little cheat-sheet reminding itself never to utter the unutterable, the law engages with the theatricality of its blind spot, the staging of its operations and the spectacle of justice, without ever leaving the familiarity of its closure.

Index

www.ingramcontent.com/pod-product-compliance
Lightning Source LLC
LaVergne TN
LVHW020413220926
848484LV00017B/2560/J